Loyalty Marketing
for the Internet Age

Loyalty Marketing
for the Internet Age

How to Identify, Attract, Serve, and Retain Customers in an E-commerce Environment

Kathleen Sindell, Ph.D.

DEARBORN™

TRADE

A **Kaplan Professional** Company

This publication is designed to provide accurate and authoritative information in regard to the subject matter covered. It is sold with the understanding that the publisher is not engaged in rendering legal, accounting, or other professional service. If legal advice or other expert assistance is required, the services of a competent professional person should be sought.

Senior Acquisitions Editor: Jean Iversen Cook
Senior Managing Editor: Jack Kiburz
Interior Design: Lucy Jenkins
Cover Design: DePinto Studios
Typesetting: Elizabeth Pitts

Library of Congress Cataloging-in-Publication Data

Sindell, Kathleen.
    Loyalty marketing for the Internet Age : how to identify, attract, serve, and retain customers in an e-commerce environment / Kathleen Sindell.
        p.   cm.
    Includes bibliographical references and index.
    ISBN 0-7931-4033-1
    1. Customer loyalty. 2. Electronic commerce. 3. Internet marketing.
I. Title.
    HF5415.525 .S53 2001
    658.8—dc21
                                                                        00-010287

Dearborn Trade books are available at special quantity discounts to use as premiums and sales promotions, or for use in corporate training programs. For more information, please call the Special Sales Manager at 800-621-9621, ext. 4514, or write to Dearborn Financial Publishing, Inc., 155 North Wacker Drive, Chicago, IL 60606-1719.

DEDICATION

My gratitude to my husband, Ivan Sindell, for his advice and encouragement.

Acknowledgments

My thanks to Jean Iversen Cook, senior acquisitions editor, for her thoughtful guidance and support. Thanks to my literary agent Doris S. Michaels and all the folks at the Doris S. Michaels Literary Agency for their encouragement. My appreciation to everyone who worked behind the scenes, especially all the people who are listed on the credits page. Thank you for making this book happen.

I deeply appreciate my editorial assistant, Reuven Goren, who coordinated copyright permissions, verified Web sites, and coordinated the multiple tasks necessary to deliver this book on time.

A special thank you to my brother-in-law, Gerald Sindell, for his profound counsel on everything relating to the business of publishing.

Contents

Introduction

Welcome to *Loyalty Marketing for the Internet Age: How to Identify, Attract, Serve, and Retain Customers in an E-commerce Environment,* a comprehensive guide that provides clear instructions, success stories, and action plans for high-level decision making. With the assistance of this book, traditional brick-and-mortar companies can develop plans for their transition to the Internet. For professional Web-based dot-com companies, you'll discover ways to fill in the holes of your existing plans and manage a customer-centric business. For businesses that combine brick-and-mortar and click-and-mortar, this book can assist you in developing a complete view of your customers, so that you can build customer loyalty and decrease marketing costs.

Some e-commerce management books are compilations of management consultant war stories that don't include Internet addresses for easy reference. Others focus on how several big-name companies should improve their online businesses but don't show how their unique stories can help you with the specific issues your company is facing. There are also e-commence books that assume you are fluent in "geek speak," the technical terms that only an information technology professional can understand. *Loyalty Marketing for the Internet Age* is different. It is designed for professional managers who aren't interested in management consultant or technological hype. It is a practical manual that addresses today's challenges of transforming organizations and processes using technology to identify, attract, serve, and retain customers in the new global economy.

In writing this book, I assumed:

- You want to discover how to leverage the Internet by identifying and profiling users, prospects, and customers. And, you want to personalize your product or service offerings, as well as acquire and retain online customers for increased profitability.
- You want to identify ways of increasing revenues by using new Internet business models. You aim for increased sales opportunities through online self-service and Web-based call centers. You have a high interest in extending your sales force by indirect selling through Web portals and affiliate programs.
- You are interested in finding out about the latest tools and technologies to make your online (and offline) customer service outstanding and to identify your best and worst customers. With this knowledge, you can focus on your high-value customers and build customer loyalty.

WHY YOU NEED THIS BOOK

Customer loyalty is often the difference between success and failure for a business. To build loyalty with online customers, businesses often have to struggle to overcome organizational and technical barriers that hinder developing customer connections. To dissolve these barriers, your e-corporation must create new relationship strategies that will allow it to build ongoing dialogues with customers. This, in turn, will allow you to tailor products and services to individual buyers and to configure offerings for specific types of customers. For many firms, building customer loyalty in this manner may seem like an unattainable goal.

Loyalty Marketing for the Internet Age provides specific, easy-to-follow directions to assist you in gaining customer loyalty by creating and implementing cost-effective strategies to strengthen the bonds of customer loyalty in the e-commerce environment. It is designed to be a reference book for high-level managers who want to reap the benefits of the online revolution. Each chapter stands alone and provides the information needed for making high-quality management decisions about basic e-commerce customer loyalty issues. You'll find out how to recognize and identify customers; how to create a "corporate memory" of each customer; and how to begin online customer dialogues. With your customer knowledge, you'll be able to make customers an offer they can't refuse and one that will bring them back for more.

HOW TO USE THIS BOOK

Most professionals will read this book in large pieces, diving in long enough to solve a particular problem or research a certain issue. *Loyalty Marketing for the Internet Age* is structured in such a way that if you want to read it through from beginning to end you can. I begin by showing how the Internet has radically changed the competitive landscape and end by introducing you to ways to build the infrastructure you'll need for your own online continuous loyalty solutions.

Some of the topics I cover include:

- Gaining an understanding of how you can use technological and managerial solutions to leverage the Internet to increase customer loyalty
- Discovering how to measure the lifetime value of your online customers
- Getting a hold of how to lay the groundwork for transitioning your company to the Internet
- Seeing how you can zero in on customer needs and loyalty types
- Becoming aware of how to develop online customer loyalty and retention strategies
- Looking into how you can increase profits despite commoditization
- Gaining an appreciation of how treating different customers differently can lead to more profits
- Discovering the best and most appropriate customer relationship marketing practices to retain your customers
- Identifying different types of online customer loyalty programs
- Uncovering how to develop your own online customer loyalty action plan

- Becoming skilled at gathering customer information for Web site personalization
- Uncovering how you can simplify customer interactions in order to increase customer satisfaction and lower operating costs
- Taking advantage of new technologies for Web-based call centers
- Becoming skilled at segmenting your customer base to identify your best and worst customers
- Identifying how you can retain your most profitable customers by anticipating and meeting their unique needs and desires

SPECIAL FEATURES OF THIS BOOK

Customer loyalty is not about being first but about getting it right. Once you have sold a product or service to an online customer, you'll want that customer to return again and again to offset your acquisition costs and to increase profitability. *Loyalty Marketing for the Internet Age* demystifies electronic customer relationship management (eCRM) and shows business professionals how eCRM is both a business strategy and class of enterprise application. Both small and large business leaders will benefit from an understanding of how to leverage the Internet to develop, nurture, and manage multiple relationships with their customers.

Loyalty Marketing for the Internet Age has many special features that make it unique. Following are a few examples of how these special features can assist you:

- You won't get lost in the jungle of techno-speak. Many software vendors provide blurry definitions of what their product can and can't do. Some technological solutions are *Web-enabled* and others are *Web-based*. Use the descriptions of technological solutions provided in *Loyalty Marketing for the Internet Age* to assist you in meeting your strategic objectives; in other words, you can identify the right computer applications for the right tasks.
- Frequently, it is useful to see details about how one company achieved a specific goal. *Loyalty Marketing for the Internet Age* is packed with short loyalty marketing success stories. These vignettes illustrate how

companies similar to yours have effectively used eCRM solutions to build customer loyalty. Each success story describes the company, solution, and benefits of building customer loyalty.

- Sometimes, it is difficult to apply a specific technique to your business. *Loyalty Marketing for the Internet Age* provides hands-on action plans that can help you design, build, and manage your transition to the Internet. End-of-chapter action plans include handy checklists to assist you in focusing on the issues that count; easy-to-use questionnaires to help you identify the tasks necessary to improve customer loyalty; and scorecards to aid in measuring your success and determining how far you have to go to meet your objectives.

- The resource center at the back of the book provides data and contact information about best practices, e-commerce consultants, publications, research, and conferences. It also includes an extensive listing of the technological solutions that may interest you. These software applications are divided into major categories and indexed so you can see which products have modules that you may want to include later. In addition, the index indicates if a software product you currently own is part of an eCRM suite (and whether you may be able to easily add online capabilities to your existing technological infrastructure).

- Become skilled at the terminology used in electronic commerce by using the glossary included at the end of the book. Refer to this glossary for a set of extended definitions of words you may not be familiar with.

HOW THIS BOOK IS ORGANIZED

E-commerce will continually increase, but not all Web sites will gain the rewards they want from the Internet gold rush. New online business models are invented every day, competition is high, and customers expect more and more online capabilities. *Loyalty Marketing for the Internet Age* shows how the separate functions of sales, marketing, customer service, project management, and distribution join together in the common theme of improving customer loyalty and how relationships with your customers are influenced by the Internet. This book is divided into three parts:

1. "An Introduction to eCRM Practices on the Web" shows how the Internet has fundamentally changed the competitive landscape. You'll gain an understanding of why customer loyalty is more important than ever and why it is important to focus on the right customers and measure their lifetime value. Compare the traditional ways of building customer loyalty to the online capabilities that you can use to strengthen the bonds of customer loyalty. Find out how you can target customer needs and exceed customer expectations.
2. "The eCRM Customer Loyalty Business Process" illustrates how you can measure customer retention and develop an online loyalty and retention strategy. Discover how you can create new markets for customers with diverse needs, and how treating different customers differently can increase profits. Look into the benefits of mass customization and see how this approach can apply to your organization. Discover how you can automate the customer loyalty process and develop your own online loyalty program action plan. Look into how hiring the right employees can increase customer loyalty.
3. "The eCRM Customer Loyalty Infrastructure" shows how you can personalize your marketing efforts and gather customer information. Understand how you can manage leads, so that you can virtually sell anything and extend your sales force using affiliate programs. Uncover how you can organize customer data to provide superior online customer service and support by dividing your customer base into segments. Find out how to make your Web site secure and protect customers from privacy intrusions. Zero in on Web-based call centers and check out the latest online technologies. Discover how you can develop eCRM projects by creating a service vision, operating strategy, and service concept and by targeting customer segments.

FEEDBACK, PLEASE

If you have any comments, suggestions, or questions, please feel free to contact me by e-mail at ksindell@kathleensindell.com.

The Benefits of eCRM

In this day and age, customers have a lot of choices. They don't have to be loyal to any one company and whether satisfied or dissatisfied, they may be ready to defect. On the other hand, loyal customers are often the most profitable customers and worthy of management attention. Loyal customers do not require acquisition costs, tend to purchase more products or services, and frequently try out new products. For any corporation, a growing number of loyal customers will tend to lower operating costs. And, loyal customers provide referrals.

In the competitive e-commerce marketplace, customer retention (that often-talked-about "stickiness" issue) is a critical success factor. For example, for every 20 online loan applications, the lender can expect one completed transaction. This chapter illustrates how online and offline customer loyalty is achieved by knowing the unique needs of your company's customers. Once you identify your customers, you can develop and use models (similar to those detailed in this book) that will strengthen the customer loyalty bond. Moreover, you need to focus on your "best" customers, that is, customers who contribute the most to your company's profitability. This highlights the fact that not all customers are the same and that it is important to meet the unique needs of your various customers. Fredrick Reichheld (1996) sums up the benefits of customer loyalty by saying: "Consistently high retention can create tremendous competitive advantage, boost employee morale, produce unexpected bonuses in productivity and growth, and even reduce the cost of capital."

UNDERSTANDING THE IMPORTANCE OF CUSTOMER LOYALTY

To remain competitive in this complex, global environment, companies must develop a customer-centric approach, which is key to creating customer loyalty and retention. A customer-centric approach is important to your company's bottom line, especially if your competitors are perceived by customers as being equal to your company. The following will quickly illustrate the power of loyalty-based management as a highly profitable alternative to business as usual:

- In many industries, one of the largest costs is attracting new customers.
- It costs four to six times more for an organization to attract a new customer than to retain one.
- There is a very strong correlation between high customer retention rates and sustainable high profits.
- Regardless of whether your firm is a traditional company (brick-and-mortar), a combination company (click-and-mortar), or a Web-based company (dot-com), when customers say they are satisfied, there is no statistical correlation that says they will remain loyal to the company. Mere customer satisfaction is not enough.
- Referred customers have on average a 25 percent higher retention rate within the first three years than customers who come from any other source.

- Reducing customer defections by as little as 2 percent is often equivalent to cutting costs by over 10 percent.
- Customer retention, not sales volume, market share, or being the low-cost supplier (e.g., Wal-Mart) is frequently the only factor that correlates to long-term profitability.
- For many companies, sustaining a 5 percent improvement in the organization's customer retention rate can nearly double profits in five years.

THE ECONOMICS OF CUSTOMER LOYALTY

Fredrick Reichheld (1996) reports that U.S. companies lose half of their customers every five years. He goes on to declare that this loss stunts corporate growth by as much as 35 percent. No company can afford to give their customers away, especially in today's environment of intensified competition due to globalization of the economy, little or no growth in the total base of potential customers, and the high cost of acquiring new customers.

According to Reichheld, many companies can boost profits by as much as 100 percent by retaining just 5 percent of their customers. So, unless you are willing to radically rethink how your enterprise interacts with its constituents, you may be in danger of giving your customers to the competition. It's to your advantage to begin to focus on the need to make customer loyalty more convenient than customer disloyalty.

For e-corporations, the economics of customer loyalty cannot be ignored. According to Sean Dugan (2000), the cost of acquiring an online customer, depending on the industry, ranges from $30 to $90. This is a high cost for getting a user to visit your Web site to make that first purchase. However, recent research by Primix Solutions indicates that the average newly online customer spends $187. If the company's customer acquisition cost is $40, and the company's gross margin is 20 percent, then the company is spending $40 to acquire $37 in business. This isn't a very good business model. However, if the customer comes back just one time, the situation is reversed and any repeat purchases promote more profits.

FIGURE 1.1   Relationship Impact

Relationship Impact	Low Service	High Service
Sales	8%	16%
Market Share	<3%>	8%
Return on Equity (ROE)	5%	30%
Return on Sales (ROS)	1%	11%

Source: Adapted from PIMS Strategic Planning Institute, Cambridge, Mass.

SOURCES OF CUSTOMER LOYALTY

Customer loyalty is developed over time. It comes from a series of favorable customer experiences that increase the consumer's comfort level, trust, and allegiance. *Customer loyalty* can be defined as the customer's belief that your company is the one to go to first for products they already use and for other products they may need in the future. Companies that offer a high level of customer service often have a high level of customer loyalty. Figure 1.1 compares some of the key financial ratios of companies with high and low customer levels of service. The PIMS study shows that companies with high levels of customer service enjoy:

- Double the sales growth of low service companies
- Positive market share growth
- Six times the return on equity
- Five times the advantage in return on sales

Note: PIMS (Profit Impact of Market Strategy) is designed to measure the relationship between business actions and business results. PIMS is frequently used by senior executives, taught in business schools, and used in academic studies. It was originally the result of a large-scale study developed for the General Electric Company in the mid-1960s that was expanded in the early 1970s by the Management Science Institute of Harvard. Since 1975, the Strategic Planning Institute of Cambridge, Massachusetts, has continued the development and application of PIMS.

THE PATH TO CUSTOMER LOYALTY

Studies by Jupiter Communications (www.jupitercom.com), an Internet research firm, indicate that online customer loyalty is often based on customer service. Survey results show that 72 percent of online consumers say customer service is critical to them. Although no comprehensive solution currently exists, Jupiter analysis shows that there is a compelling rationale to justify using technology to handle presales product inquiries, after-sale first-level support, and general Web site service requests. For example, Web sites generating more than 15,000 service incidents per month should consider implementing chatter bots (small computer programs that "talk" with customers) and systems for the auto-response of e-mail (see Chapter 10).

The implementation of these and other online capabilities can lead to a high level of customer service, which can lead to customer satisfaction. But remember, even satisfied customers can defect. Your organization needs a strategy that does more than target satisfaction and corporation efficiency. In a Gartner Group (www.gartner.com) trade press release, Dr. Harry Hoyle, vice president for Dataquest's The Interactive Home: Technology & Infrastructure U.S. program, said, "The primary key to overall consumer satisfaction with online purchasing to date is the ease of placing orders or reservations. Clearly this is critical to the future of e-commerce, for when an online experience is consistently more satisfactory than in the physical world, and at the same or lower price, consumers' habits are likely to change permanently. But it is crucial to remember there is no second chance to win customer loyalty." In other words, e-corporations that are committed to building and sustaining unbreakable loyal relationships over the customer's lifetime must be committed to delivering stellar customer service, even if it can't be seen immediately on the firm's profit-and-loss statement.

Consumers use certain products and services regularly; for example, gas stations provide automobile servicing and repairs. However, some consumers drive past the nearest gas station to take their cars to automobile dealerships for regular maintenance. In the grocery store, consumers regularly purchase the same brand of peanut butter and jelly (it may even be the brand their mothers used). Some consumers drive several miles out of their way to shop at a favorite bookstore. What makes these individuals so loyal? Often the companies use a two-prong approach to customer loyalty that is based on customer and product differentiation:

Product Differentiation

- A superior product, often a product or service that is high quality, consistent, and attractively priced
- Product or service delivery that is on time and within budget
- A "fix it now, talk about it later" policy.

Customer Differentiation

- Consistency and reliability
- Generosity of spirit (e.g., liberal return policies)
- Personalized services
- Each customer cherished and appreciated

The Importance of Customer Differentiation

Customer differentiation requires you to know the customer. This involves being familiar with each customer's uniqueness and includes an understanding of what makes one customer different from another. "Knowing thy customer" is vital to creating customer loyalty. In identifying your customer's uniqueness, attempt to:

- Identify inherently loyal customer segments, such as the mature market or certain affinity groups.
- Pinpoint marketing opportunities across various customer segments.
- Measure customer profitability, sometimes called customer value (detailed in Chapter 2).
- Develop pricing and delivery strategies that drive marginally profitable and unprofitable customers toward profitability (and loyalty).

This "know thy customer" approach is necessary for value-added marketing, a key component of customer loyalty. Knowing the customer allows you to offer special prices to specific groups, based on their value to your company. For successful loyalty programs (ones that offer rewards or price discounts), you need to know which customers require or deserve loyalty program membership.

Additionally, knowing the customer allows targeted marketing: The more information the company has, the easier it is to offer personalized care that translates into customer loyalty. However, this doesn't mean that each customer is treated the same. In fact, each customer should be treated according to his or her individual characteristics, needs, wants, and desires. This, in turn, increases the value of each customer.

Product Differentiation

Value-added marketing is a customer-centric strategy with the goal of offering a set of customer benefits and services that meet and exceed the customer segment group's expectations. The importance of value-added marketing cannot be underestimated. Group EFO, a research firm located in Weston, Connecticut, states that in 1992, 83 percent of new products failed to clear the performance hurdles set by their developers. This costly error was likely due to the company not knowing the unique needs of their customers.

Once customer needs are identified, they must be met with appealing products. An appealing product has the right mixture of financial and nonfinancial benefits. In any industry, new value-added products or services are often the cornerstone of a successful customer loyalty program. The following are a few examples of online value-added products that are personalized for individual use:

- *Simple products and services.* Individual Inc. (www.individual.com) is an online newspaper clipping service that delivers news by whatever method the client has chosen when the client selects from a wide variety of categories.
- *Complex products and services.* Most individuals do not want to work their way through thousands of design options. Therefore, Anderson Corporation (www.andersonwindows.com), a window manufacturer located in Bayport, Minnesota, collaborates with customers in custom-designing products. The resulting database of window configurations helps Anderson understand how its business is performing.
- *Big-ticket items.* Autoweb (www.autoweb.com) refers buyers to dealers, and CarsDirect (www.carsdirect.com) sells cars to consumers.

Recently, the two companies launched a cobranded service that lets customers get just what they want. The collaboration of the two business models cuts out auto dealers and allows consumers to purchase cars they want online and not the cars "offered" by dealerships. The profitability of this partnership is not limited to the original purchase. A car buyer, over his or her lifetime, can generate thousands of dollars of business (financing, service, and referrals) as well as repeat purchases.

- *Digitizable products and services.* Yahoo! recently launched Yahoo! Photos (photos.yahoo.com), the result of a partnership with Shutterfly (www.shutterfly.com), the all-digital online photo service chaired by Jim Clark, founder of Silicon Graphics and Netscape Communications. Visitors to the site are able to upload, store, and share digital images as well as develop digital film and receive prints with color and sharpness enhanced by Shutterfly's VividPics technology. High-quality digital prints are an individualized, value-added service that may soon become a standard offering of integrated online photo services. However, at the time of this writing, Yahoo! Photos is the only game in town.

- *Online services.* Medmarket.com (www.medmarket.com) is a total e-business solution that precisely targets all aspects of the medical and health care industries. Medmarket.com has created the new medium for offering the medical community the most comprehensive site online for conducting business-to-business transactions as well as providing consumer/end-user opportunities. Medmarket services include an online product guide that showcases the newest and most advanced medical products; the latest in regulatory affairs information and listings of the services available from regulatory affairs, quality assurance, and clinical services firms; and the practice management area that serves traditional medicine and clinical environments by presenting product and service information that is of interest to medical professionals.

- *Luxury and specialty products.* Coldwell Banker (www.coldwellbanker .com) shows they are not your ordinary Realtors by providing online assistance for consumers interested in purchasing a second home. Coldwell Banker offers a book titled *Road Map to your Vacation Prop-*

erty Dreams and has developed the Resort Property Network for vacation properties. At Coldwell Banker's Resort Properties Web page, select one or more of the vacation market types (Lake & Stream, Ocean & Shoreline, Mountain, or Desert) that may interest you. Next, select the vacation market (by state) and the property price range that matched your budget. Coldwell Banker also offers time-share vacation properties.

A good example of a company offering specialty products is Gay Pharmacy.com (www.gaypharmacy.com), an online drugstore that offers over 30,000 products. GayPharmacy.com combines high-quality online service and guaranteed complete privacy for the lesbian, gay, bisexual, and transgender communities.

- *Retailing services.* America Online (AOL), located at <www.aol.com>, and Sears, Roebuck and Co. (www.sears.com) have a marketing alliance. In Sears's 858 department stores, customers can use a version of AOL's software to realize a futuristic vision of smart appliances and the "connected" home. AOL includes Sears on its Web sites for viewing by its more than 20 million subscribers.

THE CUSTOMER VALUATION FEEDBACK MODEL

According to Reichheld (1996), today's accounting methodology does not identify the value of customer relationships. Customer relationships are your firm's most valued asset; however, not all customers are created equal. The customer valuation strategy considers more than customer retention or customer profitability. Customer value represents the optimal economic return that can be anticipated from each customer over the lifetime of that customer's corporate patronage. Figure 1.2 illustrates the components used to evaluate customer value. This approach can show management that customers previously considered to have low or no value may be ranked as highly valued due to unanticipated bonuses. In other words, using a customer valuation approach provides a different understanding of market segmentation.

FIGURE 1.2   Customer Valuation Feedback Model

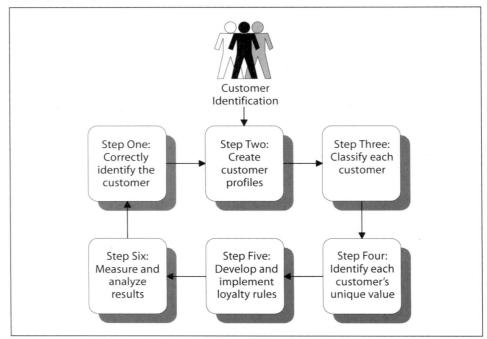

Source: Adapted from Todd Cotton, "Evolutionary Fusion: A Customer Oriented Incremental Life Cycle for Fusion," *Hewlett-Packard Journal* 47, 1 August 1996.

Figure 1.2 shows the six steps used in the customer valuation feedback system. Each step in this reiterative process can assist you in increasing customer loyalty and profitability:

Step 1. *Correctly identify the customer.* For many companies, this is not an easy task. For example, if your company sells parts to a manufacturer, is the manufacturer the customer or is the manufacturer's customer the end customer?

Step 2. *Profile each customer.* The customer valuation model is used to determine the profile of each customer's potential value.

Step 3. *Classify customer.* Sort customers based on their potential value to your company.

Step 4. *Identify what makes each customer different.* Spot what is the unique situation of a customer at any point in time.

Step 5. *Define and implement your company's loyalty rules.* Create rules that prescribe the actions to be taken when these unique circumstances have been identified.

Step 6. *Measure and analyze the outcomes.* Track customer response to advertising campaigns and special promotions.

When all six steps are completed, make the appropriate adjustments and create a customer profile again. Start the customer valuation process again by identifying customers.

Using a reiterative feedback system is vital to fine-tuning the customer value model and to controlling risks. For example, breaking the customer base into segments (a company can have hundreds of customer segments) can assist sales and marketing personnel in managing customer relationships in cost-effective and profitable ways. Additionally, when "grading" customers, look at three factors: (1) actual revenue, (2) potential incremental revenue, and (3) the probability of achieving the increment. Based on the customer's profile, you can:

- Develop a cost-effective program for customer contacts.
- Sort customers by profitability and risk of defection.
- Understand the unique needs of your customers.
- Invest in individual customers based on their customer value.

The results of the customer valuation model may indicate that a certain customer or group of customers is more profitable than expected. On the other hand, results may show mixed success, indicating that your firm is not delivering the unique value-added products you think it is. Careful analysis of the customer valuation model can show how your company should change its marketing approach or loyalty program.

E-COMMERCE IS BOOMING

American businesses are learning that market share, service quality, and customer empowerment do not guarantee a winning hand. The new key to success is customer loyalty, when linked to value and profits. This means that for your business to be successful today and tomorrow, you must be a customer-centric enterprise that uses e-business and customer relationship management (CRM) technologies. This new approach is called electronic customer relationship management (eCRM). Thus, *eCRM* can be defined as leveraging the Internet to develop, nurture, and manage multiple relationships, including customers, partners, and suppliers. This represents a shift from a focus on customer service (often considered a cost center) to a focus on customer relationships (a profit center).

The difference between customer service and CRM can be summarized as follows: customer service is usually a reactive function with a goal of efficiency, and CRM is a series of continuous customer interactions with the goal of increasing a customer's long-term value to your organization and developing and retaining customers through increased satisfaction and loyalty.

The traditional focus of CRM is managing and increasing the customer value by building business-to-customer relationships, often on a one-to-one basis. This process tends to be costly because of the need to develop and implement cross-divisional communications to fulfill customer needs. A recent study by AMR Research, an independent research company, indicates how quickly American businesses are shifting to a customer-centric approach. The AMR study predicts the CRM market will reach $16.8 billion by 2003, with a compound growth rate of 49 percent from 1998 to 2003. In contrast, eCRM uses the Internet to integrate and simplify the CRM processes, which reduces operating costs while enhancing the customer experience, a key success factor to increasing customer loyalty.

Among other things, the eCRM process focuses on acquiring customers and retaining customers. According to Thomas Stewart (1995), the cost of acquiring a new customer is often five times more costly than retaining an existing customer. In fact, for many industries, developing existing customer relationships often has a bigger payoff than high-priced customer acquisition marketing campaigns. This illustrates how building customer

FIGURE 1.3   Overview of Electronic Customer Relationship Management (eCRM) Functions

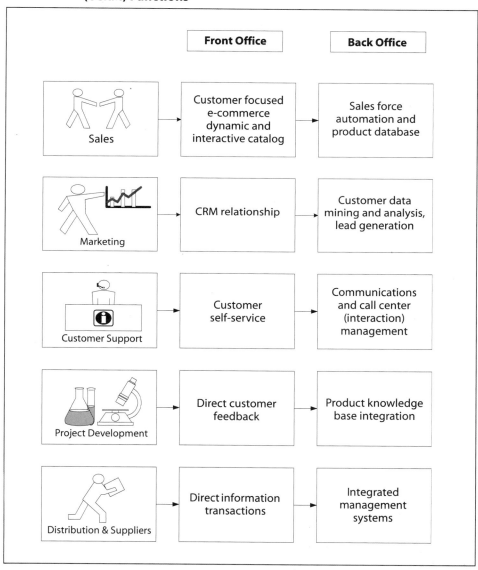

Source: Adapted from "e-Everything: Technology-Enabled Customer Relationship Management," copyright 1999 by Web Associates (wwwa.com).

loyalty is a profit center, not a cost center. Figure 1.3 shows an overview of how eCRM functions cut across major corporation divisions to maximize customer value.

Figure 1.3 shows the five primary corporate divisions (sales, marketing, customer service, research and development, and delivery and supply channels). Also shown are the eCRM functions for the front and back office. This eCRM matrix is designed to prevent divisional "silos" that can result in poor customer service and inventory stock-outs. To sum it up, Figure 1.3 illustrates how your business cannot rely on just one tactical strategy (such as customer service, reward programs, or data mining) to be successful. A true customer loyalty strategy must cut across the major corporate divisions and incorporate numerous tactics to accomplish its single purpose: Deliver a superior value proposition to individual customers.

DELIVERING SUPERIOR VALUE

It is very difficult to define superior value, but there is one thing that it isn't: It is not business as usual. In other words, you can market vanilla products and services under fancy new buzzword names using different types of mass media. The real way to deliver superior value (and to create customer loyalty) is to offer differentiated solutions one customer at a time. Harvard Business School's Michael E. Porter (1998) recently pointed out that the only sustainable competitive advantage comes from being different.

Considering customers as valuable assets to the organization is a relatively new approach. Developing customer value means focusing on customer relationships and understanding how to strengthen the loyalty bond, recognizing and acting on the customer's uniqueness, and developing benchmarks to estimate the potential value of the company's eCRM initiative. Creating real customer value involves a commitment to continually measure the results of the eCRM strategy.

Today, many companies, from diverse industries, are focusing on building customer loyalty with expectations of being rewarded by superior market share growth, good financial results, and long-term profitability. Internet-based CRM (eCRM) automates the CRM function and allows customers to interact with the company 24 hours a day, 7 days a week. Again the hurdle of integrating CRM functions across divisional lines comes into play. And, eCRM joins the functions of marketing, sales, customer service, the development of new projects, and delivery. With eCRM, the goal of creating and providing a seamless experience between different departments and business units is achievable and often cost effective. For example, with eCRM you can easily provide Web-based mass customization and loyalty marketing programs to bind your e-corporation and the consumer in a learning relationship. Over time, this ongoing relationship gets "smarter" as you and the consumer interact with each other. And, this allows you to collaborate with the customer to meet his or her unique needs.

Motorola provides a good case study of how an e-corporation uses Web-based loyalty marketing. At Motorola, the sales representative begins by working with the customer to design a pager that meets the customer's needs and preferences. The sales representative then electronically sends the specifications to the factory. Motorola's pager factory in Boynton Beach, Florida, builds pagers one customer at a time. From 29 million possible combinations, the factory manufactures the customer's customized pager within a few hours. Motorola uses mass customization to provide individually customized goods and services and a loyalty marketing approach that elicits information from each customer about his or her specific needs and preferences.

SUMMING IT UP

- Companies regularly lose half of their customers every five years. This statistic shows the need for managers to focus on the corporation's biggest asset: the customer.
- Customer loyalty is built over time. It is based on favorable customer experiences, trust, and allegiance. Companies that offer high levels of customer service often have a high degree of customer loyalty.
- You need to understand the unique needs of your customers and the customers' value to your organization. This way, your marketers can tailor customer loyalty programs that reward the right customers and drive up profits.

- An effective way to build customer loyalty is to use eCRM (electronic customer relationship management). With eCRM, you can leverage the Internet to develop cost-effective ways to cultivate and manage multiple relationships with customers, partners, and suppliers.

ACTION PLAN

DEVELOPING A CUSTOMER LOYALTY QUICK-START ACTION PLAN

Why do some customers sing the praises of a product or service and purchase it over and over again? Customer loyalty can give you a competitive edge. Focusing on customer value can assist your organization in targeting your "best" customers for special pricing and loyalty programs. This builds customer loyalty and increases corporate profits. Check out the following activity and get started on your customer loyalty action plan.

The following checklist provides a conceptual framework for converting raw data about transactions into two kinds of meaningful and useful information. First, what are the customers' current needs and how well are those needs being met? Second, what are the customers' emerging needs and how well is the company positioned to meet those needs?

Understanding How Customers Interact with the Company's Product or Service

✓ Why does the customer use the product or service?

✓ How does the customer use the product?

✓ What problem does the product or service solve for the customer?

✓ What additional or new problems does the product or service create?

✓ How can the product or service be easier to use?

✓ How can the product or service be expended to reduce this customer's problem?

Understanding the Customer's Values

✓ How does the customer define success?

✓ What does this customer see as its distinctive competence?

✓ What are this customer's problems?

✓ How can the company make this customer more successful?

✓ What does this customer value?

✓ What changes does this customer see coming in his or her environment?

Understanding the Customer Loyalty Bond

✓ How does this customer make his or her selection decision?

✓ How much of the total product budget does this customer spend with the company?

✓ What does the company have to do to increase their percentage of this customer's budget?

✓ How does the company compare to the competition?

✓ What does this customer see as the company's distinctive competence?

✓ Under what circumstances might the company lose this customer?

Source: Howard Butz, Jr., and Leonard D. Goodstein, "Measuring Customer Value: Gaining the Strategic Advantage," *Organizational Dynamics* 24 (1 January, 1996): 77-78.

REFERENCES

Butz, Howard E., Jr., and Leonard D. Goodstein. 1996. Measuring Customer Value: Gaining the Strategic Advantage. *Organizational Dynamics* 24 (1 January): 77-78.

Cotton, Todd. 1996. Evolutionary Fusion: A Customer-Oriented Incremental Life Cycle for Fusion. *Hewlett-Packard Journal* 47 (1 August): 25-39.

Dugan, Sean M. 2000. Opinions: Net Prophet: The Best Loyalty Program for Your Web Site May Be Better Customer Service. *InfoWorld* 22, 15 May.

Gartner Group's Dataquest Says 88 Percent of Consumers Rate Online Buying Satisfactory Despite Delivery and Customer Service Problems. 1999. *Business Wire,* 7 September.

Kerley, David, Lucas Graves, and Seamus McAteer. 1999. Automating Service: Reducing Supporting Costs Through Bots and Agents. *Jupiter Communications Vision Report* (www.jupitercomm.com), March.

Meltzer, Michael. 1998. Using the Data Warehouse to Drive Customer Retention, Development, and Profit. *NCR* (corporate publication): 4.

Porter, Michael E. 1998. *On Competition.* Boston: Harvard Business School Press.

Reichheld, Fredrick F. 1996. *The Loyalty Effect: The Hidden Force Behind Growth, Profits, and Lasting Value.* Boston: Harvard Business School Press.

Sales & Marketing: Once Again Know Thy Customer's Business. 1999. *The Network Journal,* 30 November, 23.

Stewart, Thomas. 1995. After All You've Done for Your Customers, Why Are They Still Not Happy? *Fortune,* 11 December, 180.

Thomas, Lynn. 1998. Customer Loyalty and Retention Primer. *Rough Notes* (www.rough notes.com/rnmag/february98/02p60.htm), September, 1.

2

The Challenges of eCRM

IN THIS CHAPTER

▼ Defining customer loyalty

▼ Focusing on the right customers

▼ Understanding your customers (not all customers are alike)

▼ Measuring lifetime value

▼ Recognizing traditional ways to build customer loyalty

▼ Building customer loyalty with Web site capabilities

This chapter begins by defining customer loyalty and by explaining the different types of customer loyalty. You'll discover how categories of customer loyalty can be affected by emotional, environmental, and governmental factors. Customer loyalty also varies from customer to customer and industry to industry. This chapter will show how it doesn't pay to expand certain types of customer loyalty, and how important it is for your company to focus on the right customers. Taking the time to differentiate customers can also lead to more profit and less marketing cost. Often companies are surprised at the wide range of "customer values." This chapter shows how you can determine a customer's lifetime value through collecting the proper data. At the completion of your review, you may be surprised to learn that as little as 20 percent of your customer base results in 100 percent of your firm's profits. These are the customers to focus on. I continue by exploring the traditional methods of building customer loyalty and conclude with a survey of the types of online capabilities your e-commerce firm needs for higher levels of customer satisfaction and higher rates of customer retention.

A company that is pursuing a policy of electronic customer relationship management (eCRM) has reporting systems that allow access to information for the corporation's marketing, sales, customer service and support, research and development, and fulfillment and delivery divisions. Executives now have to change how they manage the "visibility" of these divisions. For example, more and more customers use e-mail to contact various corporate divisions to make inquiries or complaints. Once the e-mail messages are sent, customers expect almost instant replies.

Customer expectations drive corporations to increase online capabilities to accommodate these requests and other needs. Customers have certain expectations about what type of response they expect from your company. Often this is an unrealistic requirement for instant gratification. However, in the e-commerce marketplace customers make the rules and companies must comply. This requires management to know their customers' needs, wants, and desires. Therefore, to build customer loyalty managers need to be constantly updated so they can accurately measure and analyze their company's responsiveness to customer commitments.

DEFINING CUSTOMER LOYALTY

According to a recent report by Deloitte Consultancy, customer loyalty is the critical driver of shareholder value around the world. Dictionaries often define *loyalty* as "the state of mind or an attitude in which the customer has a desire to purchase a product or service offer in preference to a competitor's alternative" or "loyalty is having or showing continued allegiance; faithful to one's country, government, brand, etc." This emotionally based definition takes into consideration the depth of customer loyalty. In general, the strength of each customer's loyalty varies from consumer to consumer and industry to industry.

In the business environment, loyalty can be defined as the consistency of customer behavior and further refined into the following seven categories of loyalty. This survey of loyalty classes shows the different types of customer loyalty and how some types of customer loyalty are more desirable than others.

Monopoly loyalty. No other choices exist. For example, due to government regulations there is only one supplier and no other alternatives. These are often low-attachment, high-repeat purchase consumers, because there are no other options.

- A utility company is a good example of monopoly loyalty.
- Many of Microsoft's (Microsoft.msn.com) products have monopoly loyalty. One customer describes himself as being a member of the "Bill Gates $100 a Month Club," because it seems to him that he has to upgrade his various Microsoft products at least once a month to remain current.

Inertia loyalty. The customer is not willing to seek alternative suppliers. These are low-attachment, high-repeat purchasers who feel little satisfaction with the company. These customers are easy pickings for competitors if they can demonstrate the benefits of switching to another company. Companies that have inertia loyalty need to focus on changing the customer's perception of the company by differentiating their products or services.

- A good example of inertia loyalty is a manufacturer who always orders a specialized part from the same vendor.
- Procurement officers demonstrate inertia loyalty when they always use a certain vendor because they are familiar with the ordering process.

Latent loyalty. With latent loyalty, consumers are low-attachment, low-repeat business customers. The customer wants to purchase the product or service but internal purchase policies or environmental factors may make it difficult to make repeat purchases.

- The customer wants to purchase from the vendor, but the vendor only offers free shipping if the customer makes a purchase of, let's say, $150 or more.
- The consumer wants to patronize the business but situational factors may result in low-repeat purchases. For example, a working couple frequently goes out to dinner. The wife likes Greek food, but the husband is a vegetarian and doesn't like Mediterranean food. Consequently, the couple only goes to restaurants that they can both enjoy. To exploit the couple's latent loyalty, the restaurant should offer a few American or vegetarian dishes.

Convenience loyalty. Customers have low attachment and make many repeat purchases. This type of loyalty is very similar to inertia loyalty. Again, convenience loyalty customers are easy pickings for the competition.

- Customers are repeat purchasers because a company is easier to deal with than others due to location.
- Let's say that the office manager of 20 years always handles the purchase of office supplies and, as a matter of habit, always orders from Staples (www.staples.com)—that's convenience loyalty.

Price loyalty. Price-conscious consumers evaluate alternative suppliers and are loyal to the retailer with the lowest price. These low-attachment, low-repeat customers are considered "no loyalty" consumers who cannot be developed into loyal customers.

- Companies that always use CompareNet (www.comparenet.com) or My Simon (www.mysimon.com) to purchase the lowest-priced HP Laser Jet printer cartridges are good examples of customers with price loyalty.
- Consumers who don't see the difference between types of facial tissues will always purchase the facial tissue with the lowest price.

Incentive loyalty. The company offers a loyalty reward program for consistent consumer behavior. This type of loyalty is similar to inertia loyalty, because consumers tend to be low-attachment, high-repeat purchasers. When the incentive is gone or used, the customer may move on to another company that has the same or better incentive program.

- Travelers who always select American Airlines (www.aa.com) because of the frequent-flyer program are showing incentive loyalty.
- Customers who always shop at one of the Safeway grocery stores because of the frequent shopper club are demonstrating incentive loyalty.

Premium loyalty. Typically, this is emotional or brand loyalty and often includes a high level of attachment and repeat purchases. For many businesses, this type of loyalty is the ultimate. Customers are very emotional about the benefits of the product or service. These customers are constantly talking about the benefits of a product or service and recommend it to others.

- A customer who takes his new Sony laptop computer to a friend's house and brags about the new features is demonstrating premium loyalty.
- Customers who want to purchase Nike shoes regardless of where they shop are demonstrating premium loyalty.
- A photography buff who always buys Kodak 35 mm film is showing premium loyalty when he disregards other kinds of Kodak films.

Anne Fisher, Wilton Woods, and Robert Steyer (1985) analyzed the customer loyalty of consumer products. At the time of the 1985 study, Bayer aspirin had the largest market share, and Tylenol had the most loyal customers. However, in 1997, the *Washington Times* reported that private-brand labels (Longs Drugs, CVS Drugs, Rexall Drugs, and so on) and Tylenol commanded the largest dollar market share of over-the-counter headache remedies, with Tylenol accounting for 23 percent of the market. Bayer ranked near the bottom with a 4 percent share of the market.

FOCUSING ON THE RIGHT CUSTOMERS

It is the customer who determines what is value added or not. And it is this value-added proposition that strengthens the loyalty bond. The best way to create a bond between you, the producer, and the customer is to exceed the customer's expectations. This creates the perception of added value and results in customers making repeat purchases and recommending your products or services to others. Consequently, to be successful your company needs the right customers and the right value-added proposition.

Today's customers want quality, price, performance, speed, convenience, and service. The combination of these factors is considered "value." High value correlates with high market share. Companies that offer high value build customer loyalty. Loyal customers make repeat purchases and more referrals. However, what customers value today can change tomorrow.

Not understanding what customers want or need can lead to disaster. In the past, some companies assumed that they knew what their customers wanted and failed to meet their emerging needs. A good example is the U.S. auto industry. When gasoline prices started to skyrocket in the 1970s, manufacturers failed to respond to the consumers' desire for smaller, more fuel-efficient cars. Foreign carmakers filled the void and staked a claim in market share.

NOT ALL CUSTOMERS ARE ALIKE

Knowing who your best customers are and who are the money losers can help you develop loyalty marketing strategies that will increase customer profitability. This means asking the right questions and translating raw data into actions. On the simplest level, you need to know:

- Who are your current customers?
- How are they segmented into different loyalty categories?
- What is the customer's purchasing volume?
- What is the growth rate of customer purchases?
- What is the duration of the customer relationship?
- How profitable has this relationship been?

Answers to these questions may show that a small percentage of the customer base provides the largest profits. For example, at British Airways about 35 percent of the customers provide 65 percent of the company's profits. At Banc One of Columbus, Ohio, the top 10 percent of its customers provided all of the bank's profits, and 80 percent of the bank's customers were money losers.

Although this information may be relatively easy to gain, other factors also affect customer loyalty. For example, customer knowledge collected in this process can be used to create a sense that your organization knows its customers. Today, many customers believe an organization may know something about them—their checkbook balance or their purchase history, for example. However, most customers desire some continuity in their relationship with an organization every time they move from one division to another.

Gathering this basic data may be time consuming, but the rewards in profitability and marketing cost savings can be huge. For instance, Texas Nameplate (www.nameplate.com) identified its top customers and implemented a program to visit these customers at least once a year to discover what the company could do better or differently. The strategy paid off, and Texas Nameplate's gross margins rose from around 50 percent in 1994 to 59 percent in 1998. The company's net margins doubled as well. Additionally, Texas Nameplate's market share grew both regionally and nationally.

Knowing the unique habits and needs of your top or prime customers can assist you in defining how you will seek the next round of prospects, and you won't waste time and money on the wrong prospects. A qualified prospect must match several of the habits and characteristics of your best customers. Turning these prospects into first-time customers and lifetime online customers is the primary objective of the e-corporation. Jeff Sweat (2000) notes that to achieve this goal, companies often have to combine a number of customer relationship management tools. For example, Chipshot.com (www.chipshot.com), a new online golf retailer, implemented an e-mail automatic response system by Kana (www.kana.com), uses Synchrony's (www.synchrony.com) customer service software, and is personalizing the Web site with BroadVision software (www.broadvision.com). Synchrony is helping Chipshot.com tie its CRM applications with its call center. In this way, the call center can see all interactions between the company and the customer. (For more information about automatic e-mail response systems and call centers, see Chapters 10 and 12, respectively.)

MEASURING LIFETIME VALUE

Understanding the differences in your firm's customer base is key to measuring customer loyalty. When customer loyalty is evaluated in this way, it is sometimes called *measuring customer value* or *the lifetime value* (LTV) of the customer. FISI-Madison Financial Marketing, a subsidiary of the Cendant Corporation, evaluates the lifetime value of bank customers by looking at:

- Average deposits, less reserves
- Interest rates paid
- Income from monthly service charges, fall-below minimum deposit fees, and not-sufficient funds fees
- Account opening and closing costs
- Annual variable operating costs, including FDIC insurance fees and value-added benefits
- Retention rate or average account life

The information listed above is used to calculate cash flows and to determine which customers offer the bank the most profit. The total is then discounted by the bank's required rate of return to today's dollars, which provides the net present value (NPV) of the customer's relationship with the bank. (The required rate of return is often equal to the return on an investment with a small amount of risk.) Next, marketing and customer acquisition costs are deducted from the NPV. See the two examples in Figure 2.1. These simplified examples from FISI-Madison show how measuring the lifetime value of customers can assist you in planning customer acquisition campaigns. (For a more detailed explanation of calculating the lifetime value of customer relationships, see Chapter 14.)

FIGURE 2.1   FISI-Madison's Examples of How to Calculate Lifetime Value

---

Example #1: Let's say that John Doe opens new checking and savings accounts at the bank. Using the information listed above and the present value tables, if John stays with the bank for two years, his lifetime customer value is $55 based on the cash flow analysis of the items listed earlier in this chapter. In other words, the NPV of John Doe's account is $69 less $14 in marketing costs ($69 –$14 = $55). However, if John stays with the bank for eight years, his lifetime value rises to $284.

Example #2: Suppose the marketing department wants to implement a direct marketing campaign to attract 600 new checking, savings, and CD account holders. The database provides the following information:

Account Type	Year Open	Account Life	Present Value
Checking	1	6	($ 3)
Savings	2	4	$140
CDs	3	2	$ 44
		Total	$181

The marketing campaign is expected to cost $30,000 or $50 per new account holder ($30,000 ÷ 600 = $50). To decide if the marketing plan is profitable, deduct $50 from the customer's expected NPV ($181 – $50 = $131). In this case, the resulting lifetime value is $131, indicating that the planned marketing project is profitable and a "go."

Source: Adapted from FISI-Madison (www.fisi-madison.com/pa/strategiest/mlvoac.htm), 20 March 2000.

TRADITIONAL WAYS TO BUILD CUSTOMER LOYALTY

Industry leaders understand that measuring improvements in product attributes, quality, and service is not enough. The result is a focus on customer satisfaction, but customer satisfaction alone is not enough. Satisfied customers often switch to other companies. It doesn't pay to have satisfied customers, it pays to have loyal ones. In the past, the rules for building customer loyalty were clear. Dividing the corporation into the five major divisions (discussed in Chapter 1) shows how each major corporate division in a traditional (brick-and-mortar) business can assist the firm in developing customer loyalty.

Offline Sales

- Offer a guarantee.
- Communicate with customers regularly.
- Be enthusiastic.
- Create fun and excitement.
- Show customers how to save money.
- Seek customer feedback early and respond quickly.
- Offer new customer promotions.

Offline Marketing

- Offer helpful suggestions.
- Publish FAQ answers.
- Say "thank you" in many ways.
- Hold a customer appreciation day.
- Recognize long-term customers.
- Personalize all company-to-customer communications.

Offline Customer Support and Service

- Make realistic promises.
- Listen to the customer.
- Respond promptly.
- Answer all telephone calls.
- Use excellent telephone etiquette.
- After the sale, send information that details how to use the product.
- Show customers your full range of products and services.

Offline Project Development and Management

- Make it easy to do business with you.
- Make your business look unique.

- Make on-the-spot decisions.
- Introduce something new.
- Use a value-added strategy.
- Build up a customer database and use it to develop customer relationships.
- Develop clubs (or something similar) to make repeat purchases into a service.
- Develop value-added promotions (get the product or service and something more).

Offline Distribution and Suppliers

- Make invoices simple.
- Ship promptly.
- Don't bill credit cards until the merchandise is shipped.

ONLINE CAPABILITIES FOR BUILDING CUSTOMER LOYALTY

Gaining and holding customer loyalty is the key competitive advantage in the e-commerce marketplace. According to Bob Wayland, a vice president with Mercer Management Consulting: "The paradigm has shifted. Products come and go. The unit of value today is the customer relationship." In this new e-commerce economy, there is one unbreakable rule for implementing eCRM systems: The more complex the business, the more difficult and expensive to implement. However, once the system is deployed, an eCRM service delivers low dollar cost customer transactions, provides low-cost marketing research, serves customers automatically, and automates the fulfillment and delivery process.

Individualized online services result in better customer experiences and greater rates of customer retention. With more technology, you are able to increase customer "touch" and know individual customer preferences and behaviors. Virtual service representatives (VSRs) can bring individualized customer service. With VSRs, your company can bring the best personal information that is relevant, helpful, and meaningful to a customer in a way that hasn't been so readily available before. Companies that have this type of capability (and other related online capabilities) can build competitive advantages with electronic customer relationship management (eCRM). Just as loyalty varies from industry to industry, the value of these online capabilities also varies. One thing remains the same: Your online company needs to treat different customers differently to ensure customer loyalty. With eCRM technologies, you can easily differentiate customers and gain a real knowledge of each customer's unique behaviors, needs, and desires.

Figure 2.2 shows how online capabilities relate to the major divisions of an enterprise. Each of the online capabilities shown can assist you in enhancing customer experiences to strengthen the bonds of customer loyalty.

Online Sales

- *Persuade users to register.* You can persuade consumers to provide personal information through a variety of means, including registration pages that allow access to higher-quality information or specific data and online contests. (For details and examples, see Chapter 6.)
- *Recognize users and call them by name.* Many Web sites use data from a customer's registration, "cookies," or other small programs to recognize returning customers with a personalized greeting. (For more information and examples, see Chapter 6.)
- *Different interfaces for different demographic groups.* Offer customers personalized promotions, bargains, or discount coupons for repeat purchasers. (For details and examples, see Chapter 8.)
- *Personalized content.* Content can be customized according to products the user has purchased or specified. (For details and examples, see Chapter 8.)
- *Users decide how to respond.* Users can decide when and how they receive and respond to sales information. (For details and examples, see Chapter 8.)
- *Customizable Web experience.* Users can customize the home page of your Web site, so they see the information that matters to them first.

FIGURE 2.2 Overview of Corporate Divisions and Online Capabilities

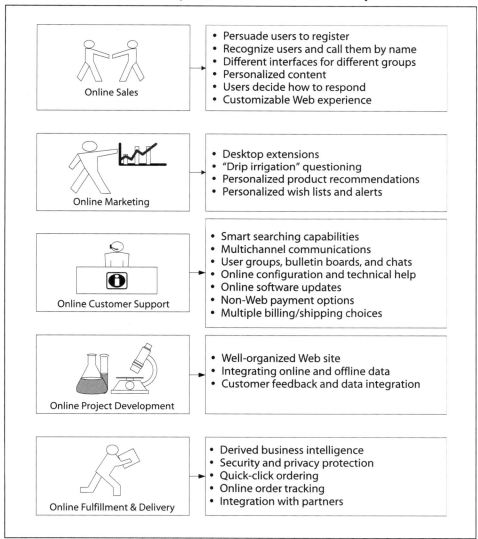

The layout of the information can be customized as well. (For more information and examples, see Chapter 8.)

Online Marketing

- *Desktop extensions.* Depending on the permission allowed by the end-user, a desktop extension could provide additional data about user preferences and activities. This intelligence is then used for detailed customer profiling. (For details and examples, see Chapters 8 and 11.)
- *"Drip irrigation" questioning.* Recognize that customers do not like to complete long user surveys. Therefore, present consumers with limited questions as they progress through the Web site. Each piece of data is gathered to provide a meaningful customer profile. (For more information and examples, see Chapter 8.)
- *Personalized product recommendations.* Keep track of what the consumer purchased and make recommendations of similar items that the customer may be interested in purchasing. For example, let's say a customer purchased a book several months ago and the author has a new release. When that customer revisits the Web site, the new title may be recommended. (For more information and examples, see Chapter 10.)
- *Personalized wish lists and alerts.* If a customer is seeking a book that is out of print or a dress that is currently out of stock, he or she can create a "wish list" that alerts the customer when the item is available. (For more details and examples, see Chapter 6.)

Online Customer Service and Support

- *Smart searching capabilities.* Allows keyword searches, multivariable searches, and searches for products or for solving problems. This allows personalized searching and step-by-step customization for products that have lots of options or require custom quotations. (For more information and examples, see Chapter 8.)
- *Multichannel communications.* Customers can reach your company via e-mail, fax, and telephone. E-mail messages are promptly responded to using individuals or automatic responders, which often use artificial intelligence. (For more information, see Chapter 10.)

- *User groups, bulletin boards, and chats.* Many Web sites build community (and customer loyalty) by offering user groups, message boards, special events, or forums. Some Web sites allow three-way communications between the customer and the company and among customers themselves via a multilanguage bulletin board. (For details, see Chapters 5 and 6.)

- *Online configuration and technical help.* Online product configuration support includes support guides and interactive questionnaires that help customers quickly solve product or software problems and return to productivity. Online technical help provides self- and auto-diagnoses, in addition to providing in-context help information that empowers customers to solve their own problems. (For more information and examples, see Chapter 9.)

- *Online software updates.* You can provide automatic software updating and direct interaction through connected devices, such as the Web site and the desktop. With the end-user's permission (for details, see Chapter 11), information can be automatically sent to a user's desktop application without the user needing to instigate the action. This allows you to update software transparently. (For more information and details, see Chapter 9.)

- *Non-Web payment options.* Offer different ways to pay, so customers do not have to send credit card information into cyberspace. For example, credit card information can be faxed, sent in two separate e-mails, or posted using the U.S. mail. (For details and examples, see Chapter 11.)

- *Multiple billing/shipping choices.* Accommodate customers who have special invoicing instructions or several delivery times and places. (For more information and details, see Chapter 11.)

Online Project Development

- *Well-organized Web site.* A well-organized, interactive Web site can provide new sales opportunities by providing insights into customer behavior. Many Web sites are organized around what the customer needs or wants to see first. The organization can be based on some type of market segmentation (small business owner versus large business), so that customers feel that their needs are being understood. (For more information, see Chapter 10.)

- *Integrating online and offline data.* Allows customers to get answers to questions about their personal situations. For example, let's say a customer sends a free-form e-mail to his mortgage lender in which he provides his Social Security number, wants to know the pay-off amount of his mortgage, and asks if the mortgage lender can beat a certain interest rate. The lender automatically reads the e-mail message, accesses several databases, and replies to the customer without human intervention. (For more information, see Chapter 10.)

- *Customer feedback and data integration.* Includes Web site feedback forms, desktop message inquiries, and yes/no questions following sales transactions and support activities. Feedback is combined with other marketing research and analyzed to continually improve online services. Forward-thinking businesses incorporate data from many corporate divisions into the customer's online experience. Many companies provide personalized Web pages called corporate portals that allow customers to access information and communicate via e-mail with the company. (For more information and examples, see Chapter 10.)

Online Fulfillment and Delivery

- *Derived business intelligence.* Combine the preferences and interactions of similar customers, then make customer recommendations based on the analysis. The more information you have in the database about the customer, the higher quality the recommendation. (For more information and examples, see Chapter 13.)

- *Security and privacy protection.* Top-rated Web sites often have prominent security and privacy statements to reassure customers how their information is being handled. Companies often outsource their automated back-office operations to third parties. These companies frequently handle charge cards, credit approvals, and other parts of transactions. Some companies hire a third-party program to assure customers about the use of their data. (For more information and examples, see Chapter 11.)

- *Quick-click ordering.* Retains the customer's credit card information, shipping address, and delivery instructions. (For more information, see Chapter 10.)
- *Online order tracking.* This methodology allows customers to view their order history online and to track online orders. (For more information and examples, see Chapter 10.)

SUMMING IT UP

- The proper management of your company's multiple customer relationships builds customer loyalty. The level of customer loyalty will often dictate the profitability of your enterprise.
- How your company backs up its commitments frequently determines whether the customers will remain loyal or switch. After all, customers are only a click away from defecting to another company.
- Customer loyalty comes in many shapes and sizes. Knowing what category customers are in can assist in fine-tuning the process of products and services to create added value. Added value is the cornerstone of repeat purchases.
- Not all customers are equal. Knowing which customers are "best" and which are "worst" can help you develop loyalty strategies that will increase profitability.
- There are easy-to-use methodologies for determining the lifetime value (LTV) of a customer. The measurement of customer value can assist the company in reducing marketing costs.
- There are many traditional ways to build customer loyalty. Building customer loyalty online requires a different set of capabilities.

WHAT COMPANY ASSETS CAN BE TURNED INTO E-SERVICES ON THE INTERNET?

To take full advantage of the new e-services, you need to look at your organization from a different perspective. Often, a 180-degree change of view is not enough, but looking at the company through a different lens can make all the difference. Answering the simple set of core questions in this action plan is the first step in that direction and the beginning of even the most ambitious e-corporation effort. The information from this activity may indicate that your company's transition does not have to be complicated or radical.

Answers to the following core questions provide an analysis of the company's true assets.

I. What does the company own today that could be turned into an Internet-based service tomorrow?

1. Our products or services?

   _____

   _____

2. Our people's know-how? Our franchises? Our customer database?

   _____

   _____

3. Our libraries? Our storage network?

   _____

   _____

4. Our customer service abilities? Our world-class billing process?

_____

_____

5. What are our hidden strengths?

_____

_____

6. What are our core competencies?

_____

_____

7. What are our hidden assets?

_____

_____

II. Can we add e-services on top of our current products and services?

In our business, how can we turn a one-time sale into an e-service annuity revenue? (Hint: If we were Ford, we'd try to sell e-services along with every car we sold. If we were Sony, we would sell e-services for music fanatics with every Walkman.)

_____

_____

_____

_____

_____

_____

Source: Adapted from "An E-Services Strategy Book: The Internet Chapter 2," corporate publication of _Hewlett-Packard,_ 19 May 1999 (www.hp.com).

REFERENCES

e-Business System Requirements. 1999. Corporate publication of Webridge (www.web ridge.com).

e-Everything: Technology-Enabled Customer Relationship Management. 1999. Corporate publication of Web Associates (wwwa.com).

An E-Services Strategy Book: The Internet Chapter 2. 1999. Corporate publication of Hewlett-Packard, 19 May (www.hp.com).

Evaluating the Sticky Factor of E-Commerce Sites. 1999. Corporate publication of Rubric Enterprise Marketing Association, 30 June (www.rubricsoft.com).

Fisher, Anne B., Wilton Woods, and Robert Steyer. 1985. Selling: Coke's Brand-Loyalty Lesson. *Fortune,* 5 August, 44-55.

Graham, John R., 2000. 27 Ways to Strengthen Customer Loyalty. Online publication of Graham Communications (www.smartbiz.com/sbs/arts/jrg1.htm), 18 May.

Griffin, Jill. 1995. *Customer Loyalty: How to Earn It, How to Keep It.* New York: Simon & Schuster.

Gromley, J. Thomas, III, Stan Dolber, Stephen J. Cole, Hayle Chun, and Jason Gatoff. 1999. The Demise of CRM. *The Forrester Research Report,* June, 1-14.

Hurst, Mark. 1999. Holiday '99 E-Commerce: Bridging the $6 Billion Customer Experience Gap. Corporate publication of Creative Good, September (www.creativegood.com).

Hurst, Mark, and Emily Gellady. 1999. White Paper One: Building a Great Customer Experience to Develop Brand, Increase Loyalty and Grow Revenues. Corporate publication of Creative Good, September (www.creativegood.com).

Smith, Wes. 1999. Frontier: Digital Manager: Winning Is Everything. *Business Week* 3626 (26 April): F22-34.

Sweat, Jeff. 2000. Customer Knowledge: Vendors Lend a Hand to Integrate Systems. *Information Week,* 10 April, 56.

Making the Transition to the Internet Age

If your company is not on the Internet, it may be starting late. Technology allows every consumer to access the Internet with Web TV, a Palm Pilot, a cellular telephone, and other devices that are yet to be invented or released. Wireless Internet access is available in some parts of the nation and will become more widely used in a year or two. Consumers can complete online transactions anytime, anyplace, and just about anywhere they want. E-corporations that focus on customer loyalty can create long-term, profitable relationships with online customers by making every transaction more valuable to each individual consumer and assisting the customer up the learning curve to complete online transactions more effectively and efficiently.

This added value builds customer loyalty and drives e-corporation profits. However, transitioning to the Internet can be a risky proposition, if it is not done correctly. If you want to cash in on escalating e-commerce profits, you must be ready to change every division, every product, and every function in your organization. Once the new system is deployed, your company should be prepared to be in a constant state of development to remain competitive.

E-COMMERCE THREATS AND OPPORTUNITIES

In the grand scheme of things, every enterprise will be targeting the same customers. Company products will have to offer real performance advantages and flawless customer service. Customers will be given (in an entertaining way) the information needed to make knowledgeable purchasing decisions. Efficiency and low prices will not hold customers. Web sites that offer personalized "touch" features and are consumer-friendly will thrive. For example, early entrants like American Airlines (www.aa.com) have created barriers through branding long-term relationships. The American Airlines Web site creates a customized home page and provides an extensive consumer profile for each user. This profile includes flying habits, information about the consumer's frequent-flyer program, and data about any special needs. Consequently, customers return again and again because they don't have to set up another user profile.

American Airlines and others show how the Internet fundamentally changes the relationship of supplier and consumer. For example, car shoppers are now arming themselves with online knowledge about dealer costs and manufacturer/dealer rebates before showing up at a dealership. These knowledgeable consumers are forcing dealerships to change how they interact with their customers. In the future, the Internet will continue to affect offline customer interactions.

How companies interact with customers online is fundamentally changing customer expectations about convenience, speed, comparability, price, and service. For businesses, there is no other channel where revenues are growing as fast as on the Internet. For most companies, choosing not to have a presence on the Internet is tantamount to committing business suicide.

VISIONING THE E-CORPORATION

In the mid-1980s, James L. Heskett of the Harvard Business School developed a Strategic Service Vision based on four elements:

1. The service delivery system
2. The operating strategy
3. The service concept
4. The targeting of market segments

Heskett concluded that companies achieve high profitability by having either a "market focus" or an "operational focus," such as United Parcel Service's insistence that all packages it handles in its consumer and retail delivery service weigh less then 70 pounds and have a combined length and girth of 130 inches. According to Heskett, organizations that achieve both a market and operating focus are unbeatable. The Strategic Service Vision ties both marketing and operating functions together and assists in the value-cost leveraging situation, which results in increased profits.

The theoretical overview of the Strategic Service Vision is useful for strategic planning purposes for your company to transition to the Internet. The four relationships of the Strategic Service Vision can be adapted for the e-commerce environment in the following manner:

1. *The e-Service delivery system.* Management must envision what features are important to your e-business.
2. *The e-Operating strategy.* Management must determine what elements of the strategy are important and what results are expected. (For more information about online customer expectations, see the action plan at the end of this chapter.)
3. *The eCRM service concept.* Gain an understanding of what the customer perceives as a good online buying experience.
4. *The targeting of e-market segments.* Identify the various segments of the customer base and determine the importance of each segment.

This chapter focuses on laying the foundation for the e-Commerce Strategic Service Vision. The four elements of e-Commerce Strategic Vision are detailed in Chapter 14.

LAYING THE GROUNDWORK FOR A SUCCESSFUL TRANSITION

The key to building a successful e-corporation is to conceptualize the project as a business strategy, not a technology plan. The goal of your e-corporation is to change customer service from a labor-intensive, expensive postsales operation to a strategic initiative on which your company's future profits depend. Don't let the primary goal of transitioning to the Internet get lost in all the details. In short, the successful implementation of your e-corporation will result in:

- Increased revenues due to better customer satisfaction, which delivers higher rates of customer retention
- Higher revenues due to the extended reach of your e-commerce–based transactions
- Increased sales due to real-time marketing campaign analyses
- Additional revenues created by new sources of presales and after-sales transactions
- New sales due to the enhanced value of deliverables, which result from improved customer and business relationship management

One way to map a successful Internet customer loyalty approach is to look at your customer base and the type of customer loyalty your company enjoys. Following are examples of the types of online capabilities customers often expect from different types of online businesses. Although this overview is fairly simple, the mechanics of implementation are complex. Keep in mind that it's likely your e-corporation will have to identify, track, and interact with individual customers and then reconfigure products or services to meet the needs of those customers.

UNDERSTANDING E-CUSTOMERS

In many organizations, customer values have a broad range. According to Colin Marshall, chairman of British Airways: "We know that 35 percent of our customers account for more than 60 percent of our sales. Using database-marketing techniques, we have focused more of our marketing effort on retaining those customers and increasing our share of their business. That's why our advertising spending is proportionately smaller than that of our competitors." (Prokesch, 1995.)

Companies like British Airways (that have a few top customers who are responsible for the majority of the firm's revenue) have the most to gain from implementing customer-focused marketing. These companies have what's called a steep "skew." The steeper the skew, the more opportunities there are for reducing marketing costs by focusing on top customers. For example, if *1 percent* of the top customers are responsible for 25 percent of company profits, then fostering relationships with these top customers will protect 25 percent of the company's profits. If *10 percent* of the top customers are responsible for 25 percent of company profits, then it is ten times as costly to achieve the same results.

ZEROING IN ON CUSTOMER NEEDS AND LOYALTY TYPES

For varying reasons, some types of products and services do not develop any type of customer loyalty, while other products and services create a fierce loyalty that has customers singing their praises. Customers with no loyalty have no attachment to the product or service and are low repeat purchasers. Customers in the convenience-loyalty category are repurchasing frequently but have a low attachment to the company. This could be due to location or customer inertia. Customers in the latent-loyalty category may be highly attached to the company but are not frequent repurchasers. Often, the rate of repurchase depends on customization or increasing the variety of the company's products or services. Customers with premium (sometimes called brand) loyalty are enthusiastic about the product or service and repurchase at a high rate. Frequently, these customers recommend the company's products or services to others. Figure 3.1 is a customer loyalty differentiation matrix based on buyer behavior and shows examples of companies that fall into the loyalty categories described above, divided by either uniform or diverse customer needs.

For example, companies in Group VII include airlines, whose customers have consistent needs (passengers want to travel safely to their destinations) and frequently have a high attachment, or premium loyalty, to a

---

FIGURE 3.1   Customer Loyalty Differentiation Matrix

Category of Loyalty	Industry Examples	
	Uniform Customer Needs	Diverse Customer Needs
Premium loyalty	Group VII Airlines Manufactured packaged goods **	Group VIII Computer systems ** High-end hotel chains Legal and professional services** Auto manufacturers Large department stores
Convenience loyalty	Group V Commoditylike services ** Book publishers Travel agents	Group VI Pharmacies Small retailers Tax return preparation
Latent loyalty	Group III Niche goods Exercise equipment	Group IV High-end industrial equipment* Information and entertainment ** Apparel for consumers
No loyalty	Group I Gas stations Dry cleaners Mass-marketed items	Group II Mortgages Digital publishers Janitorial services *

---

*Business-to-business enterprises
**Either business-to-business enterprises or business-to-consumer enterprises

specific airline. (For a definition of premium loyalty, see Chapter 2.) In many cases, this premium customer loyalty is due to high reliability ratings, frequent-flyer programs, or offers of the lowest fares available.

Figure 3.1 goes on to illustrate how companies like book and music stores often have customers in Group VI. These customers may have diverse needs. The range of customer valuations is a fairly flat skew; that is, it's unlikely that 10 percent of top customers are responsible for 50 percent of the store's profits. It is often easy for this type of company to increase profits by reducing the costs of interacting with customers. One way to do this is with a Web site. Adding a Web site that handles customer preferences, wish lists, or requests for e-mail alerts allows companies to build customer loyalty by creating relationships with customers. For example, about 60 percent of Amazon.com's (www.amazon.com) business is from repeat customers. This is twice the rate of brick-and-mortar bookstores.

To sum it up, each of the eight groups illustrated in Figure 3.1 requires different online capabilities due to customer needs and category of customer loyalty. As a general rule, a company with a customer base with uniform customer needs will not increase profits by offering customers more choices. On the other hand, a company with diverse customer needs can greatly benefit by offering customers a variety of products and services. Therefore, companies in the eight different groups require different online capabilities. The following detailed examples illustrate what may be appropriate online capabilities for specific types of companies.

Suggested Online Capabilities for Groups I and II

There are many profitable companies that meet uniform and diverse customer needs but do not have a loyal customer base. Examples of these companies are illustrated in Figure 3.1. Price-conscious e-customers in Groups I and II don't like 30-second commercials and marketing hype. They want simple-to-navigate Web sites that meet their needs with real information and easy ordering.

Companies in Groups I and II need to interact with their customers to discover how to expand customer needs and meet that demand. For example, let's say a mortgage bank customer sends a free-form e-mail message with his or her Social Security number to the bank. The customer wants to know the payoff amount of his or her mortgage and whether the bank can match the quoted interest rate of another bank. Mortgage banks with online/offline data integration can automatically search the offline database and find the requested information. The bank's "smart" e-mail response system sends an automatic e-mail message to the customer with informa-

FIGURE 3.2   Suggested Online Capabilities for Groups I and II

Group	Suggested Online Capabilities
Group I No loyalty/uniform customer needs	Persuading users to register Privacy and security statements Recognizing users and calling them by name
Group II No loyalty/diverse customer needs	Online customer support Well-organized Web site Web site search feature Personalized content Users decide how to respond

tion about the mortgage payoff amount, the interest rate the bank can offer, and the name and contract information for a loan officer.

Figure 3.2 details other examples of suggested online capabilities for companies in Groups I and II.

Group I companies have customers with uniform needs and no loyalty. Group I customers are often savvy online consumers who use special product comparison Web sites such as Bottomdollar.com (www.bottom dollar.com), My Simon (www.my simon.com), and CompareNet (www .compare.net) to do the Web surfing for them. Other customers go directly to sites like Staples (www.sta ples.com) and Office Depot (www.office depot.com) to check out prices for themselves.

Group II companies tend to have customers with diverse needs and no loyalty. Mortgage banking sites, such as Countrywide (www.country wide.com), offer online applications and use aggregator sites to prescreen customers. Aggregators like Quicken Mortgage (www.quickenmortgage .com), E-Loan (www.eloan.com), and Lending Tree (www.lendingtree .com) receive thousands of customer visits per day. Consumers go to the aggregator's Web site and complete a home loan application form, which is sent to multiple lenders so they can render a decision. Next, the consumer is presented with three lenders who are ready to do business. The benefit to the consumer is faster approval time and lower loan costs.

FIGURE 3.3   Suggested Online Capabilities for Groups III, IV, and V

Group	Suggested Online Capabilities
Group III Latent loyalty/uniform customer needs	Different interfaces for different demographic groups "Drip irrigation" questioning Personalized product recommendations Multichannel communications Online configuration and technical help
Group IV Latent loyalty/diverse customer needs	Non-Web payment options Multiple billing and shipping choices Derived business intelligence Quick-click ordering Online order tracking History of online purchases Personalized content Users decide how to respond
Group V Convenience loyalty/uniform customer needs	Integration of online and offline data Persuading users to register Privacy and security statements and protection Recognizing users and calling them by name Online customer support Well-organized Web site Web site search feature

Suggested Online Capabilities for Groups III, IV, and V

Figure 3.3 shows examples of the types of online capabilities that may be appropriate for companies in Groups III, IV, and V. It is the goal of all traditional and e-commerce businesses to try to move customers to the premium-loyalty category. To move customers in this direction, companies must determine the value of each individual in their customer base, create detailed customer profiles, and understand each customer's preferences and behaviors (see Chapter 4). In addition to having a good understanding of what is important to the customer, companies understand what's important to the market in general and how others perceive their products or services (see Chapter 5).

Group III customers tend to have uniform needs and latent customer loyalty. Companies in Group III frequently have uniform customer valuations and needs; that is, a small portion of the customer base is not responsible for the major portion of company profits. Companies in Group III are prime candidates for niche marketing. Niche marketers use online technology to define the most likely customers for the products they want to sell. A good example of a Group III company is Bowflex (www.bowflex.com). To survive in this highly competitive e-commerce environment, Group III companies have to relentlessly innovate and deliver unparalleled service.

Group IV customers tend to have diverse needs and latent customer loyalty. A good online strategy is to proactively interact with customers to create different products and services based on consumer feedback and customer needs differentiation analyses. A good example of a Group IV company is the Gap. The Gap (www.gap.com) online store not only offers apparel for men and women but also for children and infants, as well as maternity apparel.

Group V customers tend to have uniform needs and convenience loyalty. A good example of a Group V company is BizTravel (www.biztravel.com). Companies in Group V can increase customer loyalty by keeping an attitude of true helpfulness delivered in new and different ways. Even with commoditylike items, companies can stand out from the crowd by offering benefits such as capturing customer preferences, providing online software updates, configuration and technical help, or multiple billing and shipping options.

Suggested Online Capabilities for Groups VI, VII, and VIII

Figure 3.4 shows the suggested online capabilities for Groups VI, VII, and VIII. These groups often have customers who require advanced online capabilities such as customizable Web experiences, one-click ordering, and customizable products. Customers may also expect targeted discounts or special promotional offers, cross-selling, and up-selling options

FIGURE 3.4   **Suggested Online Capabilities for Groups VI, VII, and VIII**

Group	Suggested Online Capabilities
Group VI Convenience loyalty/diverse customer needs	Customizable Web experience Targeted sales promotions, gift certificates, and discounts Mass customization of products and services Desktop extensions (with appropriate permissions) Personalized wish lists and alerts User groups, bulletin boards, and chats Automatic online software updates Full, seamless integration with partners Customer feedback and data integration Different interfaces for different demographic groups
Group VII Premium loyalty/uniform customer needs	"Drip irrigation" questioning Personalized product recommendations Smart searching capabilities Multichannel communications Online configuration and technical help Non-Web payment options Multiple billing and shipping choices Derived business intelligence Quick-click ordering Online order tracking History of online purchases
Group VIII Premium loyalty /diverse customer needs	Personalized content Users decide how to respond Integration of online and offline data Persuading users to register Privacy and security statements and protection Recognizing users and calling them by name Online customer support Well-organized Web site Web site search feature

based on their individual profiles. When e-companies deliver these features, the enhanced customer experience can't be matched offline.

Group VI customers tend to have diverse needs and convenience loyalty. A good example of a Group VI company is I Go.com (formerly 1-800 Batteries), the "Mobile Technology Outfitter" (www.igo.com). The company is located in Reno, Nevada, and supplies batteries and accessories for laptops, cell phones, and camcorders. Customers are already doing business at a distance, so ordering online isn't much of a stretch.

Frequently, Group VI customers need to quickly find the product they are seeking, order, and leave. Web site transactions are usually completed within three or four minutes. Group VI companies can reduce customer defections by offering smart site-searching capabilities that can make product searches more efficient and convenient—making it inconvenient to switch to another company.

Group VII customers tend to have uniform needs and premium customer loyalty. For all companies, premium loyalty is the best possible kind of customer loyalty. Customers make repeat purchases and sing the company's praises to other potential customers. These e-corporations can dramatically increase the odds of a completed transaction, if the user can get an answer to a question immediately. With the answer in hand, the customer can complete the transaction without leaving the Web site.

The requirement for an immediate response places a huge demand on Group VII companies. Sites must prepare for user feedback by automating transaction-tracking systems and answering questions on the spot. Group VII companies often watch out for individual customer needs. In the past, the butcher knew which cuts of meat customers liked and made recommendations that were relevant to each customer's taste. In virtual space, online brokerage Charles Schwab (www.schwab.com) uses a virtual sales agent (VSA) to bring back this type of customer service. The Schwab VSA brings some of the very best personal information that is relevant, helpful, and meaningful to customers in a way that hasn't been available before. The Schwab VSA is designed to offer immediate, context-specific customer support by answering customer questions via the Web site. Answers are instantaneous, requiring no e-mail or special browser plug-ins. Customers get the answers they want with no-wait service, 24 hours a day. This automated system allows companies to allocate more marketing dollars to their "best" customers; that is, those customers who are likely to provide the company with greater profits.

Group VIII customers tend to have diverse customer needs and premium customer loyalty. This means that the customer is already sold on the brand and is a high repeat purchaser. Mass-customized products are ideal for this group. A good example is Dell (www.dell.com). Dell allows customers to build their computer system online and then track the status of their purchase right up to delivery.

Companies in Group VIII can easily expand their reach with strategic alliances to other businesses that can provide complementary services. This in turn assists Group VIII companies in acquiring new customers.

WORKING WITH CUSTOMER EXPECTATIONS

The key driver to online business success is the customer experience. The customer experience is a strategic issue that involves all the major divisions of your e-corporation—sales, marketing, customer service and support, project development, and distribution and suppliers. To be competitive in the e-commerce marketplace, the strategy you implement must limit the scope of the online capabilities so that the customer experience does not become too diffused or inefficient. Fuzzy or conflicting strategies make good customer experiences impossible.

Many companies survey customers before launching their Web sites. As a result, their online systems help them deliver the products and services that meet real customer needs. In other words, discover what customers believe are the "ideal outcomes" gained from doing business with your e-corporation, and your company can use these ideal outcomes to define itself. Next, define the core competencies and capabilities at which you need to excel (if you are to deliver ideal outcomes).

According to William H. Davidow and Bro Uttal (1989), good customer experiences result when the corporation meets or exceeds the customer's expectations. Anything less than that means the product or service is "bad." Do what is expected and the product or service is "good." Exceed by a vast amount of what's anticipated, and the product or service is "excellent." This means that it is essential for your organization to set the customer's expectations at the correct level; for example, customers of high-priced hotels always expect luxury service, anything less is unacceptable.

Often, customers develop expectations based on their experiences with competitors and similar companies. Consequently, the customer will perceive your company as "bad" if the quality of service is less than what's offered by other companies. However, customers with different educational and economic backgrounds interpret your company's service position in different ways. What seems like "personal service" to one customer may be perceived as "no service" to another. To correct this situation, carefully segment your customer base, so that targeted segments receive different service messages. (For details, see Chapter 13.)

The key to a successful customer experience is to create expectations that your company can deliver: Inform consumers of what to expect and exceed the promise. Keep in mind that not all customers are equal; that is, not all customers want, deserve, or expect the same high level of service. You can position customer expectations by:

- Segmenting customers based on customer needs and type of customer loyalty, and by using your Web site to offer products or services that meet the needs of the customer base.
- Using your Customer Valuation Feedback Model (detailed in Chapter 1) to research the needs of the customer base and by paying close attention to customer feedback.
- Using the e-corporation's strategic service vision (discussed in Chapter 14) as a blueprint for setting customer expectations at the right level. Do not promise what can't be delivered; make certain that there are no blurry or conflicting strategies that would hinder a good customer experience.

SUMMING IT UP

- The time to get on the Internet is now. Choosing not to have an online presence can be business suicide. However, before going online it is important to develop an e-commerce strategic vision that is not fuzzy or contradictory.

- To lay down the groundwork, understand your customer's needs and type of loyalty.
- Using your company's knowledge of its customer base, you can determine the types of online capabilities that are appropriate for your online business.
- When determining the appropriate online capabilities for your e-corporation, keep in mind that not all customers have the same value to the organization. Some customers need (and deserve) a different level of online customer service than others.
- One of the important elements of laying a foundation for your e-corporation is to position customer expectations at the right level. Tell customers what to expect and deliver more than what's anticipated.

ACTION PLAN

CUSTOMER EXPECTATION CHECKLIST

The most difficult part of specifying requirements for your e-corporation is that no matter what you plan or discuss, customer expectations are not going to match in every case. Knowing what customers expect is often the key to e-corporation success. Designing an e-corporation to meet customer expectations can be a challenge. Often the only way to move customers away from a price focus is to make certain that the customer's expectations are being met or exceeded in other areas. The following checklist shows the 13 top customer expectations that can create solid relationships and move customers up the loyalty ladder. When these expectations are met, they help create solid relationships and build customer loyalty.

Do You Meet Your Customers Expectations?

✓ Does your e-corporation provide real information that can be used to make a purchase decision?

✓ Does your e-corporation provide a selection of purchase options so the customer can make an informed choice?

✓ For e-corporations with complex products, does your customer get a customized online presentation that provides information in an easy-to-compare format? (This creates a dialogue about the customer's preferences, needs, and desires and is the beginning of a learning relationship with the customer.)

✓ Does your e-corporation offer a wide variety of communication channels for the customer (telephone, fax, e-mail, and so on)? Can the customer contact the e-corporation anytime, anywhere?

✓ Does your e-corporation offer cutting-edge technology? What online capabilities does your company's chief competitor offer? (Remember, being behind the technology curve sends a negative message to customers and prospects.)

✓ Is your e-corporation responsive? Can your e-corporation respond instantly to questions, feedback, requests, and complaints? (This is one area where overkill may be appropriate.)

✓ Does your e-corporation make it easy for the customer to buy?

✓ Can online customers pay for their purchases in a variety of ways?

✓ Does your e-corporation provide privacy and security for all customer transactions?

✓ Does your e-corporation provide a "seamless" relationship? In other words, when the online customer moves from one corporate functional area to another, does he or she have to start a "new" relationship?

✓ Does your e-corporation provide new ideas? (New ideas indicate that the company is alert, progressive, and ahead of competitors.)

✓ Does your e-corporation meet its commitment to the online consumer? Does your e-corporation make big promises but fall short on the delivery of those promises?

✓ Does your e-corporation offer adequate solutions to customer complaints or problems? (For example, if a customer purchases a product online, can he or she return the product to an offline store?)

Source: Adapted from John R. Graham, "Selling Strategies," *Institutional Investor*, January 1998, 8.

REFERENCES

Callahan, Charles V., and Bruce A. Pasternack. 1999. Corporate Strategy in the Internet Age. *Ongoing Research,* corporate publication of Booz-Allen Hamilton (second quarter): 1-2.

Davidow, William H. and Bro Uttal. 1989. Service Companies: Focus or Falter. *Harvard Business Review* (July-August).

Graham, John R. 1998. Selling Strategies. *Institutional Investor* (January): 8.

Hamel, Gary, Jeff Sampler, Patty de Llosa, Jane Hodges, and Len A. Costs. 1998. The E-Corporation More Than Just Web-Based, It's Building a News Industrial Order. *Fortune,* 7 December, 80-86.

Heskett, James L. 1986. Managing in the Service Economy. *Harvard Business Review* (November-December): 30.

Jordan, Peter. 1998. Part 2: E-Business Building Block —Three Steps to Help You Put Your Clients on Their Way to Electronic Commerce Success. *VarBusiness,* 12 November, 70.

McNabb, Paul, and Michael Steinbaum. 2000. Reclaiming Customer Care: The Milkman Returns. *Cambridge Information Network,* corporate publication of Cambridge Technology Partners, 28 March (www.cin.ctp.com).

Peppers, Don, and Martha Rogers. 1997. *Enterprise One to One: Tools for Competing in the Interactive Age.* New York: Doubleday.

Peppers, Don, Martha Rogers, and Bob Dorf. 1999. Is Your Company Ready for One-to-One Marketing? *Harvard Business Review* (January-February): 3-12.

Pine, B. Joseph, II, Don Peppers, and Martha Rogers. 1995. Do You Want to Keep Your Customers Forever? *Harvard Business Review* (March-April): 103-114.

Prokesch, Steven E. 1995. Competing on Customer Service. *Harvard Business Review* (November-December): 105.

Walsh, Brian. 1998. Features: Building a Business Plan for an E-Commerce Project. *Network Computing,* 15 September, 69.

Improving E-customer Retention

How can you keep customers forever? Find out how to retain your best customers and create exit barriers for your online customers. Check out e-customer retention success stories and see how financial services entities are using the Internet to strengthen customer loyalty. Discover how to measure customer retention and get a hold of which customer defections are controllable and which are not. Gain an understanding of the basics of a customer retention strategy and uncover how you determine if it's worth the price. Finally, discuss how customer satisfaction and customer loyalty rely on top-notch e-customer service.

KEEPING YOUR CUSTOMERS

All corporations want to keep their existing customers forever. However, few companies are implementing strategies that target customer retention, because most companies focus on acquiring new customers. Companies that do have retention programs often do not have accurate metrics to measure the success of their retention efforts. Greg Gianforte (2000) of Right Now Technologies states: "Companies that don't develop effective e-services wind up spending far more on customer support than their competitors—as much as 20 times more per incident." Consequently, companies with poor e-services get frustrated customers and find their call centers flooded when they introduce a new product or experience problems with an old one.

However, customer satisfaction doesn't mean that customers will not switch to a competitor. According to Fredrick Reichheld (1996), between 65 percent and 85 percent of customers who choose a new supplier often state they were satisfied or very satisfied with their old supplier. This indicates that customer satisfaction does not ensure customer loyalty. In "Five Keys to Keeping Your Best Customers" (1996), a researcher presents his findings about offline customer retention. I've summarized the five keys as follows:

1. *Identify core customers.* Not understanding which customers are the most valuable to your organization can be hazardous to the bottom line. Marketers may try to promote products or services that are designed to satisfy everyone but fail to satisfy anyone.
2. *Measure what matters.* Often, companies measure customer retention by repeat purchases. Unfortunately, studies show a weak correlation of customer satisfaction to repurchase behavior. Additionally, lack of complaints does not guarantee a high retention rate.
3. *Analyze defections.* After you know which customers you want to keep, analyze the group that decided to defect. According Harvard Business School professors Thomas Jones and Earl Sasser (1995), one company regained 30 percent of its lost customers by contacting them and listening to their concerns. Jill Griffin (1996) suggests telephoning lost customers and asking the question, "What can we do to win back your business?" Then, listen to the customer's requirements. In response, tell the customer about the changes you have made and ask again for the customer's business.

4. *Implement mass customization.* Customization can often be built into your firm's business system. For example, AutoZone (www.auto zone.com) has 2,800 stores in 40 states; it is the nation's top auto parts chain. The company sells parts, maintenance items, and accessories under brand names, as well as under private labels. AutoZone serves both do-it-yourself customers and professional auto repair shops. Each store carries a selection of parts skewed toward the vehicles that dominate that market area. Employees can instantly access the repair or sales history of any customer at any outlet. In this way, the company uses inventory management to address the diverse needs of its customers and shows its ability to tailor services to individual requirements.

5. *Meet unspoken needs.* Learning about the customer's unspoken needs happens over time and through customer interaction. Satisfying unspoken needs and going beyond customer expectations comes from understanding what makes relationships tick.

CREATING EXIT BARRIERS FOR ONLINE CUSTOMERS

With the advent of e-commerce, customers have started to demand higher quality, lower prices, and higher levels of service. Even customers who say they are satisfied frequently don't behave that way. E-corporations that aim at improving customer retention are wise to incorporate the five customer retention strategies listed previously in their customer retention programs. However, e-corporations also have other issues they need to deal with to reduce online customer defections. Steve Diorio, a principal of IMT Strategies, in an interview with David Sims, states that the way to keep online customers is to erect exit barriers. According to Diorio, there are nine ways to keep customers and bring them back:

1. *Enhance the e-customer learning curve.* Customers may be familiar with your company's product but need an easy-to-use Web site to develop expertise and confidence. A good example of how an e-corporation helps the customer learning curve is Amazon.com (www.amazon .com). When new customers click on the Help icon at Amazon.com, they discover help fo first-time visitors, search tips, ordering instruc-

tions, payment information, shipping information, guidance to managing their accounts, and book selection suggestions. Answers to the top five questions are listed, along with specific suggestions about how to complete different online tasks. This assists customers up the learning curve.

2. *Integrate processes.* Customers want a seamless customer experience that is quick and high quality. If your Web site uses third-party intermediaries, make certain the process is truly integrated, so your e-corporation appears to be a "holistic" enterprise. A good example is the supply chain management at Wal-Mart (www.walmart.com). By collaborating with suppliers, Wal-Mart controls expenses. This way, Wal-Mart can offer low prices and value every day; customers do not have to wait for a sale to realize savings. This collaboration is done behind the scenes, ensuring a seamless customer experience.

3. *Personalize the online experience.* Start using all the information your company has gathered through click streams, tracking buyer behavior, and the customer's stated preferences. Use the information to segment the customer base and cross-sell. Again, a good example is Amazon.com, which employs software applications that use collaborative filtering to make individualized recommendations. These recommendations allow Amazon.com to cross-sell and up-sale their offerings. (Collaborative filtering uses algorithmic techniques to infer what may be of interest to users based on a comparison of their preferences.) Customized recommendations provide a personalized customer experience.

4. *Provide online mass customization and product selection.* You can prevent or reduce the number of customers exiting by offering a vast variety of products and services through partnerships, mass customization, and price incentives. For example, individuals can custom-build and order computers using the Dell online store (www.dell.com). Dell breaks down the production process into independent subprocesses, which provide the flexibility needed to manufacture mass-customized computers that meet the individual needs of a specific customer. Dell employs a whole list of technological advances to make this customization possible. With computer-controlled factory equipment and industrial robots, they can quickly

readjust assembly lines. Bar code scanners make it possible to track every part of the computer, so the customer gets all the features he or she desires. Databases store trillions of bytes of information, including each customer's computer selection. Software for logistics and supply-chain management coordinate every step of manufacturing and shipping.

5. *Reduce risk and increase trust.* Internet users, experienced and newbies alike, need to be assured about online privacy and informed that their credit card information will not be used for other purposes. After all, no one wants personal information sold to direct mail marketers. CBS Market Watch (www.cbsmarketwatch.com) is a good example of an e-corporation that provides customers with information about their privacy policy. Many individuals track their portfolios online at MarketWatch. Without a doubt, these customers do not want this data made public or sold to third parties. To assure customers that this does not occur, the MarketWatch privacy policy states that the company will not "willfully disclose any individually identifiable information about you to any outside source without your express consent." The privacy statement goes on to explain how the company stores and collects information about customers. This helps to develop customer trust.

6. *Institute online loyalty programs.* The Internet started as a commercial-free initiative; consequently, this freebie culture is still part of the Internet. Customers often expect to receive something free if they purchase. For example, if you purchase a book at Barnes and Noble (www.barnesandnoble.com), you'll receive a promotional discount at affiliated sites, like 1-800-Flowers (www.1-800-flowers.com). When you use your Barnes and Noble promotional code for a discount at 1-800-Flowers, the company offers you another promotional discount on your next flower order. For most customers, after two successful purchases at 1-800-Flowers, when it's time to buy flowers for a third occasion, they are likely to start shopping at 1-800-Flowers.

7. *Establish an online brand identity.* Garden.com (www.garden.com), shown in Figure 4.1, is a Web site that sells "everything under the sun," and MotherNature.com's (www.mothernature.com) natural products and healthy advice are good examples of establishing a

FIGURE 4.1   Product aggregation and online content make Garden.com stand out from the crowd.

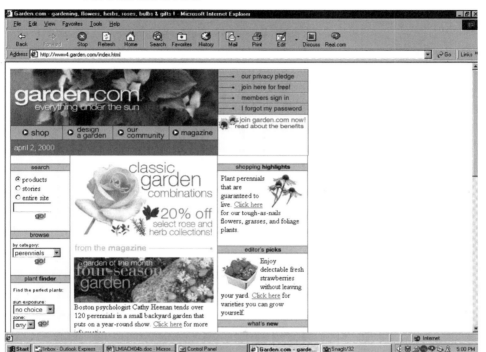

brand's value through online content and product aggregation. MotherNature.com does not manufacture the products it offers. The company is a purveyor and has built a brand name and customer following based on its brand identity.

8. *Collaborate with related companies.* You can expand your reach and keep customers' attention by maintaining an ongoing, value-added dialogue with them by using supply chain partners. A good example of related vendor collaboration is Priceline.com (www.priceline .com). Sellers—some of the biggest names in the business of travel, hospitality, cars, and financing—participate because they always have more than they can sell; Priceline.com provides buyers. Over the last several years, this collaboration has resulted in over two million online transactions.

FIGURE 4.2   Starwood Hotels strengthens customer loyalty with advanced hospitality online services.

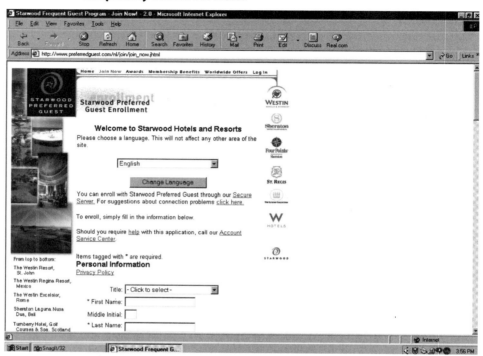

9. *Create online standards.* One way to be perceived as the industry leader is to establish the standard. This often means improving the customer's online experience by providing cutting-edge technology or revolutionary management policies or practices where the consumer doesn't expect it. For example, at Southwestern Airlines (www.ifly swa.com), travelers don't have to enter a PIN number to make a reservation. The company also appears to have a lot of flexibility, because it allows customers to make reservations for one-way tickets. Companies that make their standards known are easy to do business with and increase customer retention.

Recent studies surprised many hospitality professionals by indicating that the "best" hotel customers are individuals (not participants of conventions, conferences, or special events). Consequently, Starwood Hotels (www.starwood.com) wanted to strengthen customer loyalty by offering their best customers (individuals who have stayed at least five times at any Starwood Hotel) advanced online services, including the ability to check the balance of reward points known as Star Points and how to redeem those points online.

LOYALTY MARKETING SUCCESS STORY

Starwood Hotels

▼ **COMPANY:** Starwood Hotels & Resorts Worldwide, Inc., has over 700 hotels in 72 countries. Each year, more than 40 million customers stay in Starwood Hotels and Resorts. Starwood wanted to use Web technology to create a cutting-edge customer service and loyalty platform.

▼ **SOLUTION:** The company's loyalty program, Starwood Preferred Guest, presented an online solution that strengthened customer loyalty by offering advanced online services, including the ability to check the balance of reward points (known as StarPoints) and the ability to redeem these points online. Members are offered such advanced services as transferring StarPoints to airline miles and redeeming them for gift certificates with top retailers or for rooms. The Web site also offers members a rich array of information, including special hotel offers by geographic area and information related to weather, hotels, and membership benefits.

▼ **BENEFITS:** Starwood Preferred Guest can now harvest information about their members from one database instead of many separate databases (customer information, reservation system, and property management information). The new system integrates Preferred Guest, customer call center, and front desk at all hotels. Starwood is able to leverage its underlying base of customer data. Overall, the online program did the following:

- Strengthened customer loyalty because of easy access to loyalty program information
- Resulted in a multi-million-dollar reduction in the cost of communicating with Preferred Guest members and increased customer satisfaction

- Lowered enrollment costs and increased consumption of hospitality services among Starwood Preferred Guest members.

▼ **TECHNOLOGY:** The company used a variety of IBM products; for example, connectivity and access to the Enterprise data was accomplished by utilizing the MQSeries commercial messaging application program, DB2 Universal Database Family of database management tools, CICS transaction processing engine, and other packaged and custom business applications. All the business-critical real-time data necessary to develop the required business functionality resided in the IBM DB2 Universal Database running on an IBM S/390 Enterprise Server.

Source: Adapted from "Starwood Hotels: Raising the Bar on Customer Service through E-business," a corporate publication of IBM (www2.software.ibm/casestudies), 20 March 2000.

CUSTOMER RETENTION EXAMPLE: THE FINANCIAL SERVICES INDUSTRY

According to Jeff Resnick (1996) of Opinion Research Corporation International (www.opinionresearch.com), satisfying customers in the financial industry is one of today's greatest challenges. Financial institutions have to compete with others that offer similar services and with non-banks such as brokerages, mutual fund companies, and independent financial advisors. All of these financial services entities are competing to offer better services, lower fees, more products, and bigger investments. However, financial services entities cannot buy customer loyalty with pricing. For example, Charles Schwab Inc. (www.schwab.com) charges the highest price for online trading and is the largest online brokerage in the world. Schwab shows how e-corporations with a high level of customer loyalty can charge prices that are 4 percent to 7 percent higher than competitors', which often results in two to three times more profit. Overall, financial services e-corporations need to be innovative, build lasting relationships with current customers, and acquire new customers.

ABSA Banking Group, Ltd. (www.absa.co.za) is a good example of how customer loyalty can affect the bottom line. ABSA Banking Group is listed on the Johannesburg Stock Exchange and is the controlling company of the largest banking and financial services group in South Africa. ABSA provides a full range of retail and corporate banking, insurance, financial, and property services through extensive local and international networks in the corporate, business, and personal finance markets. The firm is committed to proactively understanding each client's needs, requirements, and business situation.

ABSA's corporate goal is to provide customers with innovative and useful solutions, utilizing the full capacity of its resources, not only in the Asia Pacific region and South Africa, but also in other key financial centers around the world. In August 1999, however, Sasha Planting, a writer for the *Financial Mail* (www.fm.co.za), stated that four of ABSA's banking institutions lost 9 percent of their market share in three years, despite the fact that the financial services market had grown in those key areas. Planting says this was due to the infiltration of foreign banks, unburdened by a brick-and-mortar infrastructure and social obligations. These foreign players started to take ABSA's best commercial and private customers by offering them personalized service, sophisticated products, and global skills. ABSA, realizing their market was under threat, identified customer retention and customer acquisition as their key strategic targets. The company set out to build customer loyalty by developing personal relationships with its customers.

Soon, ABSA learned that implementing a stand-alone call center did not assist them in achieving their goal of building a relationship with every customer. Building a vast data warehouse of information also didn't help the situation. The company had no idea how to leverage the information they gathered. For example, the credit department often hounded customers with healthy bank account balances to pay small credit card payments or to pay off small loans. The negative effect was sizable. The bank realized they had to change their business model before they could implement a technological solution. Additionally, the bank had to change its mindset from managing their traditional lines of business to managing customers—and customer expectations.

Finding the Right Focus

ABSA's dilemma is not unusual, according to a survey of 150 U.S. retail-banking executives conducted by the Information Research Practice of Unisys Worldwide Information Services (1995). The Unisys report shows that banks that achieve their greatest success in customer retention are those that:

- Focus explicitly and consistently on customer retention, even in the face of pressures to cut costs and grow market share.
- Recognize and emulate nonbanks as primary competitors for customers' funds.
- Use information technology resources to create and integrate an information infrastructure that enables the bank to both understand customers' needs and values and enable its frontline employees to use that information to cross-sell new products to clients more effectively.

The Unisys Customer Retention Report goes on to point out that 93 percent of banks see customer retention as a key goal but often don't act on that realization:

- Respondents stated that employees did not spend more time on customer retention than any other activity. However, studies show an increase of 2 percent of customer retention can have the same profit impact as a 10 percent reduction in operating costs for banks.
- Not all survey respondents measure retention. About 30 percent of respondents do not measure customer retention, and most banks defined retention by the number of customers maintained.
- Banks often ignore the real competition. About *57 percent* of the banks that consider nonbanks (brokerages and mutual fund companies) as their chief competitors had retention rates of 90 percent or better. About *34 percent* of banks that viewed other banks as their top competitors had retention rates of 90 percent or better. This indicates that when the real competition was not targeted, higher rates of customer defection resulted.
- Banks do not have the right information for retention. Although banks have some key data about customers (mortgage, credit lines, and checking and saving accounts), they do not know which competing products their customers own. They also do not know their customers' values (e.g., preferences for electronic banking or convenience). And, they do not know how often customers use specific channels such as traditional branches or telephone or online banking.

In the past, banks interacted with their customers and had strong relationships that were based on personal connections, which often resulted in lifetime relationships with the bank. Now, day-to-day banking is often handled at ATMs, by direct deposit of payroll checks, and drive-through windows. In the near future, Citibank Australia (www.citibank.com.au) expects the Internet to be their primary means of communication with their customers. Therefore, the bank launched Australia's first interactive Web site in the banking and finance industry. This initiative is part of the bank's strategy for preparing its customers for electronic banking and for completing other business transactions online. Additionally, this activity will help ensure that, as time goes on, customers who are seeking more online financial services will not defect to non–brick-and-mortar competitors.

LOYALTY MARKETING SUCCESS STORY

Citibank Australia

▼ **COMPANY** Citibank Australia has a long history of being at the technological forefront of Australian banking. In 1994, Citibank Australia opened Australia's first advanced-thinking, machine-only banking facilities. These two-way video Personal Banking Centers are linked to a home office and allow individuals to open accounts, apply for loans, make deposits or withdrawals, and access all normal banking functions. Operating hours are seven days a week, 7:30 AM to 9:00 PM. Citibank Australia then launched Australia's first interactive Web site in the banking and finance industry. This initiative is part of the bank's strategy to coach its customers to participate in electronic banking and to complete other business transactions online. The problem was how to get customers to visit and use the interactive Web site.

▼ **SOLUTION** Citibank Australia's management decided to position the Internet site as a one-stop shopping Web site for new and existing customers. This is a nontraditional move to attract banking customers, but it is Citibank's way of taking steps to achieve the goal of one billion customers by the year 2010 and of preparing customers for the future in electronic commerce.

▼ **BENEFITS** The Web site is designed to offer customers real-time information on news, economic updates, sports updates, interest rates, travel updates, and other services. Customers can download applications for Citibank's products and services. Overall:

- The Web site is Citibank Australia's first step in building customer loyalty by distinguishing itself from other financial institutions by offering online services beyond its products.
- Customers can handle their finances from a distance, when it's convenient for them, and at any time day or night. For example, customers can use electronic banking, access information on products, fill out applications, and e-mail them to the appropriate Citibank branch office.
- Visits to the Web site provide Citibank with information for building a profile on each customer.

Source: Adapted from Sasha Planting, "Customer Retention Strategies: Banks Fight to Retain Customer Loyalty," a corporate publication of Financial Mail, August 1999 (www.fm.com.za).

MEASURING CUSTOMER RETENTION

According to customer-retention consulting firm Harris Black International (1998), customer retention measures how many customers, contacts, or products are left at a specific point in time relative to the starting point. Harris Black International suggests that the best data to use is actual purchase data rather than customer questionnaires, which provide less accuracy when measuring customer retention. The Harris Black formula is:

$$\frac{\text{Customers at end of period T1} - \text{New customers acquired during period}}{\text{Customers at the start of period T0}}$$

Let's use an example from the insurance industry. Let's say that 10,000 homeowners have insurance policies that are in place January 1 (T0). At the end of the year (T1), there are 8,500 of the original polices. The company has added 2,000 new policies for a total T1 policy base of 10,500.

- Looking at the beginning and ending policies, it appears that the customer base increased by 5 percent (10,500 ÷ 10,000 = 1.05).

FIGURE 4.3   Citibank Australia uses its Web site to create a learning relationship with its customers.

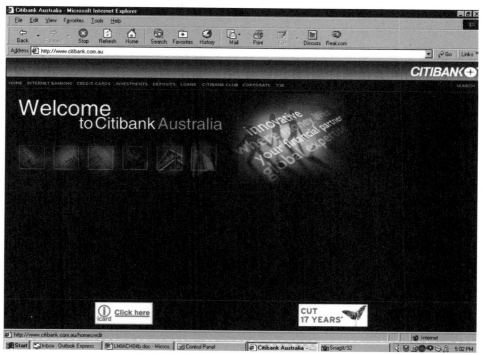

Source: Citibank, a member of Citigroup.

- Using the Harris Black formula, we can calculate a lapse rate of 85 percent: 10,500 (customers at end of period) – 2,000 (new customers acquired during period) ÷ 10,000 (number of original policies) = 8,500 ÷ 10,000, or a lapse rate of 85 percent.

Is an 85 percent lapse rate good? There are no benchmarks, standards, or targets for customer defections. Consultants at Harris Black International state: "All things being equal, improving a company's retention rate should continue as long as the marginal cost of saving a customer is less than the marginal cost of acquiring a new customer." In our example, the company should try to win the business of those 1,500 policyholders who left the company.

Controllable and Uncontrollable Customer Defections

Typical reasons for offline customer defections are poor service, pricing, or moving out of the area, in addition to customers no longer requiring your product or service or receiving a better offer from a competitor. Knowing why a customer defected is important to targeting your company's retention strategy and requires your company to use accurate customer retention metrics for measuring customer retention. Correctly measuring customer retention allows you to evaluate retention improvement efforts and create a deeper understanding of the economic value of customer retention. For example, the customer retention metric used in the Harris Black formula does not address two issues:

1. What is a true defection? Customer defections can be categorized as controllable and noncontrollable. In our example, a closer look indicates that of the 1,500 defections, 1,100 were controllable and 400 were out of the company's control, because customers no longer needing the homeowner policies were terminated for cause, or moved to locations not covered by the insurance company.
2. What time frame is appropriate for measuring customer retention? The appropriate time frame for the company is the purchase cycle. Harris Black International provides this example: If a company is measuring the retention rate of owners for a certain car in a calendar year, the base should not be the total number of car owners but the number of owners who are in the market for that particular car that year. This is called calculating the "purchase consideration window."

According to Fredrick Reichheld (1996), every company has customers that do not contribute to its profitability. On the other hand, valuable customers may be classified as dispensable based on inaccurate information. For example, some customers who were once considered outstanding become dispensable because by the time they are ready to leave, a good portion of their "wallet" or "budget" has already moved to a competitor. These partial defectors look like unprofitable customers. This can often mislead a company into not making the improvements necessary to retain the customer.

Reichheld provides this example of how a company can make efforts to retain their "best" customers and let their "worst" customers go. A leading credit card company built a computer system that let its telephone representatives instantly evaluate any customer who called to cancel an account. The system was based on the potential profit from the customer's entire wallet, not the company's current share. The credit card company had information about the customer's entire wallet from electronic credit bureau reports. The telephone representative could offer the customer appropriate incentives to entice him or her to stay. The credit card company learned which offers provided enough value to keep customers. (In other industries, companies make it their business to collect similar data, such as the Nielsen rating for television viewers.)

DEVELOPING AN ONLINE LOYALTY AND RETENTION STRATEGY

Marketing research company ActivMedia (www.activmedia.com) observes that once a customer decides to make an online purchase, the process of building customer loyalty begins. ActivMedia suggests that you encourage repeat purchases by attracting the attention of new e-customers through creating awareness of the Web site:

- *Use offline sources such as traditional advertising, public relations, and word of mouth.* For example, office-supply and big-ticket-item e-customers require information about the features of specific products. Paper-based magazine articles and editorials often motivate investment product e-customers. For example, *Bloomberg* magazine is a paper-based publication of Bloomberg (www.bloomberg.com). Bloomberg's paper media products promote its online products and services. The goal is to stretch the customer loyalty bond so loyal offline customers are also online customers.
- *Online sources are useful for Internet users seeking specific products.* Good examples are collectibles and hobby purchases. For these e-customers, search engines and directories can assist the e-corporation in building Web site awareness. (ActivMedia recommends that entities

without brands use this approach.) For example, Ruby Lane (www
.rubylane.com) is an online resource for finding, buying, and selling
antiques, collectibles, and fine art. Listing several items with Ruby
Lane is a good way for new online antique businesses to attract their
target audiences. Seeing the new business repeatedly listed at Ruby
Lane will attract the attention of new e-customers.

- *Use branding to create awareness.* About 80 percent of e-customers know
  what they want to purchase and where they want to shop, illustrating
  the importance of having a well-known brand name. Branding for online consumer apparel is very important. Here, marketers aim to link
  certain fashion lines (fit, lifestyle, and so on) to a particular brand
  name. Brooks Brothers (www.brooksbrothers.com) is a good example
  of a brand that specializes in business apparel. It is loyalty to the
  Brooks Brothers brand that attracts customers to the Web site and
  keeps them coming back.

- *Use synergy of offline and online purchasing.* Many e-customers have
  purchased a company's products offline in the past. For example, Rec-
  reational Equipment Inc. (www.rei.com) has both offline and online
  stores. Let's say that you want to purchase a Kelty Yellowstone tent
  that accommodates six people. The offline store just sold the last one
  and is now out of stock. However, in the store you can go to a kiosk
  and access REI online and order your tent on the spot. Success. You'll
  get the tent you want without having to drive to another store. That's
  the synergy of offline and online purchasing.

E-CUSTOMER SATISFACTION VERSUS E-CUSTOMER RETENTION

Most business leaders agree that a company's most valuable asset is its
loyal customers. This realization comes at a time when many companies,
especially manufacturing firms, find new customers increasingly hard to
acquire. It also derives from a growing body of work by consultants, aca-
demics, and practitioners that points out how a relatively small percentage of a company's customers often account for a large portion of its
profits. Good customer service can lead to customer satisfaction, but even

satisfied customers can defect. This means that your organization needs a strategy that does more than target satisfaction and corporate efficiency. For example, the *Internet Retailer* (1999) reports that while most e-corporations are experts in electronic storefronts and marketing, they are novices when it comes to customer service. According to the *Internet Retailer,* consumer advocates, CEOs of consumer complaint organizations, and e-customers would flunk most of the Internet's 15,000 merchants on the quality of their customer service. According to Thomas Jones and W. Earl Sasser Jr. (1995), four basic elements affect customer satisfaction:

1. *A good product or service.* The product or service is exactly what the customer expects all competitors to deliver.
2. *Basic support services.* The company makes its products and services easy to use by offering assistance and order tracking.
3. *Counteracting a bad customer experience.* The company has a recovery process that counteracts the customer's bad experience with the firm's product or service.
4. *Extraordinary services.* The company excels at meeting the customer's personal preferences, appeals to his or her values, and solves problems in a way that makes the product or service seem customized.

Setting the Stage: The First Online Purchase

According to the Boston Consulting Group (www.bcg.com), consumers who have had a satisfying first purchase experience online are likely to spend more time and money online. The satisfied first-time purchaser (over a 12-month period) typically engages in 12 online transactions and spends $500. In contrast, the dissatisfied first-time online purchaser will only spend about $140 online on four transactions.

"The first online purchase experience is the moment of truth for consumers and retailers. It is the beginning of a brand connection," said BCG Senior Vice President Michael Silverstein. "Unfortunately, too many consumers are finding that shopping online offers convenience fraught with compromise. The frustrations and failures that are commonplace in these early days of electronic retailing could be the kiss of death for the brands of Internet retailers."

"Online consumers are not a very forgiving lot, maybe because purchasing online is so new for most of them that they are in a constant state of evaluating it," noted BCG Senior Vice President David Pecaut. "The stakes are high for online retailers who do not deliver." The Boston Consulting Group goes on to say that consumers identified many "compromises" or barriers to shopping online.

Using Customer Service Personnel to Increase Repeat Purchases

In a recent study by Net Effect of Hollywood, California, of the top 25 e-commerce sites, including Amazon.com and Dell.com, 90 percent of these e-corporations do not have immediate plans to hire a full-time customer service manager, let alone install a Web-based customer management system or real-time shopper assistance program. This is remarkable, considering the results of a study conducted by Bob Tyrrell, chairman of The Henley Centre (1997). Tyrrell states that using his organization's customer service model, a satisfied complainant is likely to be more loyal than a customer who experienced no problem (91 percent loyalty versus 87 percent) and nearly twice as loyal as a dissatisfied complainant (91 percent loyal versus 41 percent).

This points out the importance of your customer satisfaction and loyalty. Overall, e-customer quality service can be divided into three categories:

1. *Selecting the product or service.* Most e-customers know what they want to purchase online. Therefore, they expect understandable product information and quick responses to their faxed, telephone, or e-mail queries. You need to empower customers so they can quickly find answers via the Web site. This can be achieved by providing your company's toll-free telephone number and other contact information, clearly stating store policies, providing online answers to frequently asked questions, and Help buttons. Track redundant questions and make the appropriate changes on the Web site.

2. *Purchasing the product or service.* About two-thirds of e-customers abandon their purchase attempts. This is often due to difficulty in navigating Web sites and not being able to locate answers to product or service questions. Therefore, your e-corporation should track customer service activities and monitor customer needs. Don't forget that the nonavailability of products or the lack of capacity for services is also a major source of frustration for customers and creates a bad customer service image. For example, many customers order a product or service online only to receive an e-mail several hours later stating the order cannot be filled.

3. *Lack of after-sales support of the product or service.* Some Internet retailers take up to five days to respond to customer complaints. Often, after-sale online assistance is not available and e-corporations frequently lack automatic e-mail responders for simple inquiries about refunds, returning merchandise, or other frequently asked questions. For example, many e-customers have been dismayed to learn that after purchasing a product online it could not be returned to the offline store.

Calculating the ROI of Your Customer Retention Program

According to the Business Research Lab of Hauppauge, New York (www.busreslab.com), a customer retention program consists primarily of three elements: (1) focusing on satisfying current customers, (2) measuring why customers leave, and (3) planning for efforts to prevent targeted customers from leaving once they state their intentions. The Business Research Lab provides the following example of how a customer retention program can quickly increase your company's profits.

Here's an example of calculating your return on investment for implementing a customer retention program: Let's say your company spends $50,000 to acquire 2,000 new customers per year. This is an average per-customer acquisition cost of $25. If the customer base is 8,000 customers with a 20 percent turnover rate, your company loses 1,600 customers per year and has a net gain of 400 new customers. If the customer retention program can reduce the 20 percent defection rate to 15 percent, the company will retain 400 customers per year (and increase the net gain to 800 customers). To reach the goal of a net gain of 800 customers per year, you'll have to pay an additional $50,000 in advertising expenditures. This example quantifies the value of your firm's customer retention program. This metric indicates that it is likely that your customer retention program does not have to be expensive to be successful. For example, a simple retention program can include a small survey, several written scripts to entice customers to stay, some additional employee time, and a modest counteroffer.

SUMMING IT UP

- Some offline customer retention methods apply to your e-corporation. However, you have to worry about developing innovative ways to create customer exit barriers.
- Some corporations lose customers because they don't recognize their real competitors. Additionally, corporations need to measure their customer retention and gather the right data to determine which losses are controllable or noncontrollable.
- You want to keep your "best" customers and let the "worst" customers go. Unfortunately, by the time many best customers are ready to leave, they are disguised as worst customers and no effort is made to retain them.
- Implementing an information system that gathers the right information about retention can also assist companies in determining customer preferences and needs.
- Your customer retention program doesn't have to be expensive. For example, a customer retention program can include a small survey, written scripts to entice customers to stay onboard, a few hours of employee time, and a modest counteroffer.

CUSTOMER SERVICE SENSITIVITY SCORECARD EXPECTATION CHECKLIST

Profitability depends on repeat business from your customers. While good marketing may get customers in the door, only great customer care, consistent communication, and constant product or service improvement will keep customers coming back time and time again. This book explores many of the opportunities you have to build and maintain better relationships with your customers.

How does your company stack up? Score one point for each yes answer.

Yes	No	**What's Your Customer Service Sensitivity Score?**
——	——	Do you know what percentage of your customers you keep each year?
——	——	Do you know what percentage of your customers you lose each year?
——	——	Do you know the top three reasons your customers leave?
——	——	Do you know what your customers' number-one expectations are?
——	——	In the last three months, have you personally contacted at least ten former customers to find out why they defected?
——	——	Do you have written customer service quality standards?
——	——	In the last six months, have you checked to see if any of your customers' expectations have changed?
——	——	Do you know how many members of your staff serve internal versus external customers?
——	——	Are any of your customer service performance standards tied to incentive programs?

Total Yes answers _____

If You Scored	You Are
7-9	A star
4-6	Just average
5-3	Definitely not customer-centric
2-1	Cruising for trouble

Note: if your company scored less than seven, your customers may not be receiving the service they deserve.

Source: Adapted from JoAnna Brandi, "What's Your Customer Sensitivity Quotient?", Corporate publication of JoAnna Brandi & Company, 25 March 2000 (www.joannabrandi.com/csq.html).

REFERENCES

Evans, Phillip, and Thomas Wurster. 1999. "Thinking Strategically About E-Commerce." *Perspectives,* corporate publication of the Boston Consulting Group, 29 December.

"Five Keys to Keeping Your Best Customers." 1996. *Harvard Management Update,* 1 July.

Gianforte, Greg. 2000. "The Insider's Guide to Customer Service on the Web: Eight Secrets for Successful E-Service." Corporate publication of Right Now Technologies, 22 March (www.rightnowtech.com).

Griffin, Jill. 1996. *Customer Loyalty: How to Earn It, How to Keep It.* San Francisco: Jossey-Bass Publishers.

How to Measure Customer Retention. 1998. Corporate publication of Harris Black International, March (www.retention.harrisblackintl.com).

Jones, Thomas O., and W. Earl Sasser, Jr. 1995. "Why Satisfied Customers Defect." *Harvard Business Review* (November–December): 88.

Planting, Sasha. 1999. "Customer Retention Strategies: Banks Fight to Retain Customer Loyalty." Corporate publication of Financial Mail (August) (www.fm.com.za).

Reichheld, Fredrick F. 1996. *The Loyalty Effect: The Hidden Force Behind Growth, Profits, and Lasting Value.* Boston: Harvard Business School Press.

Reichheld, Fredrick F. 1996. "Learning from Customer Defections." *Harvard Business Review* (March–April): 56–61.

Resnick, Jeff. 1996. "Making the Customer Retention Grade in the Financial Industry." *Marketing* (December). (Reprint available at www.opinionresearch.com/makgrade .htm.)

"The Role of Surveys in Customer Retention Programs." 1996–2000. *A Business Research Lab Tip* (www.busreslab.com).

Tyrrell, Bob. 1997. "The Cost of Losing a Customer Through Bad Service." *The Journal of Customer Relationships* 2 (Spring): 14–19. (Reprint available at www.bentleygroup.com /journal/body.htm.)

"Unisys Customer Retention Research Illuminates Key Challenges in Retail Banking." 1995. *Unisys,* Corporate publication, November (www.unisys.com).

"Why Online Retailers Are Flunking Out on Customer Service." 1999. *Internet Retailer News,* 16 July (www.internetretailer.com).

Wolhandler, Harold C., Julie Shaylor, Sue A. Shonbeck, Margaret S. Gurney, Jeanne A. Dietsch, Chris Anne Sheeler, and Tim Selby. 2000. "Capturing Online Markets: The Definitive Guide to Customer Loyalty, Executive Summary." Corporate publication of Active Media Research (Spring): 1–9 (www.activmediaresearch.com).

5

Creating New Markets for Customers with Diverse Needs

This chapter shows how your company can use the Internet to extend its reach into new markets and respond to the unique needs of its customers. Discover how your e-corporation can successfully move into new markets by following careful strategies based on effectively managing customer relationships. Read a number of success stories that detail how e-corporations have literally come from nowhere to become major market players. Look at ways to learn more about your customers, share that knowledge throughout the company, and support a corporate culture that reinforces your strategy and effectively uses technology to cross corporate divisions. This chapter discusses the current range of e-business models that are generating real revenue. Also, find out how to increase profits despite commoditization and what it takes to be customer focused without increasing operating costs. Finally, I'll show you how to zero in on "mass commoditization" to meet customers' needs and enter new markets without radically changing or adding new products or services.

YOUR E-CORPORATION: SPOTTING NEW OPPORTUNITIES FOR OLD PRODUCTS AND SERVICES

In the near past, corporations assumed that developing new markets was a big undertaking. Moreover, small companies did not have the wherewithal to consider such a venture due to the required logistics coordination, the retooling of products or services, and the need for a large physical presence. The new rules of today's e-commerce environment make these old assumptions obsolete. New markets and global virtual channels can be opened overnight to source, promote, sell, deliver, and support products and services. Louise Fickel, a writer for *CIO* magazine (1999), provides four examples of companies that used the Internet to expand and create new markets. The following examples are from the travel, telecommunications, and financial services industries.

Rosenbluth International (www.rosenbluth.com). In 1984, DuPont decided to let Neal Rosenbluth take charge of its travel business. Rosenbluth soon started talking with customers to find out how to lower travel costs. Customers wanted a more efficient travel reservation system, technology that allowed them access from anywhere in the world, consolidated management reporting, and a single point of contact for making decisions and purchases. Rosenbluth developed technology that met these customer needs. Now, Rosenbluth International has entered new markets and extended its existing markets by offering state-of-the-art online tools and responding to customers needs, such as:

- Anywhere, anytime online access to Rosenbluth International's self-booking tool, which assists customers in making reservations; finding faster, less expensive routes; ensuring compliance with corporate policies; and automating expense reporting.
- Web-based, downloadable Palm-based applications for tracking frequent-flyer miles and retrieving International travel tips.
- Access to a back-office program called Vision, which assists customers in negotiating prices with airlines.
- Alternatives for customers who don't have the time or can't afford to travel. Customers can book a TeleSuite virtual conference room in

any of 17 major cities and a few Hilton Hotels in the United States. Customers simply show up at a designated time and meet their colleagues on four-foot by eight-foot screens.

Cisco Systems Inc. (www.cisco.com). Cisco did not have the engineers and support personnel required to meet the needs of their growing customer base; therefore, in 1997 the company launched Cisco Connection Online. To keep Cisco Connection Online current, Cisco frequently solicits input via customer councils, focus groups, and e-mail. All responses are compiled into surveys that are reviewed at the executive level. Cisco Connection Online assisted in the expansion of Cisco's current market by adding ancillary and related services such as:

- Assisting customers in all parts of the customer relationship (the buying process, customer support, facts and specifications about products, and customer training). Cisco Connection Online answers about 80 percent of all customer queries.
- Offering online software downloads for customers who purchased Cisco hardware. About 90 percent of the company's software is downloaded from Cisco Connection Online.
- Assisting customers in configuring their software, pricing their purchases, tracking orders, managing service contracts, and submitting returns using the Web site's Internet Commerce Applications feature.

Charles Schwab, Inc. (www.schwab.com). Charles Schwab, Inc., realized that its customer base had diverse requirements, and that some customers were inherently more loyal and profitable than others. Schwab decided to meet the value these "right" customers required by providing access to their money anywhere and any way they wanted. To do this, Schwab had to break all the business models by deciding that the best way to meet customer needs was to let customers dictate when they wanted service and what types of services they wanted. Today, Schwab uses the best that technology has to offer and gives customers their choice of a variety of ways to reach their money. Customers now have access to their funds when and where they want (online, fax, telephone, Touch-Tone communications, or face-to-face with a broker).

Schwab provides a full menu of online investor services and customizable online tools. For example, with Stock Screener, customers decide the criteria for investment candidates. With Positions Monitor, customers monitor the performance of their investments. Overall, Schwab created a new market for online investors that combines the features of both electronic and traditional brokerages by:

- Attracting serious, committed investors with top-of-the-line Web customer support. For example, investors that want customer assistance can use Schwab's toll-free number to contact a registered sales representative for customer service 24 hours a day. You can use the same toll-free number for Touch-Tone quotes and trades. Additionally, there are toll-free numbers for stock and bond brokers. For individuals who want to meet face-to-face, there are over 300 branch offices open from 8 AM to 5 PM Monday through Friday (and some branches are open from 9 am to 1 pm on Saturday).
- Offering offline services and support. About 70 percent of new accounts are opened at offline branches, where customers can map out investment strategies face-to-face with a professional.
- Providing personalized attention for high-value customers with Signature Services (a program designed for investors with $100,000 or more in Schwab accounts, or who make 12 trades or more per month). This program includes online research, real-time quotes, and a priority phone access.

USAA (www.usaa.com). USAA serves more than three million customers—primarily members of the U.S. military and their families (a fairly uniform customer base). Its products and services include property/casualty and life insurance, banking, discount brokerage, and investment management. USAA is also involved in real estate development. USAA focuses on providing stability to members by offering them the ability to access their accounts and to do business with USAA online. Members can also telephone the company's call centers, which use technology to create a feeling that the company knows the customer. Call center representatives can use the company's Enterprise Needs-Based Sales and Service Tool to generate a customized profile of services that the member might find useful. In addition to financial services, USAA has entered several new markets:

- USAA's Alliance Services sells merchandise (computers, furniture, giftware, jewelry, and home and auto safety items) online and in seasonal catalogs.
- USAA's Member Privileges include car rental and long-distance telephone services through USAA's Buying Services.

SELECTING E-BUSINESS MODELS FOR WIDE-RANGING CUSTOMER NEEDS

In the past, managers were asked, "What business are you in?" Today, managers are asked, "What is your business model?" According to Adrian Slywotzky (1999), new challengers are using business models to gain industry leadership. For example, Compaq reinvented the business model for computer companies (to IBM's dismay), and then Dell reinvented the business model again. Southwest Airlines reinvented the business model for airlines to the consternation of American Airlines. Nucor reinvented the business model for steel manufacturers (to the surprise of U.S. Steel). All of these new business models reduced costs from 10 to 20 percent, creating new opportunities and new markets for the upstart challengers.

All of these e-corporations are successful, and each uses a different e-business model. This highlights an important point: Your e-corporation can have diverse goals and use different e-business models to achieve those goals. Selecting and understanding which e-business model is appropriate for you is critical in developing a Web site that meets the strategic goals of your e-corporation. Additionally, you need to know where your company is before you journey into new, uncharted markets; in other words, does the current e-business model work for a new market or does your e-corporation have to change to another e-business model? Gary Hamell and Jeff Sampler, writers for *Fortune* magazine (December 1998), sum up the importance of e-business models by stating: "Somewhere out there is a bullet with your company's name on it. Somewhere out there is a competitor, unborn and unknown, that will render your business model obsolete. . . .

Competition today is not between products, it's between business models, and the hottest and most dangerous new business models out there are on the Web."

Michael Rappa (2000) of North Carolina State University observes that e-commerce supports new types of business models. Rappa provides the following primer of how e-business models are shaping up. The nine e-business model types are listed in alphabetical order; however, keep in mind that new business models are being invented every day.

The Advertising Model

The advertising model is one of the most popular e-business models on the Net. Web site content is often free and mixed with advertising (which supports the Web site). The advertising model only works for Web sites with specialized high volume traffic. For example, an online publishing company selling advertising wants to keep e-customers on the site for as long as possible to see the most ads.

- *Generalized portals.* Generalized portals are supported by advertising and attract tens of million of visits per month by offering generic and diversified content or services. A good example is AltaVista (www .altavista.com), which is designed for all types of users.
- *Personalized portals.* These Web sites provide prescreened prospective customers and offer information about consumer behavior. A good example is My Yahoo! (my.yahoo.com). My Yahoo! allows users to change the layout of the Web page so it meets their interests.
- *Specialized portals.* Specialized portals attract golfers, homebuyers, and so on. Advertisers are often willing to pay a premium for this audience. A good example is Quicken Mortgage (www.quickenmort gage.com). Quicken Mortgage is designed for homebuyers seeking mortgages.
- *Attention/Incentive portals.* Corporations with complex products find it useful to use this pay-for-attention model. Good examples of these loyalty-based relationship marketing Web sites are My Points (www .mypoints.com) and Free Ride (www.freeride.com).

FIGURE 5.1   The bargain discounter e-business model, used by Buy.com, is an online shopper favorite.

- *Free model.* These high-volume Web sites give something away for free (usually high-quality content) and provide corporations with advertising opportunities. Good examples are InvestorGuide (www .investorguide.com) and Blue Mountain electronic greeting cards (www.bluemountain.com). With these Web sites, advertisers pay the cost for providing free information or services.

- *Bargain discounter.* Here, goods and services are often sold at cost or below cost. The Web site owners seek to make a profit through advertising revenue. Shown in Figure 5.1 is Buy.com (www.buy.com), a good example of this business model. At Buy.com, advertisers provide the cash needed so the e-corporation can offer products at below cost.

The Affiliate Model

Affiliate models do not require high-volume traffic and provide purchase opportunities wherever individuals are surfing the Internet. Affiliate programs provide purchase-point click-throughs to merchant opportunities. This is a pay-for-performance model; if the affiliate does not produce sales, it represents no cost to the merchant. Variations of the affiliate model include banner exchanges, pay-per-click, and revenue sharing agreements. A good example is BeFree (www.befree.com). Affiliated merchants pay BeFree when they send a customer their way.

The Brokerage Model

Brokers bring buyers and sellers together and enable transactions. The brokers charge a fee for each transaction they facilitate. These transactions can be between two businesses (sometimes called B2B or B-to-B) or business to consumer (B2C or B-to-C):

- *Buy/sell fulfillment.* Companies that use this model are online financial brokers like Fidelity (www.fidelity.com) that charge a transaction fee. Some brokerages work on volume and low overhead and deliver the best-negotiated price, for example, Cars Direct (www.carsdirect .com). If you have ever traded stocks online, you have experienced the brokerage model firsthand.
- *Market exchange.* Market exchanges are usually B-to-B with pricing based on offer/buy, offer/negotiated buy, or auction offer/bid. For an example of this model, see the MetalSite's Buyer Connection (www .metalsite.com), which lets buyers access information and purchase directly from steel manufacturers and service centers. You can find prime and nonprime steel. To purchase, you can bid, buy, or negotiate a deal. Online, you can order, pay, ship, and track your purchase.
- *Buyer aggregator.* For a fee, the buyer aggregator brings individual purchasers together via the Internet to act as a group, so they can receive volume discounts and other benefits. For a good example of this model, see MobShop (www.mobshop.com). The MobShop Net-

work is based on a committed principle: Discount prices should not be the exclusive privilege of large volume buyers. Thanks to the Internet, these preferred savings, once only available to large businesses, are now available to individuals and small businesses making single purchases.

- *Distributor.* Online catalog-type operations connect a large number of product manufacturers. For manufacturers, this decreases the cost of sales. Purchasers receive specific quotes from preferred distributors and get buyer-specific prices, suggestions, and substitutions. A good example of an online distributor is NECX (www.necx.com). NECX Direct, LLC, recently announced it had joined forces with Gateway Computers (www.gateway.com). This partnership supports Gateway's commitment to building lifelong client relationships through its "beyond the box" approach to offering hardware, services, and products, including a wide array of accessories, through NECX Direct.

- *Virtual mall.* A virtual mall is a Web site that hosts many merchants. Malls charge merchants setup and monthly listing fees. They provide automated transaction services and relationship marketing opportunities. A good example is Yahoo! Stores (shopping.yahoo.com). Yahoo! Stores offers a list of products, including apparel, arts, books, and computers. Click on the hyperlink to hundreds of stores that sell that type of product. You can pay for all your purchases with Yahoo! Wallet. Yahoo! Wallet has all your credit card and shipping information in a single secure place, so you don't have to keep entering the same information over and over again.

- *Meta-intermediary.* For a fee, the Web site provides merchants with back-end services, like financial settlement and quality assurance. Meta-intermediaries protect consumers by ensuring satisfaction with merchants. A good example is VirtualSellers (www.virtualsellers .com). VirtualSellers.com was created to provide a complete back-end service for e-commerce. By using turnkey order processing, you can, in essence, outsource the entire process. VirtualSellers handles the design and setup of the online shopping baskets; the processing and tracking of the order; and the authentication, verification, and authorization of the credit cards. VirtualSellers even accepts checks electronically and by fax.

- *Auction broker.* The auction broker charges individuals or merchants a fee, which is usually scaled to the value of the transaction. In an online auction, a seller takes the highest bid from a buyer, that is, above a minimum or reserve price. The most popular auction broker is eBay (www.ebay.com). Auction site eBay is the world's largest garage sale. It's a place to find the stuff you want to buy, and to put the stuff you want to sell on the market.
- *Reverse auction.* The buyer makes a final bid for a specific good or service, and the broker seeks fulfillment. The brokerage fee is the spread between the bid amount and fulfillment price (and sometimes a processing fee). A good example of a reverse auction is Priceline.com (www.priceline.com). Priceline.com lets customers name their own price for airline tickets, hotels, and car rentals. If the seller agrees to your price, you've got a deal.
- *Classifieds.* Classifieds are often run by local news content providers, prices may or may not be specified, and anyone listing pays a fee. Online classified ads are big business. For example, AdOne Classified Network (www.adone.com), which was founded in 1995, is a provider of online classified solutions for the publishing industry. AdOne has formed alliances with more than 100 publishers, representing over 500 publications and a nationwide print readership of more than 37 million. AdOne hosts a network of online classifieds and has served more than three million cumulative online ads to date. AdOne's products and services help publishers put their classifieds online and enable them to generate new revenue.
- *Search agent.* Search agents seek hard-to-find information, price comparisons, or the lowest price for a specific product or service. A good example is DealTime (www.dealtime.com). DealTime is a free online comparison-shopping service that locates the Web sites offering deals on the products you want to buy. DealTime doesn't sell. DealTime lists the online merchants, auctions, classifieds, and group buying sites that match your shopping criteria, so that you decide where to shop and avoid aimless searching for online deals.

The Community Model

The viability of the community model is based on user loyalty and not high traffic volume. Users have often invested both time and emotion into the Web site and sometimes contribute Web site content. The community model may be supported by a combination of subscriptions, fees for premium services, and advertising revenue. For example, FamilyEducation.com (www.familyeducation.com), a K–12 Internet community, has among other things a service specifically designed for teachers. TeacherVision.com provides an easy, convenient one-stop shop of resources specifically designed for teachers' needs. Another example of the community model is AOL's Digital City (www.digitalcity.com). Each of the participating Digital City sites offers community news, resources for improving race relations, and comment boards. Digital City's self-publishing tools allow members to engage in candid conversations about race with others from the community. Digital City sites also provide a link to the Western Justice Center's database of hundreds of organizations specializing in community-based mediation and intergroup dialogue.

- *Business trading community.* Sometimes known as a vertical Web community or "vortal," these Web sites offer comprehensive information and dialogue for a particular vertical market. Content may include product information in buyer's guides, supplier and product directories, daily industry news and articles, job listings, and classified ads. A good example is Buzzsaw.com (www.buzzsaw.com). Buzzsaw.com is leading the design and construction industry towards a whole new way of working. Buzzsaw offers a set of services that streamlines many aspects of the building process, from design to construction and from bidding to buying.
- *Knowledge networks.* These Web sites are either free or fee-based and provide information based on professional expertise or the experiences of users. A good free example is ExpertGuru.com (www.expertguru.com), and a good fee-based example is Guru.com (www.guru.com). Guru.com is designed to assist solo practitioners. Guru.com makes finding work easier by allowing professionals to post online resumés and to browse a database of freelance projects. To reduce the

hassle of running a solo business, Guru.com made it easier to access service, support, and guidance by setting up community discussion areas where professionals can find answers to their most vexing questions.

The Infomediary Model

Infomediaries provide e-corporations with data about consumer behavior and buying habits. Some infomediaries buy and sell information to other businesses, such as Net Zero (www.netzero.com). In return for their patronage, users get free Internet access or hardware. Additionally, infomediaries work in the opposite direction and provide consumers with useful information about Web sites. A good example is Gomez Advisors (www.gomez.com). Gomez provides a view of online customer experience by combining industry-specific expertise, objective and extensive Internet evaluation methodology, and high-quality community ratings and reviews of online businesses. Specifically, Gomez Advisors provides information, free of charge, about banks, brokers, credit cards, homebuying, insurance and mortgages, travel, shopping, autos, dynamic pricing, health, computers, and office equipment. At Gomez.com, you can discover who the best online broker is, where you can buy boots, and what the best online toy store is.

- *Recommender system.* This system allows Internet users to exchange opinions (both good and bad) with each other about the quality of products, services, and sellers. Recommender system agents monitor user habits and thereby increase the relevance of their recommendations and the value to the collector. For example, in the past the Helpful Online Music Recommendation Service (HOMR) recommended musical artists.

  There are also automatic recommendation systems. For example, ClickTheButton (www.clickthebutton.com) offers a personal Comparison Cart that finds deals on several products at once. With the click of a button, consumers add items to their Comparison Cart as they browse the Web. When they're ready to buy, ClickTheButton calculates the best total prices on the combination of items chosen, including tax and shipping, and then leads consumers to store order pages.

- *Registration model.* Many high-quality content sites require "free" registration. This allows tracking of the individual's user patterns and generates data for targeted advertising campaigns. A good example is the online version of *The New York Times* (www.nytimes.com).

The Manufacturer Model

A manufacturer model allows the manufacturer to directly contact the consumer (cutting out the wholesaler and the retailer). The manufacturer model offers cost savings, which may or may not be passed along to the consumer, and presents channel conflicts with existing wholesalers and retailers. Additionally, manufacturers gain a better understanding of consumer needs and preferences. A good example is Intel (www.intel.com).

The Merchant Model

Online merchants, sometimes called e-tailers, are online wholesalers and retailers of products and services that may not have brick-and-mortar stores. Sales may be based on list prices or auctions.

- *Virtual merchant.* A virtual merchant is a company that only operates on the Web. A good example of a dot-com merchant is e-Toys (www.etoys.com).
- *Catalog merchant.* Mail order catalogs are now online. A good example is Finger Hut (www.fingerhut.com).
- *Surf-and-turf.* Traditional brick-and-mortar stores now offer their merchandise in online stores. There are many examples of "click-and-mortar" in almost any industry. For example, Chase Manhattan Bank has branches and a Web site (www.chasemanhattan.com), Barnes and Noble (www.barnesandnoble.com) has a Web site and a nationwide chain of bookstores, and at Albertson's in Seattle and Dallas you can order your groceries online (www.albertsons.com) or go to the grocery store.

The Subscription Model

Internet users pay a monthly or annual subscription fee for Web site content that is often restricted or essential. A good example is the *Wall Street Journal* interactive edition (www.wsj.com). To drive volume and get advertising revenue, some Web site owners combine free content with subscription-based content or services. A good example of this combination is Hoovers (www.hoovers.com). Accrue Software, Inc. (1999) states the subscription model is one of the most common e-business models. However, Jupiter Communications recently noted that 46 percent of Internet users would not pay to view content on the Web.

The Utility Model

Here, Internet users pay for the bits and bytes they use. Variations of this model are Web sites that charge for papers, articles, or other content by the day, page, or article. Good examples are Lexis-Nexis (www.lexis-nexis.com) and Dow Jones Publications (ip.dowjones.com/content/pub dir/pubdir.asp).

AVOIDING THE COMMODITIZATION TRAP

According to Caroline Chauncey (1997), Henry Birdseye Weil, a senior lecturer in the Strategic and International Management Group of MIT's Sloan School of Management, says the process of "commoditization"—the descent into entrenched price warfare that erodes profit margins and chokes off funding for innovation—is inevitable in any industry. However, companies like Intel have successfully changed their business models to avoid the commoditization trap.

Intel used to make memory chips (a commodity). The company switched to processors and again was threatened by commoditization. In response to this threat, Intel changed its business model and began to market processors as a branded consumer product. (Remember the "Intel Inside" sticker that came with your last computer?) However, there are dangers in redefining the corporation. UAL, the holding company for United Airlines, the number-one air carrier in the world, had this problem not too long ago. UAL defined itself as a travel company, under the name Allegis. Allegis included hotels, car rentals, and United Airlines. No one got the connection, and Allegis was later broken up.

The Intel and United Airlines examples show the difficulties of avoiding commoditization and creating new markets. The e-commerce environment exacerbates this problem. In the e-commerce marketplace, competition and technology move so fast that marketers frequently do not have the time to gather extensive marketing data. This makes it difficult for managers to prioritize the markets they choose to address. According to Cirrus Marketing, "High-tech companies often see a small, unfilled niche within a market, create a product to fill it, and hope a sizable market will appear to support their efforts." In contrast, evolving relationships where customers feel their unique needs are understood can point to profitable new markets. Rahul Jacob (1994) states that companies can successfully create new markets by collaborating with their customers. Jacob uses Canon and L.L. Bean as examples of how innovation based on leveraged customer knowledge can avoid commoditization, extend the company's reach, and increase profitability:

- Canon Computer Systems had a database of 1.3 million customers. The database was used to target prospective color scanner customers. A direct mail solicitation asked printer owners if they were interested in a new color scanner for desktop publishing. The response rate was an amazing 50 percent. The company then offered interested consumers four free ink cartridges if they purchased the new color scanner. This example shows how Canon very quickly and quietly moved their customers to a new market.
- Figure 5.2 shows the Web site of L.L. Bean (www.llbean.com). L.L. Bean customer service representatives input customer telephone comments into the company's information system. Within days, decision makers in different parts of the organization have access to this data. As a result of this information gathering and market research, L.L. Bean introduced a successful line of children's clothing. This example shows how collecting and sharing information can result in a company successfully moving customers to a new market.

FIGURE 5.2   L.L. Bean leveraged its customer knowledge to successfully enter a new market.

Screen shot courtesy of L.L. Bean Inc.—www.llbean.com.

HOW TREATING DIFFERENT CUSTOMERS DIFFERENTLY CAN LEAD TO MORE PROFITS

Diane Brady (2000) notes that when you sit down in a car and look at the dashboard, with its various places to plug in different dials and gauges in any range of combinations, you are seeing the effects of mass customization. Your car radio can have knobs, slide handles, or radio dials. The upholstery can be any one of seven colors with your choice of leather, shiny velour, or high-grade matte fabric, giving you a choice of 21 ways to customize the interior. This, with your choice of other combinations of options, lets you customize your new car in a thousand ways. Lear Corporation, makers of automotive interiors, will even make an orange dashboard if you so desire. Due to advances in digital technology, this level of customization will cost about the same price and will not significantly delay delivery time of your new car. Today, consumers can often communicate directly with manufacturers via the Internet, where their instructions are absorbed into the production process.

According to Joseph Pine II (1996), one of the vital challenges to businesses today is being customer focused. Consequently, businesses must understand and fulfill each individual customer's diverse wants and needs, while keeping costs as low as possible. Pine notes that "mass customization" is one solution to this dilemma. Mass customization can serve a large and complex market, while efficiently responding to the needs and desires of individual customers.

Implementing a mass-customization strategy allows your company to develop dialogues (via the Internet, faxes, or kiosks) with customers to learn what they desire in products and services. This dialogue builds a relationship, which in turn strengthens the bond of customer loyalty. Ideally, mass customization assists customers in selecting the optimum product or service for their needs and then, as time goes on, to adjust that product or service as their needs change. However, the product or service may not be personalized in any way. In other words, numerous mass-customized products and services can be standardized commodities surrounded by customized service.

Many new companies, in an attempt to meet customers' needs, have invented new extensions of their programs or new products. However, just adding products for the sake of adding products is not the answer. In many organizations, managers do not have any incentives to question product-line extension strategies. John A. Quelch (1994) notes that marketers argue for more line extensions to serve an increasingly segmented marketplace, and sales managers use new line products to justify hiring more salespeople. Manufacturing managers are concerned about the complexity of production, and the finance department has a clear interest in cost control. The information systems needed to cull the data that would justify a more focused product line are often not in place. Quelch says this approach frequently results in hidden cost increases and weakened brand images.

One way to avoid unnecessary costs and operation complexity is to select one of Joseph Pine's (1996) four approaches to mass customization. Pine's approach harnesses the power of information technology to assist your company in effectively meeting the unique needs of its customers:

1. *Collaborative mass customization.* Your company collaborates with customers to determine their needs. This is an excellent approach, because many customers find it difficult to articulate what they want and grow frustrated when forced to select from a plethora of options. For a good example, see the Loyalty Marketing Success Story of Pitney Bowes that follows.

2. *Adaptive mass customization.* Your company offers one standard, but it is customizable product or service that is designed so users can alter it themselves. This approach is for your company if your products perform in different ways on different occasions; for example, the Motorola pagers discussed earlier.

3. *Cosmetic mass customization.* Your company presents a different standard to different customers; in other words, your product is packaged and presented to a certain set of customers. Different features and benefits are highlighted, and the customer's name is placed on the item, for example, company logos on shirts or conference logos on tote bags.

4. *Transparent mass customization.* Your company provides customers with unique goods or services that they do not realize have been customized for them; for example, a real estate agency unbundles its services and creates a menu of specific services and prices. The customer requests specific real estate services (no marketing, limited advertising, no open houses, etc.). The agency inconspicuously customizes their offerings within a standard package and presents the customer with a unique package of services.

The story of Pitney Bowes shows how the company transformed its organization to be competitive in worldwide communication channels by creating collaborative mass-customization solutions to meet customers' diverse needs. Pitney Bowes has gone beyond postage meters and now provides unique solutions to customer-specific problems.

LOYALTY MARKETING SUCCESS STORY

Pitney Bowes

▼ **COMPANY:** Pitney Bowes (www.pitneybowes.com) and postage meters have always gone hand in hand. However, with the Internet age, the company's former Chairman George Harvey began planning for a future where fax, e-mail, voicemail, and the Internet would surface as the world's leading messaging systems. With these new communication channels, Pitney Bowes's competition rapidly increased. To remain competitive, Pitney Bowes needed to create new markets for its customers' diverse needs.

▼ **SOLUTION:** Pitney Bowes realized that a product marketing approach could only take them so far. Therefore, the company developed several services to meet its customers' emerging needs. One of the services assists utilities and similar companies with invoicing. Many of the customers of these companies want to be invoiced in a particular way. Pitney Bowes's invoicing service sends invoices via e-mail, online, and fax.

▼ **BENEFITS:** Pitney Bowes is convinced that the company's shift from a product-based to a customer-based culture is just an evolution of the entire corporate culture. Today, any employee who "touches" the customer is responsible for customer satisfaction.

- The management team of Pitney Bowes believes that the culture of service has become the company's primary advantage.
- Over the past 15 consecutive quarters, Pitney Bowes has posted earnings growth. Over the past two years, the company's market capitalization has grown from $7 billion to $15 billion.
- Pitney Bowes plans to evolve to meet the needs of its many customers.

Source: Adapted from Pitney Bowes, "Success Stories," Peppers and Rogers Group/Marketing 1 to 1 (www.1to1.com/tools/), 20 March 2000.

FIGURE 5.3   Pitney Bowes meets the challenge of the Internet age.

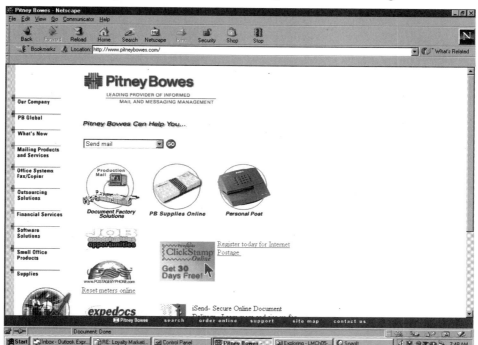

USING MASS CUSTOMIZATION TO CREATE NEW MARKETS

The rich have always enjoyed the luxury of custom-made products. With today's technology, it is possible to deliver many custom-designed products to middle-class consumers. Today's emerging new economy indicates that mass customization is not a fad. There has always been a drive to bring what consumers buy closer to what they really want. The closer a product or service meets a customer's needs, the more benefit it has. Therefore, mass customization means that customers are getting more for less. This increases customer loyalty and ensures repeat business.

According to Don Peppers, Martha Rogers, and Bob Dorf (1998), there are a number of ways to divide the corporation into modules to provide a wide range of mass-customization options that go beyond the primary product or service. In other words, you do not have to radically change your products or services to mass customize. Your enterprise can tailor the way it behaves with respect to each customer, so it appears to provide an individualized product or service. Peppers, Rogers, and Dorf provide the following examples:

- *Bundling.* Package two or more products to sell. Examples include related products (shoes and socks), consumables with products (printers and toner cartridges), and high-quantity discounts (a dozen bagels).
- *Configuration.* Without changing the product or service, preconfigure it to meet the customer's specifications, for example, telephones with preset speed dials.
- *Packaging.* Variations of the product or service are targeted for consumer types: smaller jars of spaghetti sauce for singles and couples, larger print for seniors, and multipacks for growing families.
- *Delivery and logistics.* Deliver the product at the customer's convenience. Deliver at a specific location at a prearranged time, keep inventory at the customer's location, and offer free shipping for your best customers.
- *Ancillary services.* Provide after-sale services; for example, provide automatic pickup and delivery of carpets for cleaning or computer maintenance programs.
- *Service enhancements.* Service enhancements make your e-corporation a one-stop shop for the customer, for example, next-day computer repairs or overnight laptop overhauls. For high-value customers, the fees for service enhancements can be waived, creating additional value and building customer loyalty.
- *Invoicing.* Send invoices when it is convenient for the customer. Provide invoices in a customer-determined format and offer cash discounts. Additionally, invoicing can be by fax, e-mail, or via the Internet.
- *Payment terms.* Design payment terms that are preferred by buyers, for example, smaller payments and longer terms, deferred billing and paying full price, and other types of customized payment arrangements.

- *Preauthorization.* Preset authorization and limits to meet customer needs; for example, executives can order leather chairs, but secretaries can only order $100 worth of supplies per month.
- *Streamlining services.* Restructure the accounting and shipping functions for long-term customers. This can include "low document" purchasing to reward customer loyalty. Use preapproval and preset criteria to make purchasing company products and services more convenient and time efficient.

SUMMING IT UP

- The competitive nature of business in the 1990s has led to a constant quest for ways of achieving market dominance. Implementing a new e-business model is often the answer for increased market share and entry into new markets.
- A key to the success of your e-corporation may be implementing mass customization as a strategy to redefine your products or services and to avoid being just another commodity.
- Mass customization can be defined as breaking down your organization into modules and using each module in a way that meets unique customer needs. Products and services match diverse customer needs closer than ever before and increase customer loyalty.

USING CUSTOMER INFORMATION TO UNCOVER
CUSTOMER NEEDS AND MARKET OPPORTUNITIES

With e-commerce poised to exceed $1.3 trillion early in our new century, e-business is the greatest opportunity and threat to existing business models since the industrial revolution. You'll need to use customer information to define your business strategies and assess new e-commerce opportunities. The following activity is a "thought starter" for how you can help the major divisions in your corporation spot new opportunities.

Contact the major divisions in your corporation. Ask the appropriate department to answer the questions in bold print. Answers to these questions can assist the company in spotting new opportunities.

▼ **SALES**

Current Practice: How many customers do we have and what is the size of the average basket?

New Question: What do my most valuable customers look like and how do we get more of them? What else are our customers shopping for and where? Which customers are about to leave us, and how do we keep them?

_____

_____

▼ **MARKETING**

Current Practice: What prices should we be charging?

New Question: What price maximizes the value of an individual relationship? Which customers should get discounts and when?

_____

_____

▼ CUSTOMER SUPPORT

Current Practice: Are we providing good customer service?

New Question: What media works best for communicating with our customers? How can we present offers to our customers?

_____

_____

▼ PROJECT DEVELOPMENT

Current Practice: Are we providing good customer service?

New Question: Which product is each of my customers demanding and through which channels? Given that our customers purchased certain products and services, what other ones will they buy? How are customers shopping online? Are our Web site capabilities consistent with how our customers shop?

_____

_____

▼ DISTRIBUTION AND SUPPLIERS

Current Practice: For products: How much inventory should we carry? For services: How much capacity should we have?

New Question: What assortment and sizes are our most valuable customers demanding online? What products or services are going to be sold and when?

_____

_____

Source: Adapted from "New Metrics for a New Millennium: Customer Equity," an online publication of Arthur Andersen (www.arthurandersen.com), 7 April 2000.

REFERENCES

Brady, Diane (with Katie Kerwin, David Welch, Louise Lee, and Rob Hof). 2000. Industrial Management: Automation: Customizing for the Masses. *Business Week,* 20 March, 130–33.

Chauncey, Caroline T. 1997. A Model for Maturing Markets. *Technology Review* 100 (21 November): 12–14.

Colvin, Geoffrey. 1997. Smart Manager: Value Driven. *Fortune,* 29 December, 279–81.

Cox, W. Michael, and Richard Alm. 1999. America's Move to Mass Customization. *Consumers' Research Magazine,* 1 June.

Davis, Stanley. 1987. *Future Perfect.* Reading, Mass.: Addison-Wesley.

e-Business Analysis and Accrue Insight, White Paper Part I of II. 1999. Corporate publication of Accrue Software Inc., 4 February, 1–3.

Fickel, Louise. 1999. Know Your Customer. *CIO* magazine, 15 August, 1–6.

The Five New Rules of the Electronic Economy. 2000. Online publication of *Arthur Andersen,* 7 April (www.ac.com/services/cht/cht_ecommerce_rule5.html).

Gilmore, James H., and Joseph B. Pine. 1997. The Four Faces of Mass Customization. *Harvard Business Review* (January-February): 91–101.

Hamell, Gary, and Jeff Sampler. 1998. The e-Corporation. *Fortune,* December, 80–91.

Jacob, Rahul. 1994. Selling: Why Some Customers Are More Equal Than Others. *Fortune,* 19 September, 215–19.

Loyalty Abuse: Marketers Must Remember That a Successful Loyalty Strategy Is Founded on Attitude, not Technology. 1998. *Marketing Magazine* 103 (5 October): 29.

Mische, Michael A. 1997. The Competitive Value of Innovation. *The Journal of Customer Relationships* (Winter). Online reprint available at www.eloyaltyco.com/journal/index.htm.

Peppers, Don, Martha Rogers, and Bob Dorf. 1998. *The One to One Field Book.* New York: Doubleday.

Pine, Joseph G., II. 1996. Serve Each Customer Efficiently and Uniquely. *Business Communications Review* 26 (1 January): S2-6.

Positioning: Target Marketing for High Tech Products. 2000. Online publication of Telesian Technology, 7 April, 1–5 (www.cirusmarketing.com).

Quelch, John A. 1994. Extend Profits, Not Product Lines. *Harvard Business Review* (September-October): 153–60.

Rappa, Michael. 2000. Business Models on the Web. Online publication of North Carolina State University, 7 April (ecommerce.ncsu.edu/business_models).

Slywotzky, Adrian. 1999. How Digital Is Your Company? *Fast Company,* 1 February, 94–102.

Automating the Customer Loyalty Process

▼ Discovering how to start an online customer loyalty program

▼ Identifying the types of Internet incentive and reward programs

▼ Developing an online loyalty program

▼ Finding out how to set loyalty goals and measure your success

Automating the customer loyalty process can be using a Web-based, industry-specific database tool, improving communications, or providing "soft benefits" that make e-customers feel special. This chapter shows how loyalty incentive and reward programs are more successful online than offline. Internet surfers frequently use loyalty programs at special portals, specific e-commerce Web sites, or spread throughout the Internet by promotion networks. The variety of features offered by these Internet-based loyalty programs is staggering. Because of this wide range of online loyalty programs, there are many programs that match the needs of the largest or the smallest e-corporation.

The first step in developing an online loyalty program is determining exactly what are your customers' values. This assists managers in selecting the right types of rewards for the loyalty program. Next, the objectives of the loyalty plan need to be tested. If the economics do not support an online loyalty program, your company may gain a greater return by investing in automating the sales force or beefing up online customer service and support. This chapter concludes with a discussion about the importance of setting goals for the online loyalty program and measuring your company's success.

WHY HAVE AN ONLINE CUSTOMER LOYALTY PROGRAM?

Recent reports indicate that e-commerce sites are turning over as much as 60 percent of their customers every six weeks. This led a few pundits to describe the e-commerce buying experience as an "online vending machine" and highlights the difficulty of building online customer loyalty. Some e-corporations have made their Web sites more "sticky" by introducing online loyalty programs. NFO Interactive, an online market research firm located in Greenwich, Connecticut, surveyed a representative sample of 1,905 online customers and determined that about 53 percent of all online consumers would buy more online if reward points or incentives were offered at a specific retail Web site. Moreover, 47 percent of the online consumers said they would return regularly to a specific e-commerce or retail Web site if they knew they would receive reward points or other loyalty incentives. NFO notes that only 15 percent of online consumers indicated rewards programs had no influence on their purchasing decisions.

LOYALTY AND YOUR E-CUSTOMERS

According to Richard G. Barlow (2000), chairman and CEO of Frequency Marketing Inc. in Cincinnati, Ohio, over 60 million Americans belong to frequent-flyer loyalty programs. Also, households often belong to grocery frequent-shopper programs, and credit cards with reward components are one of the fastest-growing segments of the credit card business. Rewards are even being attached to debit cards. More companies are offering loyalty programs, because it is easier and less expensive than ever before, and customers have come to expect it. This means that you cannot ignore customer loyalty programs that provide incentives such as Web currency, frequent-flyer miles, upgrades, elite memberships, and other rewards that assist in creating compelling online customer bonds.

The Guest Net Success Story below shows how a Web-based database program can facilitate loyalty among a hotel's best customers. Patrick J. Kennedy, the owner of La Mansión del Rio, realized that to be successful his hotel needed to increase customer retention by building customer loyalty. Therefore, he created a Web-based database application specifically for hotels called Guest Net (www.guestnet.com). Guest Net is an excellent example of how companies can automate the customer loyalty process. For example, if a special art exhibition will be on display in a city where a subscriber hotel is located, by using the Guest Net database software system that property can generate a list of all hotel customers with an interest in art who have previously stayed at that particular hotel or anywhere throughout the system. A special mailing targeted to this group can announce a weekend package that includes tickets to the exhibit, special receptions with the curator, and other benefits.

LOYALTY MARKETING SUCCESS STORY

Guest Net

▼ **COMPANY:** The hotel industry cultivates its "best guests" because they outspend new guests by a ratio of five to one. Additionally, it generally costs less to retain current customers than to acquire new ones. This indicates that repeat business is essential to the profitability of hotels. Patrick J. Kennedy, owner of La Mansión del Rio in San Antonio, Texas, was losing money due to a lack of customer loyalty.

▼ **SOLUTION:** Kennedy created a customer loyalty program that was so successful he standardized some of the techniques. Recently, Kennedy developed the Guest Net Information System, a Web-based service that provides domestic and international hotel subscribers with the capability of accessing customer data in real time and to begin crafting relationship management marketing programs for their best guests (anyone who has stayed at the same hotel five or more times).

▼ **BENEFITS:** Guest Net Information System provides database information and an electronic communications system.

- The Guest Net Information System compiles highly detailed guest-purchase histories and preference information, to which demographic and lifestyle information can be added.
- Subscribers have the capability to access customer data in real time, which allows hotels to personalize services, products, and experiences to match guests' needs.

Source: Adapted from La Mansión del Rio, "Success Stories," Peppers and Rogers Group/Marketing 1 to 1 (www.1to1.com/tools/), 19 February 2000.

Cultivating customer loyalty can result in a strategic advantage and competitive differentiation that can ward off the commoditization of products and services in the e-commerce marketplace. Customer loyalty programs can encourage customers to feel a connection or, better yet, an allegiance with your e-corporation's products or services. One way to do this is to make certain that your performance consistently exceeds customer expectations. Additionally, your e-corporation can cultivate online customer loyalty with:

- *Personalized Web sites that engage the e-customer.* After a purchase, your e-corporation can entice the customer to return to the Web site with follow-up (customer approved) e-mail messages about special offers and other information.
- *Ongoing customer relationships.* Your Web site recognizes the returning customer as a repeat customer and allows the customer to enroll in a reminder or alert e-mail notification service.
- *Effective customer communications.* In addition to providing customers with a way to check the status of their orders, respond to e-mail and telephone inquiries within 24 hours or sooner.
- *Rewards programs that facilitate loyalty among your e-corporation's best customers.* Remember that all customers are not created equal. If the customer invests time and effort in an online loyalty program, he or she will automatically provide you with much needed information about customer buying behaviors, desires, wants, and needs. With this information, you can distribute more rewards to your most loyal customers.

FIGURE 6.1   Guest Net provides real information in real time.

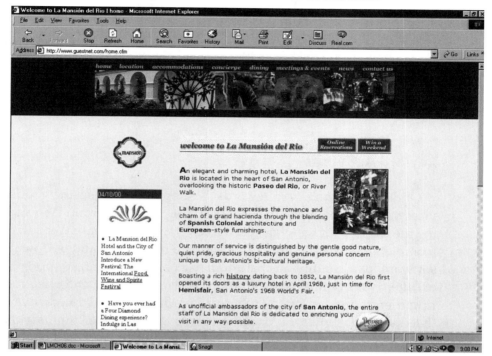

The Online "Gimme" Factor

"Web site effectiveness was once measured by the number of hits. Today, it is measured by purchases. Online consumers have the gimme factor. That is, 'I'm here at your Web site. Now make it worth my while to buy something,'" explains Lee Smith, vice president at NFO Interactive. Strategically planned loyalty programs can be powerful marketing tools to increase customer retention and build customer loyalty. NFO Interactive also notes that over 50 percent of the respondents to a recent study indicated they would happily provide personal information in return for a reward or incentive. Online rewards are generally divided into five categories:

1. *Cash*—cash-back programs, cash rebates, or receiving cash for completing certain activities

2. *Travel*—frequent-flyer miles, free or discounted transportation, and vacation packages
3. *Savings*—receiving products or services for less than full price
4. *Free stuff*—receiving a free gift, product, or service in return for completing a reward activity or based on the accumulation of reward points or Web currency
5. *Charity*—a reward activity or earned commodity can be donated to a selected charity

Reward Activities

Online consumers earn rewards by shopping (purchasing goods or services online); viewing Web sites (spending time on certain Web sites, surfing the Internet, or viewing specific advertising material); Web interactions (completing forms or surveys, receiving e-mail notifications, downloading software, participating in chat room discussions or fantasy sports leagues, or other types of interactive Internet-based activities); and referrals (referring friends and family to the rewards program). NFO Interactive reports that online consumers favor certain types of rewards. A summary of online consumer preferences based on a NFO Interactive study is as follows:

- *Products or gifts (28 percent).* These customers want to earn rewards or reduced prices for watches, T-shirts, and other items with your company or product logo.
- *Airline miles (18 percent).* In return for purchasing products or services, completing forms, or providing other customer information, these customers want frequent-flyer miles added to their frequent-flyer accounts at the airlines they select.
- *Gift certificates to retailers (16 percent).* These customers are interested in gift certificates that can be applied to new purchases or to similar products or services. For example, customers who have just purchased at Barnes and Noble also receive gift certificates or discounts for J. Crew, 1-800 Flowers, and other retailers.

- *Electronic cash (14 percent).* These customers tend to say, "Where's the money?" They want cash credited to their credit card accounts as a reward for purchasing or providing information.

TYPES OF ONLINE CUSTOMER LOYALTY PROGRAMS

Forrester Research predicts that e-corporations will spend about $6 billion a year for online incentive and promotion programs by 2002. Today, online loyalty program providers can be divided into four types; however, variations of these models and new models are constantly being invented:

1. *Portals*—loyalty programs operated by and/or for portals and other large e-commerce sites, such as AOL Rewards
2. *Stand-alone programs*—stand-alone loyalty programs and promotional tools developed by and/or for individual e-commerce sites, such as Autobytel.com, Mobalist Rewards, CDnow, Fast Forward Rewards, and CBS SportsLine Rewards
3. *Networks*—online promotion networks that are providers of loyalty, direct marketing, and promotion products, such as Netcentives
4. *Customized networks*—internally developed and customized loyalty networks that are operated on behalf of third parties, such as Maritz Marketing Research, Carlson Marketing Group, Loyalty Group, a division of Alliance Data Systems, and BI Performance Services

FEATURES OF INTERNET-BASED LOYALTY PROGRAMS

Online loyalty program providers aim to assist you in identifying and cultivating your e-corporation's most profitable customers, in addition to fine-tuning the market segments within your customer database and pinpointing what works for individual customers. To effectively reach this goal, online incentive program providers have developed several types of rewards programs.

Shopping portals. Many people believe that shopping portals have the potential to knock down the shopping "impulse barrier" and allow users to immediately buy online. Shopping portals are free shopping services that give e-customers cash-back savings with selected merchants. A good example is Dash (www.dash.com), a mobile shopping portal. Download the software and shop the Net with the company's shopping agent, called DASHbar (which integrates into your Internet browser). DASHbar tracks cash savings and provides alerts to hot deals, coupon savings, and cash shopping rewards.

Pay to surf. Some companies will pay individuals for surfing the Internet and looking at ads on the Web. The pay is about $0.50 to $0.60 per hour, but the company will pay a commission for anyone you sign up. The referral commission is about $0.10 for each hour a referral spends online. Pay-to-surf companies essentially pass on to users a portion of their revenue from selling ads. For example, download AllAdvantage.com (www.all advantage.com) software and be paid to surf the Web. AllAdvantage pays members $.50 per hour (with a monthly maximum of $25) for active use of the AllAdvantage viewbar, a panel at the bottom of the member's Internet browser displaying advertising and promotional material. Members can decide whether the viewer is active (visible) or inactive (minimized). Members also earn cash for using the referral payment system. AllAdvantage offers travel rewards and discounts of 5 percent to 25 percent when shopping at selected online retailers.

Coupons. Internet-based coupon systems are quickening for some categories of marketers and online newspapers. Online coupons have become more important as a number of deep-pocketed national online publishers—like Bell South and Bell Atlantic, to name just two—have fielded sophisticated new types of Web coupon services aimed at local advertisers and shoppers. Online coupons are savings opportunities for e-customers. For example, download Cool Savings (www.coolsavings .com) software for "Squeals of the Day," a listing of daily savings opportunities. Members can also sign up for a free e-mail notification service that provides e-mail messages about new savings and coupons in the member's areas of interest. Ecoupons (www.ecoupons.com) allows members to search for new deals and offers by zip code and category. When users find offers they like, they can save them in their eSavingsBox for future reference. Or, sign up for e-mail updates to receive notices of new deals on selected products and services.

E-mail. E-mail marketing is sometimes known as digital direct marketing. It is attractive to marketers, because it is about 20 times less expensive than typical offline catalog campaigns. It also is one of the best ways to keep customers coming back, though there are privacy concerns. E-mail promotions include e-newsletters embedded with ads, graphic-filled e-mails that look like Web pages, or simple text e-mails with links to special deals. Overall, e-mail promotions are a $156 million industry of firms that provide delivery services, list management, and lists filled with consumers who "opt in" to receive such information. Some e-corporations use targeted e-mail messages in their online customer loyalty programs. A good example is BonusMail (www.bonusmail.com), which sends e-mail messages to subscribers. When consumers click on the hyperlinks in the e-mail messages to view advertisements, they receive points. A variation of this is Email.com (www.email.com), which pays each member a small amount each time he or she reads an e-mail message, takes advantage of a Web site opportunity, or his or her referrals read an e-mail message. Members are paid by check when their accounts exceed $30.

Credit cards. A good example of an online credit card and financial service with an optional rewards program is NextCard Visa's reward points (www.nextcard.com). The program offers instant online credit card approval, a choice of customized credit card offers, personalized Picture-Card designs, and online customer service. NextCard has continued with its complete GoShopping! service, NextCard Concierge one-click shopping companion, online bill payment services, and comprehensive rewards program. Reward points earned by making purchases using NextCard can be used for travel, vacation, and hotel awards. Reward points can also be redeemed for gift certificates and free services from major department stores, Internet retailers, and restaurants.

FIGURE 6.2   Get FreeRide points you can spend like money at selected stores.

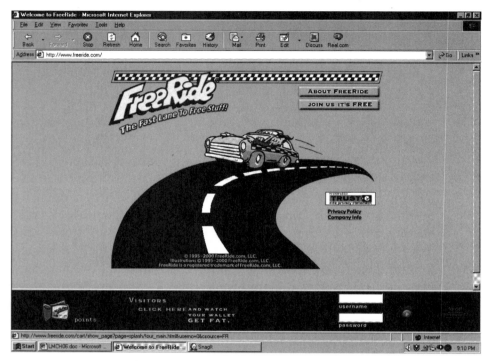

Screen shot courtesy of FreeRide.com LLC.

Web currencies. Web currencies can be earned for shopping, touring Web sites, responding to offers, reading e-mail messages, or other types of Internet interactions. Beenz (www.beenz.com) is an imperfect currency in that each beenz is sold to a Web site operator for one American cent and is exchangeable only for half a cent. The half-cent markup is made up of the currency's apparent value as a marketing tool and Beenz.com's profit. Individual consumers, though, can't redeem beenz for cash. Beenz Web currency is used for discounts, services, or goods and is held in an Internet account. It costs nothing at the moment to earn beenz; it is given away for logging on to certain Web sites.

Another example is Free Ride (www.freeride.com), shown in Figure 6.2. Free Ride allows its members to quickly earn and spend points at over 1,300 online and offline sponsors for merchandise (such as Duracell batteries, Quaker oatmeal, and Oreo cookies) or for Internet services and other products or services. My Points (www.mypoints.com) takes another approach by making strategic alliances with Internet service providers (ISPs) like Prodigy (www.prodigypoints.com). This way, ISP users can earn points good for a variety of products and services, such as travel awards, gift certificates, and prepaid phone cards from more than 50 name-brand rewards providers.

Opinions. E-corporations are interested in the opinions of prospective and current customers. Online firms like Zoomerang (www.zoomerang .com) ask panelists to participate in online surveys to earn rewards for their time and responses. CyberGold (www.cybergold.com), another opinion surveying e-corporation, pits its cash-back incentive model against points-based loyalty models. Cybergold rewards consumers with cash for responding to Web-based advertisements and programs. With more than four million members, Cybergold provides its clients with several means of reaching consumers on the Internet. In return, Cybergold members are provided with a wide selection of programs to receive the best value for their attention and activities. Members are free to spend their cash online or offline by transferring it to a Visa card or bank checking account. Cybergold's partners include Visa USA, MBNA, AOL, Earth-Link, E*Trade, and Autobytel. A user earns Internet payment currency by completing surveys, reading ads, trying out a particular product or service, and purchasing items from affiliated merchants. Rewards can also be transferred to the user's bank account or donated to nonprofit corporations. CyberGold uses technology to match ads and other online information based on the user's personal interests and demographics.

Auctions. Users earn auction rewards by placing bids. A good example is DealDeal.com (www.dealdeal.com), which specializes in auctioning computer products and accessories. DealDeal.com may be the largest online software auction. The firm offers up to 1,000 items in one single auction. Its DealBucks program rewards auction bidders when they place auction bids, complete surveys, or make referrals. After DealBucks have been earned, they can be applied during a DealDeal auction. DealBucks can be applied as 5 percent to 20 percent of the bid price, which results in a cost savings of 5 percent to 20 percent on a specific item.

Specialty stores. Until recently, some specialty stores offered reward points for purchases. A good example was Petstore.com, which was purchased by Pets.com. Before the acquisition, Petstore.com was an online retailer of pet supplies, food, and treats and had over 7,000 pet products for dogs, cats, fish, birds, reptiles, amphibians, and small animals. Petstore.com allowed customers to sort items according to brand, price, size, and color. Site visitors received reliable, easy-to-read product information prepared by a team of professional writers and product experts. Consumers could join the online community and become a Petstore Pal. If 250 Petstore Pal points were earned within a six-month period, the Petstore Pal received a 10 percent discount off all purchases for the next six months.

Sports. Online sports fans are rewarded for checking sports statistics, scores, and news. Additional points can be earned for buying products or participating in programs like fantasy sports leagues. A good example is CBS SportsLine (www.sportsline.com), which provides a personalized start page that can be customized to include news and scores for specific sports and teams. CBS SportsLine also offers points for participating in various promotions and contests. For an annual fee, users can upgrade to SportsLine Rewards Plus and receive double points and more exclusive rewards. According to Media Metrix, the 1999 fourth quarter traffic grew 95 percent over the same period last year, averaging approximately 5.5 million page views per day.

Travel Click Rewards. Frequent-flyer miles can be earned by consumers who use Click Rewards (www.clickrewards.com), a company owned by Netcentives, an online promotional and loyalty program firm. Click Rewards offers users points for visiting certain Web sites, such as Yahoo's search engine. Consumers can transfer their points into an airline frequent-flyer account or a hotel frequent-stay account. One Netcentives point equals one airline mile or hotel point. As of this writing, airlines participating in the program include American, U.S. Airways, Delta, Northwest, Continental, British Airways, and Alaska Airlines. Another example of a firm offering travel click rewards is Travel Navigator (www.travelnavigator.com), which allows members to earn points in two ways. First, users earn points when they research travel destinations or book travel, hotels, and car rentals. The second way to earn reward points is by referring friends and relatives to Travel Navigator. Members also receive discounts on vacation packages.

Contests and games. Yoyodyne (www.yoyodyne.com) uses push technology for its promotional services. Yoyodyne provides online sweepstakes and customer games that e-corporations place on its Web site. The games can be implemented in a one-to-one manner, such as Dilbert's online trivia game. Users participate in games and provide marketers with demographic and psychographic information. Yoyodyne is an interactive direct marketing company. Yoyodyne has created and implemented more than 100 promotions, including custom games and multisponsor sweepstakes, for a variety of corporate clients, such as KPMG, H&R Block, Reader's Digest, Modem Media, Prodigy, Sony Music Entertainment, Sprint, and ZDNet. Another example is SpeedyClick (www.speedyclick.com), which rewards users with SpeedyBucks for entering contests, taking advantage of special offers, and participating in other interactive activities. Users complete a claim form to redeem their SpeedyBucks for various prizes. SpeedyClick also offers an auction area and treasure hunt.

Free or low-cost online information or classes. One way to sell a company's consulting services, training or certification services, and publications is to provide online classes. A good example is the Ziff Davis University (www.zdu.com), which offers many free and low-cost online courses. This site helps the company sell its publications and training services, and allows it to develop reseller and partnership opportunities. For example, Micron customers (www.micronpc.com) can attend free online classes to learn about computers and related subjects. Micron University, in partnership with the Ziff Davis ZD University online course center, offers customers free course tuition for one year after the purchase of a PC. Micron uses the free online courses to help differentiate itself from its many direct online seller competitors, such as Dell and Gateway.

Superstores. Online superstores offer consumers savings on a wide variety of name brand products and rewards for purchasing selected products. A good example is Netmarket (www.netmarket.com). Netmarket offers a one-stop shopping site where members and nonmembers can browse eight diverse superstores to find more than 800,000 name brand products at everyday deep discounts. Members enjoy extra benefits, including free extended warranties, cash back on qualifying purchases, and a low price guarantee. Netmarket offers club members Netmarket Cash for qualified purchases. Netmarket Cash is accumulated throughout the year and applied towards future purchases or received as a cash rebate at the end of the year. Netmarket has a low price guarantee for selected Netmarket products. In addition to traditional shopping, Netmarket also offers an online flea market, auction area, haggle zone, rebate lists, and members-only bargains.

DEVELOPING AN ONLINE LOYALTY PROGRAM ACTION PLAN

When developing an online loyalty program, walk in the customer's shoes to make certain that the proposed program has value to the customer and helps you increase the customer's perceived value of your e-corporation's products or services. Next, your e-corporation must define the loyalty program's objectives and make certain that the economics of the proposed program are realistic. Finally, set goals for the loyalty program and measure the success of your efforts. (The action plan at the end of this chapter provides a summary of the issues to consider when formulating an online loyalty program.)

Understanding What Your Online Customers Really Value

Grahame R. Dowling and Mark Uncles (1998) report that companies who want to practice loyalty marketing need to know who their loyal customers are. In the past, your company could get to know its customers personally and could reward them with special services and attention. As the number of customers increase and your company becomes more complex, management is often forced to rely on database marketing and market research to monitor customer behavior and identify your firm's best customers (see Chapter 13). Retailers and packaged-goods manufacturers use database-mining techniques to fine-tune their products and services and allocate marketing resources to the right customers for a maximum return. Many companies use customer profitability analyses and calculate the lifetime value of their customers, and then divide customers into market segments (see Chapter 8). This allows your company to interact with customers in each market segment differently. Fine-tuning this approach allows you to create unique customer relationships within selected market segments. For a company with poor data about customers, a loyalty program can pinpoint customers at the point of purchase or service delivery to track their behavior and preferences. Using database technology in this way allows you to establish personalized dialogues with customers, resulting in increased loyalty.

Analysis of many of the rewards programs shows that management often does not understand what customers really value. According to Louise O'Brien and Charles Jones (1995), a loyalty program must have value to a customer if it is to be successful. Consequently, all successful loyalty programs must include the following five elements:

1. *Cash value.* The cash value of the reward must be enough to attract the customer's attention. Cash value can be rebates, cash discounts, or what a customer would have to pay to acquire the reward.
2. *Choice of redemption options.* Customers want a variety of ways to spend cyberbucks or points they have earned. For example, redemption options can include one frequent-flyer mile for each purchase dollar or cash back at the end of the year.
3. *Aspirational value.* This rewards customers for changing certain behaviors. Additionally, programs with aspirational value frequently have as much to do with psychology as economics. For example, a discount on a telephone bill does not have the appeal of an exotic free vacation.
4. *Relevance.* Customers do not want to play 20 different games or wait 20 years to accumulate enough points for a free airline ticket or other type of reward.
5. *Convenience.* Rewards linked to a credit card are convenient, because neither the merchant nor the customer has to exert any incremental effort (such as mailing receipts to the merchant).

Offering the Right Type of Rewards

Dennis L. Duffy (1997) suggests that some companies provide "promotional currency" as a reward. This is a good approach for companies that have products and services with at least two or more of the following characteristics: (1) a low involvement decision, (2) high fixed and low variable costs, (3) a gap between real cost and perceived value of the product or service, and (4) idle capacity.

Duffy goes on to state that other successful loyalty programs are often a combination of communication and soft benefits:

- *Communications.* Communications in the retail industry seek to leverage the consumer's attachment to the brand and are designed to reinforce the shopping experience. Communications benefits can include special services for members and members-only special toll-free telephone numbers. Business communications have a different goal. Business communications seek to help the customer be more successful; that is, if your company understands and solves a customer's business problem, it will build a customer relationship.

- *Soft benefits.* In the retail industry, there are often combinations of soft benefits and communications. Soft benefits relate to the customer experience with the retail brand. Soft benefits can include merchandise previews, personalized content, and invitations to be a beta tester of a new software product. Overall, the goal of the soft benefit is to make the customer feel special. To do this, your company must know what is important to the customer.

The Planet Rx (www.planetrx.com) story shows how the online pharmacy offers e-customers the special attention of a neighborhood pharmacist. PlanetRx, shown in Figure 6.3, uses a stand-alone customer loyalty program that is designed to assist the e-corporation in preempting competitors and securing the company's "first mover" advantages.

FIGURE 6.3   PlanetRx is a high-touch Web site that makes e-customers feel special.

LOYALTY MARKETING SUCCESS STORY

PlanetRx

▼ **COMPANY:** PlanetRx, based in San Francisco, is an Internet-based pharmacy focused on content, community, and commerce. It operates a distribution center and pharmacy in Memphis, Tennessee. PlanetRx processes about 250,000 purchases per month and believes that customer loyalty will be a competitive weapon as there are more entrants into the online pharmacy industry.

▼ **SOLUTION:** PlanetRx, early in its development, realized that it needed to build online customer loyalty by being "high touch." PlanetRx.com is a full-service online pharmacy devoted to all health and wellness needs. The company wants to empower customers by bringing them the products, information, and personalized service they need to make better choices about their health. For example, questions are divided into three categories: pharmacy questions (from common ailments to how to take prescription medicines); PlanetRx questions (how to set up an account, reach a 24-hour care associate, and about purchasing and shipping); and insurance questions (how does insurance work on PlanetRx and does insurance cover PlanetRx purchases?). Additionally, customers can discuss and educate themselves on their medication options. PlanetRx implemented the required technological infrastructure to handle a tremendous volume of users and transactions, in addition to data warehousing and data mining technologies to assist in automating the customer loyalty process.

▼ **BENEFITS:** Overall, the Web site uses technology to re-create the neighborhood pharmacy, where customers felt comfortable talking to the pharmacists:

- PlanetRx offers customers their own store and configures special offers based on the customers' past purchases.
- Customers feel that PlanetRx knows their needs, and the company gains by increasing customer loyalty.

▼ **TECHNOLOGY:** PlanetRx designed and built its own transaction infrastructure. The solution is a robust end-to-end commerce engine. However, IBM's software products facilitated the decoupling of transactional elements and now house PlanetRx's online catalog as well as its information related to shipping and logistics. Some of the IBM products used are:

- IBM's MQ Series for commercial messaging
- IBM's DB2, an industrial-strength database management tool for business intelligence, transaction processing and a broad range of application for all types of businesses. PlanetRx expects this product to occupy a prominent place in future business intelligence initiatives.

Source: Adapted from "PlanetRx: The Pharmacy of the Future Builds for the Long-Term Using IBM Technology," an online publication of IBM (www2.software.ibm.com/casestudies), 23 March 2000.

SETTING LOYALTY GOALS AND MEASURING YOUR SUCCESS

Online customers show a higher propensity for belonging to online loyalty programs than offline programs. Other e-corporation benefits include a global reach, the ability to use technology to understand the dynamics for customer relationship management, and increased brand awareness. According to Dennis L. Duffy, president of Cadmus Direct Marketing in Charlotte, North Carolina, over the years loyalty programs come and go. Moreover, a loyalty program is not a substitute for a good product and won't overcome a price disadvantage. After all, consumers usually make their purchasing decisions based on service and price/value perceptions (discussed in Chapter 9). Dowling and Uncles (1998) note: "For any customer loyalty program to be as effective as possible, given the prevailing competitive conditions, it must leverage the brand's value proposition in the eyes of customers (that is, the balance of benefits relative to price)." This highlights the need for your e-corporation to define the objectives of your loyalty programs. For example, how does the loyalty program increase the customer's perception of value of your product or services? What does your e-corporation want to achieve with the loyalty program? Is your e-corporation solving a problem (e.g., the lack of customer retention) or taking advantage of an opportunity (e.g., capitalizing on being the first or largest in a certain e-commerce market)?

Looking at the Economics of the Loyalty Program

Duffy (1997) suggests that a critical step in developing an automated loyalty program is understanding how the company is making money. For example, look at customer invoices to determine how much customers spend. Determine what your company's average expenses are for goods or services sold, marketing costs for new customer acquisitions and customer retention, and the average length of customer relationships. This information can be used to divide customers into market segments (see Chapter 13) and evaluating the proposed online customer loyalty program.

At this stage of the loyalty program's planning process, it is important to do a reality check. Do customers have a low involvement with the company's products and services? Do customers really want a relationship? Can the relationship between customers and your brand support a loyalty program? If the answer is no, then you should focus on building customer loyalty in other areas, such as investing in automating the sales force (see Chapter 9) or beefing up online customer support and service (see Chapter 10).

Setting Goals for an Online Loyalty Program

According to O'Brien and Jones (1995), there is often a discontinuity between loyalty program strategy and implementation. Moreover, it is often difficult to measure the full effect of a loyalty program. As seen below, over time the company can measure increases in purchase amounts, higher retention rates, and incremental upgrades. Overall, a well-designed loyalty program can target and attract valuable customer segments. At the same time, it can save your corporation money by discouraging money losers, those undesirable customers who actually cost the company money.

Jill Griffin (1995) suggests that you track the variables listed below to measure the success of the loyalty program. Using current retention rates, your company can set customer retention objectives for the next few years. The same analysis can be completed for share of customer and new customer retention rate.

- *Client base.* The client base is the total number of active customers, which includes first-time and repeat customers. (Nonactive customers are not included in this list.)
- *New customer retention rate.* This is the number of new customers who return to make a second purchase within a predetermined period of time. The time period should be equal to the buying cycle for your company's products or services. For example, hair salons are often on a 90-day buying cycle, and automobile purchases are often on a five-year purchasing cycle.
- *Current customer retention rate.* This is the percentage of customers who have met a certain amount of repurchase requirements within a

specific time period. For example, what percentage of online customers have purchased at least five airline tickets within the last year?

- *Share of customer.* This is the percentage of the customer's total budget that you have captured. For example, if you have 100 percent share of a customer, the customer spends all of his or her budget dollars with your company.
- *Average number of new customers per month.* This is the number of first-time purchasers within a one-month time period.
- *Purchase frequency.* This is the average number of times the customer purchases products or services from you.
- *Average purchase amount.* This is the average amount paid for products and services at each purchase. For example, the average purchase at eBay is $30.
- *Attrition rate.* This is the average number of customers who, for any reason, are lost each year. These customers may go inactive, move to another location, switch to another company, or be dissatisfied with the company's products or services.

SUMMING IT UP

- Studies show that about 53 percent of all e-customers would buy more online if reward points or incentives were offered at a specific Web site.
- Online consumers tend to be affected by the "Gimme" factor, that is, make it worth my while to purchase something at your Web site.
- For any loyalty reward program to be successful, it must (1) have a cash value, (2) include a choice of redemption options, (3) contain aspirational value, (4) be relevant, and (5) be convenient.
- The right type of reward for a loyalty program can include hard benefits (promotional currency), communications benefits (special services), and soft benefits (making the customer feel special).
- Successful online loyalty programs have clear objectives, recognize customer wants and values, provide an economic value to your company, and offer measurable results.

DESIGNING AN ONLINE CUSTOMER LOYALTY PROGRAM

Online businesses realize that getting "hits" is not enough. Online customer loyalty is a strategic advantage in the competitive e-commerce environment. Additionally, many e-corporations want to preempt competitors and secure their first-mover advantages. Other e-corporations want to respond to a competitor's loyalty program. Here are nine starters for designing a successful online loyalty program with a program that will stop customer defections.

Points to Consider	Description
1. Understand your online business.	Clearly identify the objectives of the e-corporation: ✓ What are the strategies to achieve that vision? ✓ Does the online loyalty program support the e-corporation's operating strategy?
2. Identify your loyalty program objectives.	The e-corporation's evolving objectives may include: ✓ Becoming the online market leader in your industry ✓ Increasing the customer base ✓ Driving traffic to the e-commerce Web site ✓ Strengthening customer loyalty ✓ Building brand awareness. ✓ Reinforcing and extending the brand.

Points to Consider	Description
3. Understand your customer segmentation.	A successful loyalty program understands how customers think and behave at the e-commerce Web site: ✓ What motivates your customers? ✓ What are your customers' interests? ✓ What are your customers' preferences? ✓ What are your customers' viewing patterns? ✓ What are the buying behaviors of your customers?
4. Design customer rewards.	Determine what are the important elements of the loyalty program, stated in terms of results produced for customers.
5. Manage customer rewards.	Manage customer rewards by determining: ✓ What are the right levels of "achievable" redemption opportunities to engage customers? ✓ How will the loyalty program move customers through the member life cycle? ✓ What is the "activation" cost of starting the loyalty program?

Points to Consider	Description
6. Select loyalty program features that help the e-corporation meet its goals and objectives.	Detailed features of a customized loyalty program depend on addressing the key objectives in the program. Decisions to make include: ✓ What is the right type of promotional currency (points, cash, and so on)? ✓ What is the right mix of rewards/redemption options? ✓ How long should it take to redeem? ✓ What are the right kinds of redeeming opportunities? ✓ How many redeeming opportunities should be offered?
7. Launch the online loyalty program.	How well is the online customer loyalty program positioned in relation to customer needs and competitor's offerings?
8. Measure your success.	To what extent is the resulting value of the online loyalty program leveraged over the cost of the loyalty program?
9. Extend the loyalty program.	What features of the customer loyalty program address the e-corporation's key objectives, and how can these be expanded?

Source: Adapted from "Netcentives Corporate Capabilities: Appendix Design Considerations," a corporate publication of Netcentives (www.netcentives.com), 15 April 2000.

REFERENCES

Allen, Cliff, Deborah Kania, and Beth Yaeckel. 1998. *Internet World: Guide to One-to-One Web Marketing.* New York: John Wiley & Sons, Inc.

Barlow, Richard G. 2000. Customer Relationship Management in the Next Millennium. Online publication of CRM Community, 1 February (www.crmcommunity.com/news/openarti cle.asp?ID=937).

Dowling, Grahame R., and Mark Uncles. 1998. Do Customer Loyalty Programs Really Work? *Sloan Management Review* 38 (22 June): 77–83.

Duffy, Dennis L. 1997. Loyalty Marketing Column. *The Relationship Marketing Report.* Corporate publication of Cadmus Direct Marketing, Inc. (July): 1–4. Online reprint available at Relationship Marketing Resource at www.relationshipmktg.com/Free%20Articles/ArticleIndex.htm.

Griffin, Jill. 1995. *Customer Loyalty: How to Earn It, How to Keep It.* San Francisco: Jossey-Bass Publishers.

Incentive and Reward Programs Spur Online Purchasing and Customer Loyalty. 2000. Online publication of NFO Interactive, 7 April (www.nfoi.com/nfointeractive/nfoipr 62899.asp).

Lach, Jennifer. 1999. Carrots in Cyberspace. *American Demographics* 21 (1 May).

O'Brien, Louise, and Charles Jones. 1995. Do Rewards Really Create Loyalty? *Harvard Business Review* (May–June): 75–85.

Sterne, Jim. 1996. *Customer Service on the Internet.* New York: John Wiley & Sons, Inc.

7

Employee Loyalty in the E-corporation

What are the keys to employee loyalty? The answer to this question is important, because loyal e-customers and loyal e-employees go hand in hand. Customer loyalty and customer relationships are built over time and require the effort of loyal employees to maximize customer productivity gains and opportunities. Additionally, seasoned employees reduce the need for training and recruiting. These cost savings can be used to beef up other areas of your e-business. This chapter establishes how studies show that long-term employees cost less than employees who are in the learning phase of employment. In other words, even if your company does not pay for formal training, a new employee is not as productive as a long-term employee.

However, don't look at employees only in terms of costs, because this disregards the value of your employees. Moreover, if your e-corporation is seeking ways to reduce compensation and implements arbitrary layoffs, you can destroy employee loyalty. In this type of environment, employees take a defensive stand and start thinking about their personal survival. Increased employee defections and office politics can also destroy or reduce the profit contribution of employees; that is, employees will adopt a mentality of doing just enough to remain employed while they look for exit strategies. One industry analyst observes that viewing employees in terms of cost is like meeting the short-term objective of losing weight by cutting off an arm. This chapter concludes with a discussion of how you can cultivate employee loyalty by changing corporate culture and creating meaningful jobs with appropriate compensation and incentives.

HIRING AND KEEPING THE RIGHT EMPLOYEES

According to Michael A. Verespej (1995), in the future we can expect even more changes in the landscape of the workplace than we have recently experienced. Individuals will be hired for skills to work on projects, not to fill job vacancies. There will be no end to individual learning. The words *worker* and *manager* will become obsolete. Executives will listen more, and the number of core workers at companies will continue to shrink. However, the most striking difference will be in the area of employee loyalty. Employees will be loyal to products, services, and customers. What's best for the company will also be best for the employees, because they will be partners in the business.

Today, your e-corporation must produce more with fewer resources for customers who demand more for less. This means that each e-corporation job must be filled with an employee who has the potential to be a superior performer but who may not possess the minimum qualifications. Bear in mind that e-corporations are relatively new phenomena. Frequently, there aren't enough experienced employees to fill open positions. Consequently, many e-corporations offer stock options and BMWs as signing bonuses, when other businesses are only required to offer a paycheck.

The solution to this situation is to hire the right people for the right job and create an environment to produce superior performance. In other words, employee selection is geared to what customers and managers think is important. Your e-corporation has to analyze its jobs and measure each job's requirements for hard skills, soft skills, behavior, attitude, and intelligence. For example, you can hire employees who easily relate to customers or computer whizzes with no interest in people but who can provide excellent service.

Employee retention consultants KeepEmployees, Inc., of Fort Collins, Colorado (www.keepemployees.com), state that many industries are experiencing a 25 percent to 30 percent annual turnover rate. KeepEmployees, Inc., suggests that you start your employee retention program by hiring people who are likely to be successful and who are satisfied with the corporation.

The savvy corporation cultivates employee loyalty by directly supporting the reasons that successful, satisfied employees stay with the e-corporation. Loyal employees often stay with the corporation because of a positive relationship with their supervisors, the opportunity to remain marketable by improving their skill sets, and making work-related decisions, in addition to sharing in the financial success their efforts help create.

PRICING EMPLOYEE LOYALTY

According to Fredrick Reichheld (1996), the economic model for employee loyalty is similar to the model for customer loyalty, because the company obtains economic benefits from employees in the same manner. That is, measure the Net Present Value of the employee by three variables: profit contribution, rate of return, and tenure. Just like customer loyalty, the value of employee loyalty increases with tenure and profit contribution. Employee profit contribution has many components; the following six are at the top of the list:

1. *Recruiting investment.* The cost of acquiring the employee includes any signing bonuses, company-paid employee moving expenses, and employment agency costs, in addition to the costs of the pool of candidates. For example, if 16 people are interviewed for two positions, then the cost of hiring the candidate includes the recruitment costs of interviewing eight applicants. Other recruitment costs may include the cost of:
   - Attracting applicants
   - Preemployment administrative expenses
   - Entrance interviews
   - Aptitude tests, skills tests, and drug tests

- Hiring-decision meetings
- An employee finder fee

2. *Training.* Training is the cost of aligning the new employee's skills and knowledge with the skill set required by the organization. This includes the time and cost of job training by other employees. Other new-hire training costs may include the cost of:
   - Information literature (manuals, brochures, policies)
   - General orientation
   - Job orientation

3. *Efficiency.* Efficiency is the measurement of the reduction in cost of completing a specific job. For example, let's say it takes an hour for a new employee to create an invoice for the first time. For an experienced employee, the same task may take five to six minutes. Other lost productivity costs may include the cost of:
   - Additional overtime to cover the vacancy
   - Additional temporary help
   - Low morale-related time wasted
   - Additional employee defections related to the departure

4. *Customer selection.* Experienced employees are much better at finding and recruiting the best customers. These customers are often tuned into the value of your company and have or will have a longer relationship with your e-corporation.

5. *Customer retention.* Long-term employees have a higher rate of customer retention than short-term employees. Experienced employees tend to mature with the customer relationship.

6. *Customer referrals.* Experienced employees are a major source of referrals and often add to the sales effort. Long-term employees frequently provide employee referrals to the organization, which reduces recruitment costs and gains higher-quality employees.

PRODUCTIVITY AND THE LOYAL EMPLOYEE

James Heskett, W. Earl Sasser, Jr., and Leonard Schlesinger (1997) note that the traditional measures of employee turnover do not include the economic impact of reduced customer satisfaction. Overall, the economic consequences of employee loyalty are hard to measure individually, but taken together the components have a powerful economic effect on value creation and corporate profits.

The economic model for employee loyalty is based on the profit contribution and the tenure of the person. Productivity is part of the profit contribution. It is a measure of the production of the person, group, or team. Technology is used to enrich jobs and improve the ability to deliver value. With education and training, technology can move employees up the learning curve and lengthen the retention of employees.

According to Fredrick Reichheld (1996), in an effort to reduce costs, employers often see technology as a way to displace people or as a justification to reduce or dampen the growth of compensation. However, a *low* cost approach achieved by measuring cost per unit can destroy value, because it does not contribute value to the *top* line. A better approach is cost as a percentage of revenues. This approach takes into consideration the growth of the top line and allows employees to drive value creation and maximize value from longer-term customers. Sanctioning employees to improve value creation improves pricing and cost as a percentage of revenues (see Chapter 9).

Employee Productivity Bottlenecks

Corporate takeovers, downsizing, and rightsizing have changed employee attitudes towards work. High levels of employee loyalty, satisfaction, and productivity often seem like unrealizable goals. Many companies inadvertently put up roadblocks to employee loyalty and productivity by:

- *Mismatching compensation and productivity.* Some employees are motivated by money and others by incentives. Incentives can range from "thank you" lunches to profit sharing. If your compensation doesn't match the employee's requirements, productivity will be dampened.
- *Hiring the wrong people.* Sometimes, the corporation's written goals do not match the employee traits valued in the corporation. Consequently, productivity is held back when workers who do not easily relate to customers end up in the front line. Frequently, the key to creating a productive e-corporation culture—one that thrives on change to define the behaviors and attitudinal traits that will carry the e-cor-

poration into the future (e.g., the ability to work in a team and entrepreneurial spirit). Individuals who exhibit these traits should be hired and promoted. If these individuals are current employees, make certain their new roles showcase these traits.

- *Inadvertently developing crazy career paths.* On occasion, career paths are short-circuited due to mergers and acquisitions, new technology, or corporate reorganizations. Therefore, workers do not see a future for themselves within the organization and start using company time to plan their survival strategies.

- *Not providing adequate training.* Often, high-salaried employees and management staff are thrown into the thick of things without any formal or informal training. This leads to bad habits and diminished employee self-worth. Productivity declines. After all, if you did not invest time in the employee, why should the employee invest time in you?

- *Using layoffs as a cost-cutting measure.* Studies over the last ten years indicate that layoffs used as a cost-cutting measure don't help a company. Often, lost time, reduced productivity, and devastated morale create hidden costs that offset any anticipated cost savings.

- *Using an inefficient organizational structure.* New technologies such as desktop video conferencing, collaborative software, and Internet/ intranet systems converge to forge the foundation of a new workplace. With an inefficient organizational structure, this new workplace will not reach its full potential of unrepressed productivity, flexibility, and collaboration.

Cures for Reduced E-employee Productivity and Low Motivation

he profitability of your e-corporation is tied to employee loyalty and productivity. When evaluating employment options, today's e-employees look at the total work environment, including critical factors such as flexibility, control over projects, and training opportunities. As part of your company's retention program, management needs to build an environment where e-workers want to stay. A good example of a company that has

FIGURE 7.1   Raytheon aims to keep its employees by implementing an aggressive employee retention program.

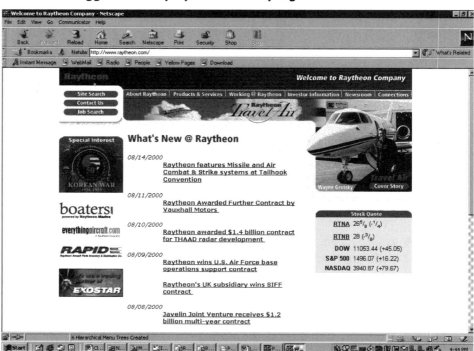

an aggressive employee retention program is Lexington, Massachusetts–based Raytheon (see Figure 7.1). Writers for *Internet Week* (2000) report that twice a year, each company officer at Raytheon delivers an employee update to the human resources department. In many cases, the report must identify employees with the highest professional potential and detail diversity measurements and employee training and developmental plans. Some senior employees, targeted as having high potential, get placed in the company's Leadership Development program to be coached for advancement. The selected employees spend a week rotating through various departments, discovering how the company works and what works for them. Also, Raytheon has several other employee loyalty programs. Overall, Raytheon has 2,400 information technology employees. As a result of the company's effective approach to retaining information technology employees, the annual turnover rate is a low 9.5 percent. This is less than half the industry standard of 20 percent, according to a recent Gartner Group research report.

CHANGING CORPORATE CULTURE AND THE E-CORPORATION

For many corporations to effectively change to e-corporations, they have to rely on successful corporate politics. Changing corporate culture involves an accurate analysis of the workforce and discovering how to navigate the sensitivities of current employees, for whom once-prized traits may become irrelevant or harmful in the new corporate culture.

The impact of eCRM technology on the corporation's culture is tremendous. Seasoned employees are proud of their work knowledge. With the implementation of eCRM systems, this knowledge, which is often a large part of job satisfaction, becomes obsolete. Additionally, long-term employees are frequently required to retrain and master a new set of skills. Many loyal employees may find it difficult to make the transition to the new e-corporation.

Not only are seasoned employees frequently resistant to change, they are also skeptical about the success of the new initiative. This skepticism often seems justified. Many corporations embrace fashionable management trends only to quickly disregard their efforts in favor of what appears to be an even-more-promising management approach. Jill Griffin (1995) provides this example: A supermarket ran a series of ads seeking to promote its friendly cashiers. "If one of our cashiers ever forgets to say, 'Thank you, have a nice day,' we will give you one dollar." A few weeks after the ad, a customer entered the store and purchased a few items. The cashier rang up the sale and handed over the change, less the friendly greeting. The customer claimed the dollar and explained the terms of the ad. The cashier smiled and said, "I don't have to give you a dollar. That was last month's campaign." This example illustrates how your corporation needs to build a larger vision about why a corporate program is in place and what results you are seeking.

KEEPING E-EMPLOYEES HAPPY ON THE DOT-COM FARM

How can your e-corporation hang onto its intellectual capital and build a strong workforce when something better is always around the corner? Roger Herman and Joyce Gioia (1998) state that a recent survey by Response Analysis of Princeton, New Jersey, identified the three most important aspects of work. Of the 1,600 respondents, about 52 percent wanted to be responsible for their work and results, 42 percent wanted acknowledgment for their contributions, and 39 percent wanted their tasks to match their strengths.

The Response Analysis survey indicates that your e-corporation needs to: (1) recognize employees as valuable intellectual assets, (2) define each employee's growth path (this may include expanding his or her skill set or mentoring for a promotion), and (3) appropriately reward employees for the financial success their efforts generate.

According to the survey, if you want to attract and motivate loyal employees, you need to give up a production-line management approach. The first step is to create a corporate culture that provides meaningful work:

- *No mindless tasks.* Workers need to feel their work is important and understand how it fits into the corporate strategy. In other words, employees want to know that their work is a valued part of the whole. Be sure that employees have access to information that will enable them to fulfill their responsibilities.
- *Making an impact.* Employees need to know how their work affects others within the corporation and the corporation's strategic goals. Management can cultivate this feeling by listening to employee suggestions for process and environmental improvements. This shows that the corporation values the ability in individuals to improve workplace effectiveness. After all, what employees know is often more valuable than what they do.
- *Responsibility for results.* Giving employees the information, responsibility, and authority to meet customer demands increases the meaning of work; in other words, trust employees to make the right decisions.
- *Success metrics.* For work to be meaningful, employees need quick and direct feedback. When workers gain feedback from internal and exter-

nal customers, they can gauge their effectiveness in meeting customer demands, solving customer problems, and making appropriate decisions. As part of the continuous feedback loop, customers evaluate employees, and the corporation supports and guides employees with ongoing coaching for better decision making.

Employee Loyalty and Dealing with the Generation Gap

According to Kayte Vanscoy (2000), what keeps employees loyal often lies beyond perks and the job itself: "Today's workers believe in the work more than ever before, but in return they expect you to believe in them." Most managers agree that employees motivate themselves. It is the manager's responsibility to determine the motivational issue for each employee and attempt to work with it. Additionally, managers need to keep in mind that what works with one population of workers may not work for another.

Vanscoy points out that what motivates workers can vary by generation. At this time, baby boomers have more power in the workforce, because they outnumber the X generation (their children) and the Y generation (their grandchildren):

- *Baby boomers are a mixed bag in the new economy.* Some baby boomers can adapt and others retreat from change. Boomers that can adapt are a good match for working in an entirely new business environment, working with reengineering efforts, and assisting your firm in transitioning to the Internet. Those who find it difficult to change are excellent in jobs that maintain and fine-tune ongoing operations. Both types are important to the organization because of their "institutional knowledge." Each can provide wisdom and skills with a new-economy outlook.

- *Generation Xers are not slackers but are fiercely independent.* They often view themselves as entrepreneurs and frequently demand flextime, stock options, and telecommuting. As individuals, they also see themselves as being in the business of themselves, value their employee contracts, and want it all, that is, a job that keeps challenging them and supports an energetic lifestyle. Keep in mind that gen Xers who can afford the risk of being on their own will require stronger enticements to stay with your e-corporation.

- *Generation Yers can work in team environments and are not as cynical as gen Xers.* Often, gen Yers have unrealistic expectations about compensation and make other demands. Traditional human resource techniques may not work. You'll have to discover what does work for each employee.

Different Compensation and Incentive Strokes for Different Folks

The relationship between job performance and rewards makes work more meaningful. Many e-corporations expect their employees to work long hours to achieve quick results. This works in a corporate culture that emphasizes individual responsibility for results, has high respect for individuals from top management on down, and provides access to information, resources, and higher management. However, one size does not fit all. At e-corporations, some employees may get special treatment. For example, at Georgia-Pacific in Atlanta, new hires with skills in SAP, Unix, and Visual Basic get signing bonuses, and many of the information systems groups have a "special dispensation" to dress casually.

Often, companies hire consultants to advise them on how flexible the corporation can be to certain classes of employees, that is, what exceptions can be made for new employees with particular skills. Nonfinancial benefits can include flexible work hours and access to training courses and conferences. Financial benefits for certain employees may also vary. Some employees may value pay hikes and others want incentives. Figure 7.2 provides a quick overview of the three primary employee incentive categories.

Figure 7.2 is divided into three categories: (1) effective incentives, (2) more effective incentives, and (3) most effective incentives. Effective incentives are the benefits that are provided by most midsized corporations. Many employees are so accustomed to these benefits that they do not recognize them as incentives (such as the annual company picnic, casual dress days, and payroll direct deposit services). More effective incentives are employee benefits that are frequently offered by larger corporations. Retirement and stock benefits plans may be offered to a selected category of employees, or selected categories of employees may receive higher levels of benefits (such as a bigger company car, a larger office, or a better retirement plan). The most effective incentives are tailored to the individual employee and offer some risk to the employee in return for the opportunity of reaping monetary rewards, recognition, and appreciation for work well done. The five programs listed in Figure 7.2 are the most popular today, but even more progressive and revolutionary employee-based incentive programs are just around the corner.

WHAT MOTIVATES SOME E-WORKERS?

To drive loyalty and customer satisfaction, you need employee satisfaction. Highly motivated employees often have a high level of job satisfaction. In the e-commerce workplace, there are many highly motivated workers, and for many of these employees, work is not just work—it is a lifestyle. Statistics from the Department of Labor show that workers in the computer and electronics industries work on average 10 percent to 28 percent more hours than other U.S. workers. Julie Schmit, a writer for *USA Today* (1996), reports that "Silicon Valley unions are rare, strikes almost unheard of and employee productivity is high."

According to Schmit, numerous employees state that the lure of new technology and the prospect of creating something new has a lot to do with their self-motivation. Sometimes it's the money that motivates e-workers. Many of the first employees of new companies reaped huge monetary rewards from stock options when their companies went public (remember Intel, Cisco Systems, and UUNet?). Even public companies use stock options as a "carrot in cyberspace." For example, when the value of Microsoft's stock slid due to an unfavorable verdict in the Department of Justice's antitrust case, Microsoft kept workers from defecting by increasing their stock options. Sometimes, it's the work that motivates employees. Given the right project, workers want to work hard. At times, this hard work is linked to fame within the industry or peer pressure (everyone is doing it). Often, it's nontraditional work hours, casual clothes, telecom-

FIGURE 7.2   **Employee incentives often give employees a good reason not to defect.**

Effective Incentives	More Effective Incentives	Most Effective Incentives
Scholarships for kids	Medical insurance	The best managers identify
Community service	Stock purchase plan	what motivates workers and
Casual dress days	Service anniversary	then design cost-effective
Sign-on bonus	Retirement plan	incentive packages pegged to
Company picnic	Dental insurance	those motivators. Some of the
Tuition refunds	Vacation	most common programs are:
Credit union	401(k) savings plan	
Jury duty pay	Day care services	
Holiday parties	Sick pay	
Direct pay deposit	Company newsletter	
Summer jobs for kids	Physical surroundings	
Subsidized cafeteria	Employee of the	
Exercise facilities	month	
Company store	Holiday pay	
Christmas bonus	Company car	
Recreational leagues	Flexible work hours	
Free/reserved parking		
Matching gifts to		
charities		

Most Effective Incentives column text:

The best managers identify what motivates workers and then design cost-effective incentive packages pegged to those motivators. Some of the most common programs are:

1. Stock options (about 35 percent of all high-tech companies offer stock options to all employees).
2. Revenue sharing (team members share a portion of revenues generated by the team or company regardless of individual input).
3. Tournaments (work is arranged so that top-performing teams earn the highest incomes).
4. Forced contracts (workers are assigned target production or revenue levels, with a guarantee of one high-wage level if the target is achieved and a lower wage level if they miss).
5. Profit sharing (workers have an opportunity to share in the team or firm profits—a form of forced contract because it depends on profit levels).

Source: Adapted from Keep Employees Inc. (www.keepemployees.com/retention.htm), 26 April 2000, and Michele Himmelberg, "Employee Loyalty & Good Business Practices: Incentives," an online publication of the *Macon Telegraph* (www.macontelegraph.com), 1999.

muting, keeping a sofa in the office, or bringing dogs to work. (One hiring criterion at an online mortgage-lending firm based in San Francisco was that the new hire's dog must get along with the other dogs in the office.)

If your e-corporation has the resources to offer extras (beyond the expected health benefits, 401(k) plans, and paid vacation time), you may want to consider this list of popular benefits. According to a survey for the Society for Human Resource Management, the following are the most popular types of perks being offered to keep employees loyal, happy, and productive:

- Professional development
- Relocation benefits
- Dependent care flexible spending account
- Flextime
- Paid maternity leave
- Cell phone or pager for personal use
- Telecommuting
- Compressed workweeks
- Fitness center subsidy
- Paid paternity leave

SUMMING IT UP

- The economic model for employee loyalty is similar to the model for customer loyalty, because your company receives economic benefits from employees in the same fashion. The net present value of employees is based on profit contribution, rate of return, and tenure.
- Changing the corporate culture is an art and a science; however, all efforts will be worthless unless you create an environment that thrives on meaningful work.
- Retaining e-employees means abandoning a production-line approach to management. You cannot afford to treat all employees the same. Old rules will have to be broken and new ones created for individual employees.

SHIFTING CORPORATE CULTURAL VALUES TO INCREASE EMPLOYEE LOYALTY AND RETENTION

Who's in charge of retaining employees? Most organizations have someone who is in charge of recruitment, but no one who is in charge of employee retention. In the past, companies like IBM had career managers for each employee. The career manager would help guide the employee in trying to achieve his or her goals. However, over time it was evident there was no linkage between ambition and achievement. The military offers another model: The commander is responsible for bringing new people on board in the proper manner by taking responsibility for their training, growth potential, and retention in the service. Answer the ten questions and discover how your organization rates in the employee loyalty department.

Here are ten questions about employee loyalty and retention issues for the management team to discuss when planning the e-corporation.

1. Is the level of trust in your organization high or low?

   _____

   _____

2. How does your e-corporation help individuals develop a sense of pride in their work?

   _____

   _____

3. When managers delegate responsibility, do they provide employees with the authority and the access to information required to get the job done?

   _____

   _____

4. Does your organization listen to employee recommendations for process improvements?

_____

_____

5. Realizing that innovation is critical to competitive success in the e-commerce environment, how does your e-corporation cultivate innovation?

_____

_____

6. Does your company offer training so employees can improve their skill sets? How does this integrate with your e-corporation's strategic plan?

_____

_____

7. What methods does your e-corporation use to show employees that it appreciates them and their work?

_____

_____

8. How does your e-corporation reinforce and reward the kinds of customer relationship-building interactions it wants to see repeated?

_____

_____

9. What are your e-corporation's five most important values? How are these values demonstrated by management and staff each day?

_____

_____

10. How does your e-corporation assess and meet its employees' needs?

_____

_____

Source: Adapted from JoAnna Brandi, "20 Tough Questions," *Florida Business to Business,* an online publication of JoAnna Brandi & Company (www.customerretention.com), October 1999.

REFERENCES

Calderon, Jack. 1996. Incentive: There Are More Ways to Pay. *Electronic Buyer News*, 2 December, 20.

Griffin, Jill. 1995. *Customer Loyalty: How to Earn It, How to Keep It.* San Francisco: Jossey-Bass Publishers.

Herman, Roger E., and Joyce L. Gioia. 1998. Making Work Meaningful: Secrets of the Future-Focused Corporation. *The Futurist* 32 (1 December): 1–6.

Heskett, James L., Thomas O. Jones, Gary W. Loveman, W. Earl Sasser, Jr., and Leonard A. Schlesinger. 1994. Putting the Service-Profit Chain to Work. *Harvard Business Review* (March–April).

Heskett, James L., W. Earl Sasser, Jr., and Leonard A. Schlesinger. 1997. *The Service Profit Chain.* New York: The Free Press.

Lewis, Bob. 1998. Opinions: IS Survival Guide. *InfoWorld* 20 (9 November): 1–2.

McKenna, Regis. 1997. *Real Time.* Boston: Harvard Business School Press.

Reichheld, Fredrick R. 1996. *The Loyalty Effect.* Boston: Harvard Business School Press.

Schmit, Julie. 1996. 90 Hrs. a Week and Loving It, Sleep and a Social Life Take a Back Seat. *USA Today*, 3 April, 01A.

Seybold, Patricia B., and Ronni T. Marshak. 1998. *Customers.com.* New York: Random House.

Vanscoy, Kayte. 2000. The Hiring Crisis: How to Find, Keep, and Motivate Employees in the New Economy and Steal the Best Ones from Your Competitors. *Smart Business* (July): 85–97.

Verespej, Michael A. 1995. A Workforce Revolution? (Forecast for 2020). *Industry Week* 244 (21 August): 21–27.

Personalizing Your Marketing

The effectiveness of Web site personalization cannot be ignored. Financial network CNNfn (www.cnnfn.com) realized as much as a 12 percent gain in the response rate to its personalized online advertising due to Web site personalization, and Microsoft's CarPoint (carpoint.msn.com) doubled the rate of its previous responses. Time and again, Web site personalization has converted window shoppers to buyers, boosted online revenues, and encouraged up-selling and cross-selling by catering to e-customer interests. Web site personalization allows your e-corporation to increase loyalty by intelligently matching products, Web site content, and offers to the right buyers, in addition to building loyal customer relationships and enhancing the Web site experience. This chapter shows how personalizing a Web site requires some planning. You'll need to decide what type of personalization is appropriate for your company's e-customers, determine your company's personalization goals, and measure the success of the personalized marketing program.

Carrie Johnson of Forrester Research (www.forrester.com) states that Web site personalization will be the guiding principle of every e-corporation for the next several years. After all, customers can easily surf the Web comparing prices, or use automated agents such as My Simon (www.mysimon.com) and Comparison Shopping Net (www.comparisonshopping.net). Consumers can even name their price at Priceline.com (www.priceline.com). The "one price fits all" approach is well on its way to becoming obsolete. According to the Forrester report "Pricing Gets Personal," about 57 percent of all online retailers are currently testing a mix of strategies to appeal to price-conscious e-customers and like "preferred" pricing for repeat customers to build customer loyalty.

CUSTOMIZATION VERSUS PERSONALIZATION

Jeremy Allaire, chairman and executive vice president of Allaire Corporation in Cambridge, Massachusetts, recently stated: "Profiling, personalization, and business intelligence technologies are the core requirements for establishing meaningful online customer relationships. For businesses to effectively compete in the new economy, they need to acquire a deeper understanding of their customer base and leverage this knowledge in key areas like customer service, support, sales, and marketing." Web site personalization can be the answer to commoditization threats by helping to make your e-corporation's Web site stand out from the crowd. Before taking this path, it is important to define the differences between customization and personalization. Web site personalization is so new that the definitions of these two terms are often not clear.

Web Site Customization

In cyberspace, customization is defined as being under direct Internet-user control. In contrast, online personalized content is usually managed by the e-corporation. It usually starts with the e-customer filling out an online registration form or answering a few questions to gain access to a higher level of Web site information or to speed up purchase transactions. Some Web sites track user clicks and analyze the "click stream." Other Web sites rely on "cookies." According to Netscape, *cookies* are a "general mechanism which server side connections can use to both store and retrieve information on the client side of the connection"; that is, a small data file is written on the PC's desktop by the owner of the Web site the user views in his or her Internet browser. The cookie file (cookie.txt) on the Internet users PC contains information the Web site owners can use to track passwords, Web pages visited, the date of the last visit, and sometimes the user's geographic location.

After the free registration (where the Web site owner gathers information about the user's name and U.S. mail and e-mail addresses), the user selects options, such as clicking on certain headlines from *The New York Times* (www.nyt.com) or entering a ticker symbol at the *Wall Street Journal* (www.wsj.com) site to track a particular stock (see Figure 8.1).

With customized pages, users can skip the parts they don't have time for or focus on what interests them. For example, at Schwab (www.schwab .com), if you have a higher interest in the performance of your portfolio than in today's financial news, you can design your customized Web page to present your portfolio information first. Since the user is in control, this is a perfect way to meet the unique needs of each Internet user. Keep in mind that the customization approach works well if users know what they will see when they click a link and also understand what they are deselecting. In other words, use your customer knowledge to carefully prepare a menu of value-added options. If your Web site offers complete coverage of what users want and need, customization is terrific. However, there are limitations to customization. If something that is of vital interest to your customers isn't included on the Web page, it can't be selected.

Often, customization can stage a positive online experience. This approach to customization provides customer value and is often the first step in creating memorable customer interactions and strong customer loyalty bonds. After all, many customers are resistant to the notion of building a personal relationship with a vendor; in other words, some users do not want a relationship with the e-corporation. In this situation,

FIGURE 8.1   *The Wall Street Journal* lets users track just the stocks that interest
them.

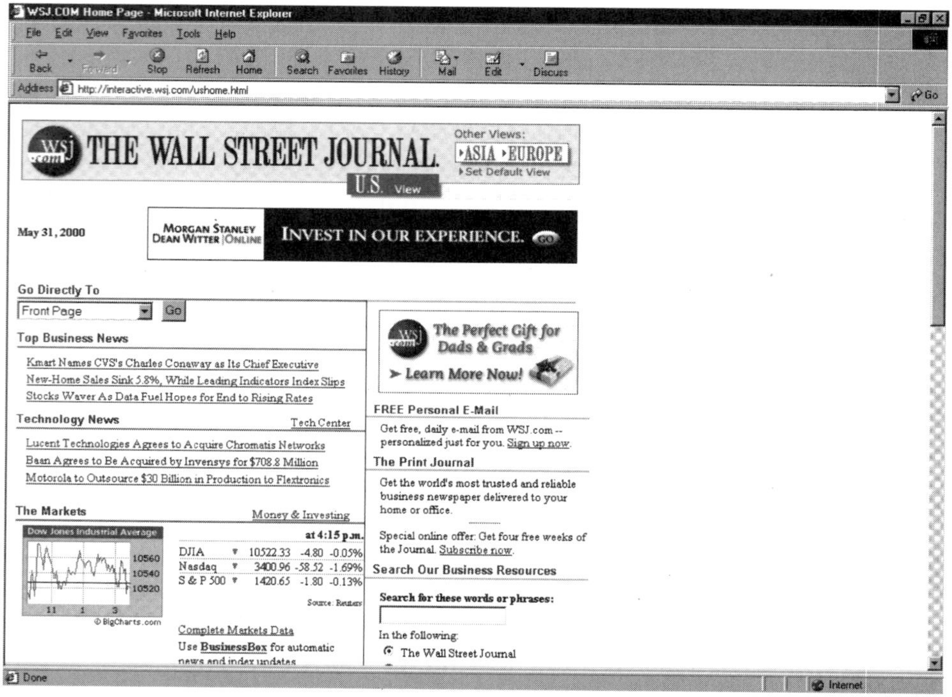

you can create customer-unique value by creating online experiences that
reach individual customers through *portals* that include:

- Web pages that are designed for a specific individual (without the
  customer's knowledge) at a particular moment in time
- Web pages with characteristics that meet the customer's individual
  needs (although some other customers may have the same needs and
  may therefore purchase the same offering)
- Web pages with just the right amount of content. The customer is not
  overwhelmed by content (sometimes called information overload)
  and gets exactly what he or she desires.

Personalization

Personalization is driven by Web sites that try to serve the e-customer with value-added offerings such as individualized Web pages at My Yahoo! (www.my.yahoo.com). Customized Web pages increase your interactivity with users and this, in turn, stimulates an ongoing dialogue that can build customer loyalty. Customized Web pages are based on some form of model that profiles the user's needs. Here, the personalized software has to "guess" what the e-customer needs. It is a little like playing 20 questions, because the same customer may have different needs and wants at different times. An e-customer can quickly get frustrated if the computer guesses wrong. Where personalization shines is in situations in which the e-customer's wants and needs are relatively unchanging and easy to describe in machine-understandable ways.

The story of 1-800-Flowers (www.1-800-flowers.com) provides a glimpse of a Web site that captivates. It uses personalized marketing to go beyond the replication of a flower shop or phone order house, enhancing the value of a possible sale by expanding what one originally thought one might want to buy and for whom.

LOYALTY MARKETING SUCCESS STORY

1-800-FLOWERS

▼ **COMPANY:** Selling flowers is a fairly low-value item. However, 1-800-Flowers is a rapidly growing $30-million-a-year online business. To overcome this hurdle, 1-800-Flowers developed a Web site that uses personalized marketing to emphasize variety.

▼ **SOLUTION:** 1-800-Flowers uses Web site personalization to go beyond replication of a flower shop by providing a Web site that captivates and expands what you originally thought you might want to buy and who you might want to buy for, thereby enhancing the value of possible sales.

The company shows a concern for customer issues and builds customer loyalty by donating 25 percent of product sales. Joint marketing deals with United Airlines provides customers with frequent-flyer miles. Notification programs automatically

FIGURE 8.2   1-800-Flowers is a master of personalized marketing.

Courtesy of 1-800-FLOWERS.COM.

remind customers of important occasions and dates. Registration gives customer bonuses, keeps track of purchases for later reuse, and provides faster service. Corporate and consumer customers can get tailored e-mail messages and product offerings that go beyond flowers (balloons, gourmet items, plants, gift baskets, and so on). Corporate customers also have account managers for personal attention.

   ▼ **BENEFITS:** 1-800-Flowers provides customers with choices, relationships, personalization, and easy transactions.

- Corporate customers can save time and money by working with their account manager.
- Customers get tailored e-mail messages and can join the preferred customer club, so they can make better purchases.

- The firm helps customers make more creative and thoughtful purchases by providing balloons, gourmet items, plants, baskets, and more.

▼ **TECHNOLOGY:** Through a remote administration system, 1-800-Flowers employees can now update products, prices, and content directly. Today, 1-800-Flowers takes over 40,000 orders per day and uses Windows NT Server 4.0 application server technologies such as MTS and IIS.

Source: Adapted from Computer Database Plus (1997), an online publication of ZDNet (www.cma .zdnet.com), 1 May 2000.

For personalization to be the most effective, you must know a lot about your customers, which puts a burden on customers that is not always welcome. Consequently, e-corporations use a technique called "creeping personalization," so that e-customers don't have to do extra work, like setting up extensive customer profiles before getting some benefit from the Web site. There are two primary ways to personalize a Web site:

1. *Business rules filtering.* Business rules–based filtering is a process of surveying e-customers by asking them to set criteria. Questions can include standard information like your zip code, gender, and type of computer you use. Web site content is delivered to meet these preset criteria. Business rules criteria can be just about anything, such as home loan interest rates for a particular state, information about new products, or services that meet a customer's needs.

2. *Collaborative filtering.* Collaborative filtering (sometimes called group filtering) provides Web site content that is relevant to users by combining their individual preferences with those of others with similar preferences. However, users often have to complete extensive registration/customer profiles to get access to the service. Examples of Web sites that use this type of collaborative filtering are AOL's Buddy List—a travel version of its instant messaging service that lets users view their buddy lists and send messages from any computer that has a browser—and My Yahoo!, which allows users to collect their favorite parts of the Web site in one place. Here are two examples of how collaborative filtering can work:
   - Let's say one user likes these two books: *The Handbook of Real Estate Lending* and *The Unofficial Guide to Buying a Home Online*. A second user likes *The Unofficial Guide to Buying a Home Online* and

Investing Online for Dummies. The collaborative filter software will recommend *Investing Online for Dummies* to the first user. In this way, Web site users "collaborate" and make recommendations to each other without really interacting.

- Collaborative filtering can go beyond book recommendations to information; for example: "Eight percent of the people who are somewhat like you clicked on this hyperlink [for a news item, product, or service], and you didn't. Would you like to click now?" This relieves the burden of personalization on the consumer for whatever personalized feature you are offering.

The success story of Gloss.com (www.gloss.com) shows how e-corporations can make online shopping a unique experience. Gloss.com uses personalization technology to provide new, inspiring, convenient, and fun content every time you visit the Web site.

LOYALTY MARKETING SUCCESS STORY

Gloss.com

▼ **COMPANY:** Gloss.com is an online destination for beauty news, prestige beauty brands, and beauty advice. Gloss.com, located in San Francisco, California, launched its Web site in the fall of 1999. The company began as an e-corporation designed to bring beauty closer to people everywhere. To be successful, Gloss .com needed to attract customers and bring them back.

▼ **SOLUTION:** The Gloss.com team comprises experts from the beauty, retailing, Internet, and editorial industries. The Web site features products in the skincare, makeup, bath and body, fragrance, hair care, home fragrance, accessories, and gift categories. The team determined the key to success was to offer users a highly personalized online experience by providing customers with constantly new content based on their consumer profiles.

▼ **BENEFITS:** Gloss.com selected a personalized marketing technology that allowed the firm to analyze online customer buying patterns. Experts used this information to decide which products to present to various segments of Web users. Customer benefits included:

- A personalized online shopping experience tailored to the needs and interests of each individual user
- Personalized cross-selling and up-selling based on each customer's buying habits
- Tools for better consumer decision making, because Gloss.com can list an unlimited number of product attributes

▼ **TECHNOLOGY:** Gloss.com uses the Blue Martini E-Merchandising System (www.bluemartini.com). The Gloss.com Web site was up and running in about 14 weeks. The cost of the software was $1 million, and consulting to get it up and running will likely cost another $1 million. The software runs on Windows NT and Sun SPARC/Sun Solaris operating systems.

DEVELOPING A WEB SITE PERSONALIZATION PLAN

The personalization approach that is best for your e-corporation depends on the needs of customers (uniform or differentiated) and the level of customer loyalty (no loyalty to premium loyalty). For example, a customized Web site may be best for your company if it has a uniform customer base and no loyalty. As you increase the use of technology-based tools, you must also provide easy access to people via the high-touch approach. Human-to-human contact through hot lines, voicemail, and e-mail systems is often the critical element in overcoming resistance to high-tech tools and for gaining acceptance. A high-touch Web site with lots of personalization features may be best for your company, if you have a differentiated customer base and premium loyalty. (*High touch* is often defined as providing lots of human-to-human contact with online technology via "call me" buttons, voice over the Internet, or text chat contact with live agents. For details, see Chapter 12.)

Keep in mind that Internet products and services are constantly being redefined, making them a moving target for marketers. Today, e-corporations do not have time for in-depth market research and testing before

FIGURE 8.3   Get your shopping experience personalized at Gloss.com.

rolling out a marketing campaign. However, bringing ideas to the market to stay ahead of the competition does not mean that you have to make multi-million-dollar decisions without any planning. Building the personalization of a Web site takes vision, planning, and a good understanding of what works online and what doesn't.

1. Understand What You Are Selling

Identify what you want to sell. For an online travel agency, the product may be travel reservations, but what people are really buying is the easy-to-use online services, an accurate user profile that speeds up reservations, and verification that the user's travel plans meet corporate guidelines.

2. Identify Customers

Take the time to focus on your e-corporation's real customers. Who does the e-corporation really need to communicate with? The procurement officer, office manager, or some other person may make the actual order or sign the checks for products or services, but the end-user or customer may be another person within the organization.

When target groups have been identified, what can you learn about them without alienating them as customers? What if your company does not have time to conduct primary research? For difficult-to-find information, there are several good online research companies that can help you fill in the blanks. Media Metrix (www.mediametrix.com), the Yankee Group (www.yankeegroup.com), and Forrester Research (www.forrester.com) are excellent sources. (For more information, see the Resource Center.) The reports from these organizations are often expensive and can range from $1,800 for a brief report to several thousand dollars. Compared to the cost of setting up your own focus group or marketing study, these think tank reports can be relatively inexpensive, and making a mistake because you don't have the right information can cost more than any online research report. (For information about related privacy issues and policy statements, see Chapter 11.)

3. Target customers

Not all customers are created equal. The clustering of customers into logical groupings according to their buying criteria and attractiveness allows you to segment and target buyers effectively. (For details about getting to know your customers, see Chapter 2.) The customer segmentation process is a valuable tool that your e-corporation can use to group and target desirable accounts for personalization. For example, your organization can use segmentation to divide customers into two groups: customer needs and e-corporation needs. The organization's needs may be growth potential, profitability, tendency to buy a broad range of products or services, or a propensity to make large purchases. Customer needs may be overnight delivery, multiple billing options, or special volume pricing. Segmentation allows each factor to be weighed according to importance and given an attractiveness score, and each account can be plotted on a matrix. (For more information about segmenting your customer base, see Chapter 13.)

Jeffery Graham (2000) provides this customer segmentation example for a car-buying Web site. For purposes of targeting customers, a qualified buyer is someone who fits a certain demographic profile, shows interest in a certain car's price, and registers for a test drive. Next, the marketer creates a matrix. The target segment, called qualified buyer, is one axis of the matrix. The characteristics for a qualified buyer—demographic fit, interest in price, request for a test drive—are listed on the other axis of the matrix.

Once customer segments are identified, you can start developing different online experiences for different customer targets. Your e-corporation must be careful in determining which customer segments qualify for what offers. Using the car-buying site example, qualified buyers may be offered a brochure and a video. Repeat customers may be offered discounts or other incentives. Customers who are just browsing may be offered an online newsletter.

Keep in mind that it is often difficult to determine the motivation of e-customers and to match the right offer to the right customer. However, if done correctly, this activity changes the focus away from cut-rate pricing. In other words, personalized marketing is not just throwing out differentiated prices to everybody. Personalized marketing is differentiating customers to reward repeat consumers and to up-sell and cross-sell products and services.

4. Set Personalized Marketing Goals

After identifying what you are selling, who your customers are, and what benefits customers want from your product or service, your e-corporation can begin setting goals:

- What do you gain from personalized marketing, for example, increased brand awareness, selling more products or services, generating leads, or reducing operating costs?
- What customer behavior will the Web site enable; for example, will it drive sales or create a knowledge base?

For measuring the success of personalization, your e-corporation needs to determine the success criteria of the initiative. Overall, the success criteria can be simple or complex. A success criterion can be converting 1 percent to 2 percent of Web site users into customers. Another success criterion is increasing the number of repeat visits. For example, Excite (www .excite.com) claims that personalization increased repeat visits by five times.

If your corporation already has a large Web site, it is unwise to convert the entire site to personalization all at once. A better approach is to divide the site into areas and convert the Web site one area at a time. The successful implementation of personalization takes a lot of thought and effort. Make sure your corporation has the technical resources needed to complete the personalization initiative once it has started.

5. Define the Business Rules of the Product or Service

Your company has a certain logic to how its products are marketed and sold. This knowledge can be used to highlight what should be personalized. This knowledge can also be used to create business rules for the processes of marketing, selling, customer support, and distribution. Document the business process and use this to determine the Web site's business rules. Following are a few examples:

- Certain information or products are only available to subscribers.
- Some customers receive free shipping or express shipping.
- If product A is out of stock, product B is recommended.
- Determine the relationship between products and information; for example, are products such as tents linked to hiking equipment?

6. Determine the Level of Personalization

Personalization is so prevalent that most users are surprised when an e-corporation doesn't use personalization technology. For example, a child can design a Barbie doll at <www.barbie.com/mydesign>. Figure 8.4 is an illustration from the My Design™ area of the Web site that shows a friend of Barbie that girls can personalize online. Thanks to mass-customization

FIGURE 8.4   Barbie.com makes personalization so simple even a child can use it.

techniques, Mattel has thousands of possible combinations. Just point and click to choose the hair color, lip and eye color, clothes, and personality characteristics. Save the profile for later or purchase the doll. Mattel will custom-make the doll and send it directly to a specified address.

As online customers become experienced Internet users, they are expecting more and more of this type of personalization. Therefore, it is a good idea to check your competition. A good place to start is Media Metrix 500 (www.mediametrix.com/top500/top500.html), an alphabetized monthly list of the top 500 e-commerce sites that attract the most "unique" visitors (multiple visits by same person are only counted once). Discover what are the hottest interactive features of your competitors. Following are other items for your consideration:

- Will your e-corporation be using the latest personalization technologies? (Many of last year's most popular Web sites can quickly lose their audiences to Web sites that have implemented newer, easy-to-use technologies, interactive customization, and personalization features.)

- What personalization features are must-haves?
- Do the proposed personalization features truly enhance the customer experience and encourage repeat purchases?

7. Assign Monetary Values to Personalization Features

As part of your personalization effort, you'll need to build a performance management system of the critical success factors. The management system will identify the most important indicators of success, show how the personalization enhancements are meeting those objectives, indicate the need for any corrections, and help your organization gain a positive return on the investment.

A cost/benefit analysis is appropriate once the level of personalization is determined. How much will it cost (including hardware, software, and support), and how long will it take to recover the initial investment? One "quick and dirty" way to determine your payback is to deduct your costs from expected revenues. For example, let's say your costs are $50,000 and your expected return is $50,000 each year for the next three years. The formula is: $50,000 ÷ $50,000 = 1 or one year for payback. Let's say costs are $150,000 and your returns are $50,000 per year: $150,000 ÷ $50,000 = 3. In this second example, your payback is three years. Once you have determined how long it will take to recover your initial investment, decide if the proposed technological solution is cost efficient. In this case, what happens to your e-corporation if you have to replace your breakthrough technological solution in two years?

Next, develop a return on investment (ROI) model that meets the needs of your organization. After determining your personalized marketing goals, set a monetary value for each metric. Many companies use sales to measure the return on investment from ad campaigns. If your average cost per new customer is $5, will your personalization goal be to pay less than $5 per new customer? Whatever the goal of each personalization feature, remember that each personalization feature needs a monetary value assigned to it. This can assist you in determining the success of your e-corporation's efforts. Figure 8.5 provides a few examples of how you can measure your success.

Keep in mind that repeat business must be entered into the success equation of your e-corporation's personalization efforts. For example, Ad-Knowledge (www.adknowledge.com), a data mining and analysis firm, states that by tracking several campaigns over the past few months, they discovered that within 90 days of showing an ad, fully 48.6 percent of the sales leads generated by a campaign came from repeat visits (above and beyond the initial visit). This type of information can be used to assist you in accurately determining the ROI of your personalized marketing efforts.

HOW TO GATHER INFORMATION FOR WEB SITE PERSONALIZATION

In most e-corporations, the customer base is a mix of users who have no customer loyalty and those who have high value and are fierce advocates of your products or services. Knowing the wants, needs, and desires of your high-value customers can assist you in developing successful personalized marketing campaigns. This knowledge, combined with the ROI analysis outlined earlier, allows you to identify which personalized marketing approaches will work for your e-corporation. It also eliminates wasteful spending and increases profits from within your e-corporation.

Often, gathering intelligence about customers is more of an art than a science. Customer data gathering is the responsibility of individuals from technology, sales, project development, and marketing. There are two steps in gathering a customer's information: The first step is gathering information before your e-corporation builds a relationship with the user. The second step is gathering more information to fine-tune customer information in an effort to match the unique needs of each individual customer.

FIGURE 8.5   Measuring Your Personalization Success

Measure of Success	Value
Personalized Online Ads: The number of online ad-driven consumers who looked at three or more Web pages of the site	Monetary Value: Determined to be equal to calling the 800 number for information about the product or service. The value is $X per visitor.
Personalized Online Coupons: The number of Web site rebate coupons presented at time of purchase	Monetary Value: $X per purchase. This is the same as consumers responding to a newspaper promotion with a rebate offer.
Sales Leads Generated by Personalization Features: Number of names generated through Web site registration, targeted contests, and promotions	Monetary Value: $X per name. The value assigned is the same as if a name were generated through traditional promotions but weighted due to the source. (This weighting could be placing a greater value on the name or reducing the value on the name.) Assuming the e-corporation developed a way to measure each of these against specific campaigns, the e-corporation could show the ROI from specific and multiple campaigns.

Gathering User Information

Your Web site cannot be personalized unless you have built customer profiles. Once you have built your customer profiles, you'll be able to answer these key questions (statistics provided by Forrester Research):

- In North America, 49 percent of all Internet consumers are male. Are your target consumers men or women?

- In North America, 47 percent of all Internet consumers have some college education. How do your target consumers compare?
- The median income of Internet consumers is $36,000. What is the media income of your target consumer?
- About 34 percent of all households of Internet consumers have children. What percentage of your target customers has children, under 18 years old, living at home?
- The median age of Internet consumers is 45 years old. Are your target customers older or younger than the median?

Your company can begin by analyzing which areas of its Web site a user visits. There are noninvasive programs, such as Aptex's SelectCast, that use a "you are what you view" technology to gather customer information. The software then takes this data to predict demographic information about Web site users.

Often, Internet users are willing to provide information or have it acquired from other sources about their needs and preferences in return for personalized messages, targeted advertisements, and Web sites personalized to meet their individual needs. For example, e-customers will usually provide information such as name, street address, and e-mail address in return for free downloads of white papers or software programs. This information flows into a new individual customer profile. However, customers demand certain restrictions on data collection activities, such as receiving advance notice of what is being collected and the choice of "opting out" of the opportunity. (For more on Internet privacy issues, see Chapter 11.)

Gathering Customer Information

Many e-corporations start customer profiles with a default or preliminary profile based on research reports and, when possible, clickstream data (records of the Web pages visited by users). When the user becomes a customer by making a purchase, transaction information is added to the profile. After the customer starts doing business with your e-corporation and there is an element of trust in the relationship, you can ask the customer to fill in or update his or her profile. This is often called incremental or drip irrigation questioning, and the following details how it works:

- *Request more personal information in response to a user or customer inquiry.* In the context of the service you provide, you can ask for more specific information. For example, you have a membership program that offers loyal customers a higher-than-usual level of service or other benefits. The customer may ask for a membership form, at which time it is appropriate for you to ask for standard information (e.g., address, contact information, etc.) and specific information (e.g., smoking or nonsmoking, driver's license number, size of car preferred, king-size or queen-size bed, and credit card number).

- *Request that the customer select from a menu of options.* Give customers the full menu and have them select what they want. For each item selected, the customer may say: "Give me more like this" or "Give me less" or "Now that I see it, I don't want it." However, for a large Web site with thousands of menu options, this is not a feasible approach. Customers become overwhelmed, leave, and don't return. An alternative is setting up a default profile, hoping it is the customer's general area of interest, and letting the customer "tweak" it. Even this approach has limitations, because many people don't know what they want until they see it.

- *Request that customers update their profiles.* If customers know they have a profile, your company should provide access to this file so customers can update and modify it. Customers can be prompted to update the profile when they visit the Web site. For example, the personalized greeting can include the question, "Have you changed your e-mail address lately?" You also can send e-mail messages to customers encouraging them to update their files. The e-mail message might say, "Thanks for being a customer for one year. Click here to update your profile and visit our Web site for a 10 percent discount on your next purchase." (For more information on personalized marketing with e-mail messages, see Chapter 10.)

- *Request that the customer leave some information about himself or herself.* Each time a customer visits the Web site, he or she is asked one or two questions and leaves more customer profile information. Often, this approach is so subtle that users don't even realize they are providing more data. For example, at Southwest Airlines you'll receive Click n' Save e-mail updates if you provide your name and e-mail address.

Gathering Implicit and Explicit User and Customer Information

Data gathering can assist you in improving the customer's Web site experience. As your e-corporation builds relationships with customers, individual profiles can be collected incrementally and used to improve the customer's online interaction with you. One requirement of data collection is that your e-corporation gather both implicit and explicit information from their customers without alienating them. This "creeping personalization" process continually increases the value you can provide customers, which in turn strengthens customer loyalty and optimizes the profitability of each customer relationship. For example, each time you visit Amazon.com, your Web site interactions are recorded and stored. The next time you log on, this data is used to provide you with a more personalized customer experience.

- *Implicit data* is data gathered at the back end of your Web site's operations by recording Web site activity with analysis application software that often uses cookies or clickstream data. These programs record what types of tools customers used and what areas of the Web site they visited.
- *Explicit data* is information from registration forms, online surveys, and order forms. For example, having e-customers provide data for a sweepstakes is a good way to begin a customer profile without asking the customer to complete a customer profile form.

There are a number of ways to analyze the data collected. Users and customers can be clustered into behavioral groups for marketing purposes; preferences can be used for product innovations; and responses of certain customers in particular segments can be used to plan marketing campaigns. Overall, customer data will likely come from any number of sources, making integration a major challenge for you.

COMPUTER APPLICATIONS THAT AUTOMATE ONLINE MARKETING

Computer applications support the business needs of both large enterprises and small dot-com companies with profiling and personalization capabilities. There are many software products to personalize your Web site:

- Enterprisewide solutions that are modules of larger applications
- Stand-alone products that integrate with legacy solutions
- Solutions for a small, simple set of products
- Solutions for high-volume, high-information stream Web sites

Overall, there are software solutions for every budget and e-commerce business model. Software products should be evaluated on how well they deliver customized reports that address your e-corporation's success metrics. In the next two sections are a few examples of the major players in the Web site personalization market. The first section includes examples of online personalization software products that cost more than $25,000. The second section covers examples of online personalization software solutions that cost less than $25,000.

Personalization Software Tools for More Than $25,000

- Aptex SelectCast 2.1 (www.aptex.com), shown in Figure 8.6, uses cookies for improving personalization. The targeting technology that Aptex employs can be used to tailor both advertising and commerce-oriented content. SelectCast watches what users do on the Web site; it is an intelligent agent server that personalizes online content based on observed user behavior. In other words, personalization is based on "you are what you view" content-mining technology. The product is designed specifically for high-volume Web sites and information streams. SelectCast 2.1 takes this information a step further by using data to predict key demographic information, such as age and gender. SelectCast does its work in real time, which enables the system to constantly fine-tune and update its profiles of individual visitors. The latest version introduces more sophisticated reporting features, enabling marketers to better tweak and target online campaigns. Customers include Infoseek, Microsoft's Expedia Travel, and CUC International, which uses the program for personalized searching, promotions, and couponing on its netMarket commerce site.

- Blue Martini (www.bluemartini.com) is an enterprise application designed to let merchandisers such as Gloss.com leverage their brand names via the Internet. Blue Martini blends mature catalog management, discounting, personalization, site management, and data mining into one powerful e-commerce package. The software is ideal for companies that want to get online fast. If your firm already has a Web presence, you'll have to redo your efforts. Also, if you plan to offer auctions, this is not the application for you. Blue Martini supports multicurrency and multilingual transactions, data mining, and clickstream and postsales analysis, in addition to catalog, discounting, and price list management features.

- BroadVision (www.broadvision.com) makes software that customizes Web sites according to each visitor's behavior, including buying habits, product and service interests, and preferences. BroadVision software then automatically adjusts the information users receive to best match their interests and needs. Both Siebel and BroadVision say their products will work together, so that you will be able to share customer information across all channels. For example, when a user interacts with your BroadVision-powered Web site, the customer information captured in BroadVision will automatically be combined with customer information in Siebel front office applications. With Siebel's front office applications, your company can provide a consistent customer experience across all channels, whether the customers interact in person, over the phone, through a reseller, or via the Internet. BroadVision's tools are designed to let your Web site recognize customers and display relevant products and services. Clients include Kodak Picture Network, US West, and The Baan Company.

- Edify (www.edify.com), which is owned by S1, develops Internet applications that enable companies offering financial services to create their own financial portals on the Internet. S1 Virtual Financial

FIGURE 8.6   Aptex SelectCast 2.1 uses collaborative filtering and predicts customer behavior.

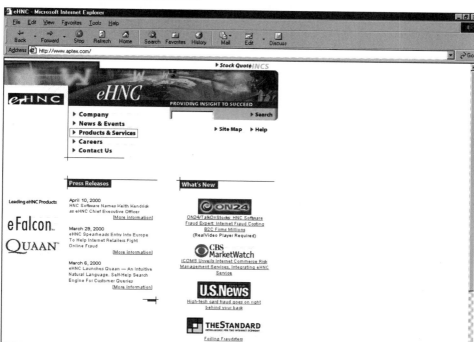

Reproduced with permission from eHNC Software. Contact Gaylin Allbaugh, product manager, at 858-799-1444.

Manager software lets customers display users' investment information in one application. Your company's Virtual Financial Manager software lets customers such as Bank of America, Citigroup, and KeyCorp display users' credit card, bank account, loan, and investment information in one application. S1 (formerly Security First Technologies) launched the world's first Internet bank in 1995, sold those operations to focus on putting other banks on the Web, and acquired Web software developer VerticalOne and banking software maker Edify. Edify is also known for its Interactive Voice Response (IVR) voicemail system and Web integration technology. Clients include Eddie Bauer, Nike, and Unisys.

- Net Perceptions (www.netperceptions.com) provides GroupLens and NT-based Net Perceptions for Ad Targeting programs. Ad Targeting uses technology licensed from Neural Applications to track information about site visitors and site usage to serve the optimal banner ad. The multistep process employs fuzzy logic, genetic algorithms, and time of day. The company claims customers have doubled their click-through rates in only three months using special percentage-improvement reports to optimize their sites. Business Week Online and Startribune.com were the first official users. This collaborative filtering solution requires other users to actively or passively rate content. Clients include Amazon.com, Musicmaker, N2K, and CDnow.

- Allaire's Open Sesame (www.allaire.com) is a cookie-based product that provides profiling and personalization technology designed to deliver highly personalized customer interaction capabilities. Open Sesame offers the ability to maintain an accurate view of the interests and trends of users and user groups so as to enable effective service and information delivery. It also connects users and customers with information in a personally meaningful way to create, service, grow, and retain online relationships. Open Sesame provides end-users with the convenience of viewing their Web sites with tailored content, including product recommendations and targeted sales promotions. The program includes learning and recommendation engine technology, implicit and explicit user profiling, individual and group profiling, real-time learning and dynamic profiling, and customer profile data-mart. Clients include Ericsson and Toronto Dominion Bank.

Personalization Software Tools for Less Than $25,000

- Allaire's ColdFusion (www.allaire.com) is a complete Web application server for developing and delivering scalable e-business applications. ColdFusion is designed to deliver the key requirements of e-commerce and enterprise Web applications such as intuitive visual tools; a high performance, multithreaded architecture; and advanced features such as just-in-time compiling and load balancing. ColdFusion ensures that your applications will scale to handle the most demanding sites, includes open integration with databases, e-mail, directories, and the latest advanced Internet security technologies for Web server security. Clients include NetGrocer and Kodak.

- Macromedia's LikeMinds (www.andromedia.com) personalization server meets the challenges of personalization by delivering highly accurate product recommendations, personally relevant content, and targeted promotions for each individual Web visitor. LikeMinds makes your Web site more convenient for online shoppers and builds trust in you as an online merchant. In doing so, it converts browsers into loyal customers. LikeMinds then closes the e-business loop by reporting on customer preferences and the effectiveness of its recommendations. Macromedia created a patented collaborative filtering technology—a click-to-close personalization solution. LikeMinds makes use of every interaction with Web visitors to fully leverage each step of the interactive sales process. It uses individual clickstream data, purchase history, explicit preferences, and product similarities to engage Web visitors with highly accurate product recommendations that help them decide what to try and what to buy. LikeMinds helps build customer loyalty because of its accuracy. Unlike other solutions, it creates an affinity group for each online visitor. (An affinity group is a collection of visitors who are most similar to the Web visitor.) Like-Minds builds a unique affinity group around each Web visitor in real time to generate recommendations that closely match that person's individual tastes. This collaborative filtering technology examines users' behavior (passively or actively), finds other users with similar behaviors, and creates a prediction or a product recommendation. Clients include Cinemax-HBO's Movie Matchmaker and Columbia House's Total E entertainment site.

- Neuromedia's NeuroStudio (www.neuromedia.com), shown in Figure 8.7, is intelligent-agent software designed to help users find information within your Web site. Your NeuroStudio Web site gives users the option of creating customized page layouts through the use of chatterbots. The intelligent agents communicate with users via two-way chat. Neuromedia provides a comprehensive suite of products and services that allows your online company to build and maintain virtual representatives, or vReps,™ that offer 24-hour automated sales

FIGURE 8.7   Type in a question and Neuromedia's vRep will respond directly with an answer.

Printed with permission from Neuromedia, the leading supplier of automated natural-language customer service representatives for the Web.

and customer service using natural language. These vReps bring "the best of the real world" to the Web by providing a dedicated on-site personality that talks to users in plain English. With NeuroStudio vReps, you can answer customers' questions, make purchasing recommendations, assist with purchase transactions, and aid in overall site navigation. The personalization program stores user data in a local database and uses either cookies or user login information for analysis. Users can store preferences, customize look-and-feel pageviews, and add new topic contents to the bot (intelligentagent).

SUMMING IT UP

- There is a difference between customization and personalization. Web site customization keeps the user in control. Web site personalization lets you as the Web site owner control the content presented to the user.
- Building a personalized Web site requires information from customer profiles. Information gathering can be noninvasive or invasive. Noninvasive data collection can include user clickstream analysis and research reports. Invasive approaches include registration requirements, contests and sweepstakes, and requesting users to select from a menu of options.
- Building a personalized Web site takes hardware, software, and organization support. There is a wide range of prices for Web site personalization programs; therefore, it is important to develop a management system to measure the success of the personalization effort.

ACTION PLAN

PERSONALIZATION OF A WEB SITE PLANNER

Some personalized Web sites are runaway hits, and others languish in the dust. Following is a planner for major Web site personalization issues. Any or all of the subjects listed on the planner may be relevant to the success of your proposed Web site.

What to Consider When Personalizing a Web Site		
Will Do?	**When?**	Learn from every move. It is often difficult to decipher e-customer motivations; therefore, you may want to analyze every click (sometimes called the clickstream) on the Web site.
		1. If the user visited two Web pages, which page did he or she visit first?
		2. The user visited six Web pages, which page did he or she stay at the longest?
		3. How often does a particular user visit the Web site?

What to Consider When Personalizing a Web Site

Will Do?	When?	
Will Do?	**When?**	4. How do you evaluate the users' Web site experience based on Web pages accessed, time spent at the Web site, items downloaded, and purchases? 5. Based on the data collected, is the user satisfied? Note: If the user is unsatisfied, he or she should be given the opportunity to approach the Web site in a new way.
Will Do?	**When?**	Remove areas of resistance. Do not require lengthy registrations, long surveys, and payment before the user knows what the Web site is all about. Newcomers can be asked to introduce themselves with greeting profiles. Next, set up activities to "pull" the user in and make it worthwhile to leave some information about themselves.
Will Do?	**When?**	Listen to the online customer. There are a number of sources that provide important customer profile information: 1. Past purchase and other customer data, in addition to derivations (data mining) performed on this data for nonreal-time personalization 2. Clickstream data (discussed earlier) and interpretations of the data 3. Customer responses to questions and preference surveys completed after a dialogue is created
Will Do?	**When?**	Give users choices and the opportunities to "opt out." Users change their preferences and multiple users can share the same computer. Give users the opportunity to view and update their profiles. Additionally, users should always have the opportunity to opt out of the personalization process. One alternative is to offer an "impersonal page" that is easy to navigate and doesn't use personalization.

		What to Consider When Personalizing a Web Site
		1. Align clicks with meaning to discover the users' interests.
		2. Include directory pages that allow users to click to topics of interest. This will indicate the user's preferences.
Will Do?	**When?**	Gather information as noninvasively as possible.
		Often, personalized Web sites present users with a list of questions. The user indicates which questions he or she agrees or disagrees with. Limitations of this approach are alienating users and receiving fictional answers from frustrated users. See how you can use "drip irrigation" or incremental questioning to let users explain their preferences.
		Sell the user on the benefits of the Web site's personalization.
		Let the user know that his or her preferences were used to personalize the Web site. Sell the worth of the personalization by quickly learning what the user values. If users are aware of the personalization, they may want to add to it, increasing the Web site's value to the user and the e-corporation.
		Note what users dislike. What users ignore provides good clues about what they like and shows how to sell products and services. Items that do not receive a lot of consumer interest can be dropped and replaced by something more attractive. Don't rely on a single personalization feature on the home page; have varieties available and properly placed in the Web site.

What to Consider When Personalizing a Web Site

Will Do?	When?	Let users say what they like and dislike.
		You never know what personalization features users will like and dislike. One e-corporation said that users described their first Web site as too ugly and too slow. This shows the value of letting users say what works and what doesn't. An instant feedback button can facilitate this process; however, some users will be willing to talk about themselves. Optional questionnaires or extended interview pieces that can be completed at the user's convenience may be useful. If there is a possibility that the personalization is off the mark, provide a "correct personalization" button for one-click corrections.
Will Do?	When?	Strive to provide instant gratification and don't let users wait for personalization.
		"Too slow" is a common user complaint. Make every effort to meet user expectations on performance. Don't make them wait; give them whatever screen you can give. A good alternative is to have a canned response, if personalization is too slow. This approach is also a good fail-safe mechanism, if something doesn't work correctly. In other words, the user gets dropped out of the personalization mode but seamlessly continues in the unpersonalized mode until the error is corrected.
Will Do?	When?	Provide a clearly stated primary policy.
		Users frequently fear that their profiles will be sold to marketing companies or shared with others. Also, users are worried about the security of their credit card information; users don't want fraudulent purchases to appear on their monthly statements. One way to allay user fears is to allow users at any point to erase the variables and methods by which the e-corporation determines their personalized content. Additionally, assure users that their preferences and credit card information are safe with the e-corporation.

Source: Adapted from Matt Calkins and Michael Beckley, "The Ten Rules of Personalization," *The Appian Web Personalization Report,* an online publication of Appian Corporation (www.appian.com), 1999.

REFERENCES

Allen, Cliff. 2000. Is It Time for a Personalization Makeover? Online publication of ClickZ Network, 14 March (www.clickz.com).

Customers Will Provide Information for Personalization. 2000. Online publication of CyberAtlas, 1 May (www.cyberatlas.internet.com).

Dean, Richard. 1998. Personalizing Your Web Site. Online publication of CNET, 2 June.

Featherly, Kevin. 2000. Personalized Pricing—Online Retail's Next Trend? Online publication of ZD Net Newsbytes, 25 April (www.zdnet.com).

Graham, Jeffery. 2000. Creeping Personalization 101. Online publication of ClickZ Network, 3 January (www.clickz.com).

Newell, Fredrick. 2000. *Loyalty.com.* New York: McGraw-Hill.

Nielsen, Jakob. 1998. AlertBox: Personalization. Online publication of ZDNet Developer, 4 October (www.zdnet.com).

Peppers, Don, Martha Rogers, and Bob Dorf. 1998. *The One to One Field Book: The Complete Toolkit for Implementing a 1 to 1 Marketing Program.* New York: Currency/Doubleday.

Seybold, Patricia B., and Ronni T. Marshak. 1998. *Customers.com.* New York: Time Business, Random House.

Siebel, Thomas M., and Pat House. 1999. *Cyber Rules: Strategies for Excelling at E-Business.* New York: Currency/Doubleday.

Zeff, Robin, and Brad Aronson. 1997. *Advertising on the Internet.* New York: Wiley Computer Publishing, John Wiley & Son.

9

Virtually Selling Everything

All sales hinge on the business proposition (or value-added proposition) of your company. However, creating a value proposition in the physical world and the virtual world is not the same. In cyberspace, value-added services that surround a product or service are often more important than the product itself. This chapter discusses how you can use technology and your customer knowledge to develop new services and products that create so much value that it spills over to employees and investors. I will also show you how to increase sales and extend your sales force with affiliate programs and how small merchants can link up with big merchants to create pop-up microstores, in addition to increasing your point-and-click sales force with portals. Today, about 20 percent of all online revenue is driven through portals. Find out if you want to participate in this potential big money game. The chapter concludes by showing you how the Internet has changed sales force automation. Get ready to check out the big eCRM software packages that include full suites of products for every part of your corporation.

CHANGE THE TRADITIONAL CHANNEL AND TURN UP THE VOLUME ON ADDED VALUE

In a 1998 interview with Internet Week, John Shedletsky, IBM's director of competitive technologies, observed: "Traditional channels will have to change; they will not go away, but they will have to add value and become information brokers and deal makers that bring customers and products together." This indicates that the first order of business for you is to determine the health of your e-corporation's business proposition (sometimes called the value-added proposition). Fredrick Reichheld (1996) asks if an airline's frequent-flyer program can really increase customer loyalty when almost every other aspect of the airline's service is undifferentiated. Can a credit card company's customer recovery unit stop customers from defecting and still charge 18 percent interest? Focusing on each of these isolated value-added efforts is not enough. Your organization must have a comprehensive business proposition that, if well executed, creates so much value for so many customers that it spills over to employees and investors. For example, sales personnel with products or services that are in high demand automatically become consultants rather than sales representatives. Overall, this is what makes creating a value proposition or revitalizing a current business proposition the basis for value, customer loyalty, and sales.

Making a value proposition for the physical world and the virtual world is not the same. According to Jeffery Rayport and John Sviokla (1995), many brick-and-mortar businesses that are transitioning to click-and-mortar are "managing two interacting value-adding processes in two mutually dependent realms, which pose new conceptual and tactical challenges. Those who understand how to master both can create and extract value in the most efficient and effective manner."

According to David Siegel (1999), the goal of an e-corporation is to increase loyalty and decrease customer churn in an environment where customers are constantly lured to other Web sites by new business propositions. An e-corporation strategy is to rely on branding, but online branding is difficult to maintain. Online customers find it difficult, if not impossible, to maintain relationships with 50 different e-corporations. Other e-corporations use a strategy that relies on Web site "stickiness," that is, the Web site's ability to attract large numbers of users. However, high volume traffic doesn't mean much if no one is buying. Siegel continues by stating that the primary concern of e-customers is the company's business proposition, not the brand. For example, if you offer a 40 percent discount and a competitor offers a 50 percent discount, your company brand won't stop customers from flocking to the competitor's Web site.

There are other difficulties in developing a value-added business proposition. For example, it is the customer, not the provider, who always defines value. Value is rooted in the personal and organizational needs of customers as they experience your products or services. Therefore, value is a function of needs being identified and satisfied in ways that meet and exceed customer expectations. Organizations have always captured customer data. However, it was only for inventory, production, and logistics to help monitor and control processes. For the most part, it was not used to identify the unique needs of individual customers; in other words, the information was not part of the value-added proposition for customers. Federal Express (www.federalexpress.com) changed that concept when it allowed customers to track packages online. The free service created added value for customers and assisted the e-corporation in building customer loyalty in a market that is constantly threatened by commoditization.

One way to add value is to use technology and customer knowledge to develop low-cost approaches to delivering extraordinarily high-value results to customers. This means using customer knowledge to invent business lines targeted to specific customer needs. For example, USAA (www.usaa.com) began as a life insurance company. Over time, the firm used the information it gathered about customer preferences and needs to develop new products, such as insurance for boat owners. By doing so, USAA created new value for customers by reducing the number of insurance companies they have to deal with.

A second way to add value is to synthesize your customer knowledge. Leverage your customer knowledge, experience, and resources to create better customer experiences at the Web site with customer-centered information, service, and support. In other words, take your knowledge of customer "hot buttons" and provide online solutions. Including customer-approved, value-added solutions like this increases customer satisfaction and builds customer loyalty bonds. Here are two examples:

1. Autoweb.com (www.autoweb.com) automates much of the overhead related to evaluating and processing auto bids and car loans. The e-corporation distinguishes itself from competitors by giving customers specialized service as an incentive. Although most of the Autoweb.com services are free, the company has two paying models: for $19.95 customers can advertise used cars in a classified section for 30 days, and consumers can receive a history of any used vehicle, including mileage and accidents reports for $12.50.

2. Purchasing hardware is easy. Knowing how to use and integrate it with existing systems is worth paying for. In the past, IBM (www.ibm .com) delivered hardware. Now IBM consulting services, such as IBM Global Services, surround IBM products with a wide variety of consulting services. These consulting services include business innovation services, integrated technology services, and strategic outsourcing services. In fact, IBM services are such a great business proposition that someone else can almost sell the product.

The story of American Airlines (www.aa.com) shows how to cost-efficiently reach millions of customers to notify them of special pricing deals that are available on short notice. American Airlines uses customer-focused sales and technology to increase customer loyalty.

LOYALTY MARKETING SUCCESS STORY

American Airlines

▼ **COMPANY:** American Airlines wanted to tell customers about the availability of deals on airfares. With two million frequent flyers registered at the Web site (of which 40 percent are members of American's elite-level frequent-flyer program), the problem seemed insurmountable.

▼ **SOLUTION:** American Airlines redesigned the Web site, so that each customer had access to his or her own custom-built home page. After logging in, customers are greeted by name, can immediately view the total number of frequent-flyer miles they have accumulated, and are shown customized news, information, special offers, and travel packages based on their individual profiles and travel histories.

▼ **BENEFITS:** American's personalization is so refined that individual customers may receive an offer for a specially priced travel package to a place they previously selected. The offer may arrive during a week when the children are out of school in the school district where the customer lives.

- If a customer's preferred destination is in the current week's offer, then a clickable Sale AAlert icon is displayed on his or her personal home page.
- American Airlines uses mass customization to render millions of different Web pages, based on specific business rules that determine how the Web site will be customized.
- Managers get instant feedback on how well the Web site is working by viewing the table of data that shows which business rules were triggered during the day.
- Without closing down the Web site, managers can manipulate 33 business rules by accessing a special control center to change the way the Web site customizes various offers for different visitors—in real time.

▼ **TECHNOLOGY:** BroadVision software is used for personalization; however, the Web site is integrated with a number of other computer systems. For example, the 36 million total AAdvantage members are tracked on an IBM DB2 mainframe. A subset of this database is copied daily to an Oracle database running on a Sun E4000 Web server to work with Web site users. When a reservation is made, it is made using the integrated booking application, which uses a set of Digital VAX computer systems to run the Sabre reservation system on a VMS operating system.

Source: Adapted from Peppers and Rogers Group, *Marketing 1 to 1 Success Stories* (www.1to1.com), 19 February 2000.

FIGURE 9.1   American Airlines has personalized its Web site to promote targeted special fare opportunities.

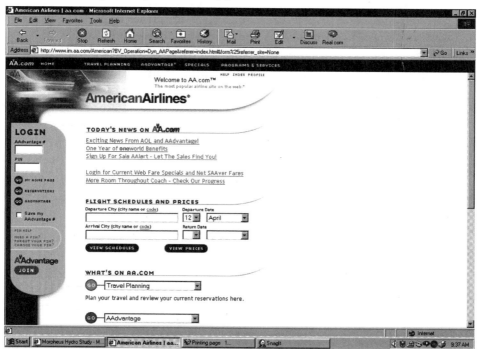

THE POINT-AND-CLICK SALES FORCE: AFFILIATE PROGRAMS

Forrester Research interviewed 50 online retailers with active affiliate programs that have been in place for at least three months. On average, these retailers have more than 10,270 affiliates that currently generate 13 percent of total online revenues. Forrester expects affiliate programs to power ahead to 21 percent of revenue by 2003. Affiliate programs are useful for small and large businesses. According to eMarketer (www.emarketer.com), about 20 percent of all online merchants use affiliate programs to build traffic. Additionally, there are more than 30 companies that offer a variety of affiliate management systems and do-it-yourself software to help businesses get started.

Dennis Berman (1999) provides this example of the power of affiliate programs: Walter W. Fredrick Associates, Inc., of Peabody, Massachusetts, is an architectural equipment and computer supplier with a three-person sales team and a Web site, which costs about $70,000. Overall, sales results have been disappointing. The firm's treasurer decided to start an affiliate program à la Amazon.com, and the firm's virtual sales force grew to 120. In other words, the firm drives traffic from other Web sites to its home page. Every time a customer links to the firm's home page at <www.ink express.com> from an affiliated Web site and makes a purchase, the affiliate Web site owner receives a 5 percent commission. In less than a month, the firm's Web site traffic increased from 5 visits per day to 182. Affiliates now drive more than half of the Web site's traffic and provide $2,800 per month in revenue. This amount is growing at a rate of 25 percent per month; however, affiliate revenue is still a lot less than the $3 million the firm grossed last year.

How Affiliate Programs Work

With an affiliate program, your e-corporation offers a commission to Web site owners for recommending your products or services. You decide how to reward affiliates:

- *Pay per click.* The affiliate is paid per visitor sent.
- *Pay per lead.* The affiliate is paid if the visitor submits predetermined information; for example, provides demographic information, joins a mailing list, or requests additional information.
- *Pay per sale.* The affiliate is paid a percentage or a flat rate for each sale generated from visitors sent.
- *Two-tier programs.* These programs are designed to give affiliates a choice of commission methods and also offer an additional commission on sales or clicks generated by affiliates that were introduced to your two-tier program. Keep in mind that anything more than two tiers is considered multiple-level marketing, or MLM, which is very different than extending your sales force via the Internet.

Usually, affiliates join your program at no cost to them. Each is allocated a unique ID code and links to your site via a banner, half-banner, button advertisement, or text link using the unique code. Your affiliate program

---

FIGURE 9.2   Examples of Affiliate Programs

Web site	The Deal	Pros	Cons	Extras
www.linkshare.com	From one Web page, members can track activity of multiple affiliate programs. Member sites can evaluate whether to affiliate with your site.	Over 150 online merchants, such as Avon, 1-800-Flowers, and many lesser-known sites.	Some merchants may take several weeks to review your site. No estimate is given on how much time the approval process takes.	If you generate significant traffic, member sites may cut you a better deal than the original terms.
www.refer-it.com	A clearinghouse of information on more than 500 affiliate programs, with descriptions and ratings.	You can browse the various programs and join them from Refer-it. Includes major players like Amazon.com and Reel.com but consists mostly of lesser-known merchants.	Refer-it is basically just a link list, so you can't use it to track your affiliate commissions.	Has a helpful guide for creating your own affiliate program.
www.amazon.com	5 percent commission on books and other items; 15 percent commission for selling specific titles on your site.	Pays higher commissions than Barnes andnoble.com. Great flexibility as to how the Amazon link looks on your site.	Buyers must jump directly from your site to a specific item for you to get higher credit.	Sales reports online at Amazon's Web site; Amazon.com has great interface flexibility.
www.barnesand noble.com	5 to 7 percent commission on books, based on sales volume; 5 percent commission on everything else.	Gives credit for items you buy yourself (unlike Amazon.com).	Does not let you work with other online bookstores.	Online sales reporting is updated in near real time; offline reports are at the Web site.

FIGURE 9.2   Examples of Affiliate Programs (Continued)

Web site	The Deal	Pros	Cons	Extras
www.beyond.com	5 percent commission on mailed software; 20 percent on electronically distributed software purchased through your site.	Any item bought through a link from your site counts.	No commissions for items you buy yourself.	E-mail reports on the 1st and 15th of each month.
www.outpost.com	3 percent cash or a 5 percent Outpost credit on software titles. You must sign up through LinkShare.	Part of the LinkShare network, so you can track sales and traffic reports at LinkShare's site.	No commission on leads that generate Outpost.com hardware sales.	Weekly e-mail newsletter with fresh ideas and promotions.

management software program tracks and measures results for both you and the affiliate, so that you know exactly what commissions are due at the end of the month. Figure 9.2 provides examples of affiliate programs and illustrates the types of deals e-corporations like Amazon.com (with over 2,000 affiliates) are offering affiliates. Each program has its advantages (higher commissions) and limitations (poor tracking). Some of the extra benefits of affiliate programs include higher commission rates for generating a significant amount of traffic and almost-real-time online sales reports.

Affiliate-program software can be purchased or custom-programmed for $500 to $25,000; however, this means that you still have to recruit affiliates. An alternative is to hire a service bureau to manage your affiliate network. Following are a few examples:

- Commission Junction (www.commissionjunction.com) is an electronic solution for tracking leads and sales and for paying commissions—all at a very competitive price. The Commission Junction Network creates revenue-sharing relationships between online merchants and Web site affiliates. This arrangement provides merchants the most cost-effective means to increase Internet store traffic by placing pay-for-performance ads on over 85,000 affiliate Web locations that are most likely to attract buyers for a particular product. Cost to start is $1,045.

- BeFree (www.befree.com) is also an affiliate network. BeFree makes tools for syndicated selling. It lets online sellers like BarnesandNoble .com and The Electronic Newsstand sell their wares on thousands of sites, embedding their goods and services into the content of some of the premiere sites on the Internet. Its BFAST system lets sellers grow, manage, and optimize affiliate networks. Through intelligent targeting, BeFree lets the same retailers capture revenue from slotting fees by selling virtual shelf space, and adds accountability to its outbound CPM (cost-per-thousand impressions) advertising with BFIT, an intelligent targeting system. Cost to start is $5,000.

- LinkShare (www.linkshare.com), shown in Figure 9.3, is a provider of advanced affiliate program technology. LinkShare's Web marketing features include a Web-based Affiliate Network with immediate access to over 30,000 potential affiliate sites, a hybrid pricing structure, dynamic direct selling, real-time distribution, and management of merchandising strategies. From privately branded programs to integrated affiliate networks, LinkShare has over 100 successful installs and program launches. Cost to start varies.

The Latest Trends in Affiliate Programs

Forrester Research reports that affiliate programs are evolving from one-size-fits-all into syndicated boutiques, commerce networks, or elastic retailers, where retail and media firms share ownership of traffic revenue, merchandising, and content. "Commerce and content companies need each other more than ever," says Jim Nail, senior analyst at Forrester Research. "Today's popular affiliate program structure will be replaced by what Forrester calls cooperative eCommerce, designed to satisfy increasing consumer demands for self-service, to diversify revenue streams, and to offer a shopping experience that will engender loyalty," according to Brian Clark (1999) of GMD Studios in Winter Park, Florida. He summarizes Forrester's "New Affiliate Marketing Methods" report by dividing the three models into the following categories:

1. *Small site to big merchant.* Syndicated boutiques will have pop-up microstores that use automated merchandising and store-building

FIGURE 9.3 With LinkShare you can track the activity of multiple affiliate programs.

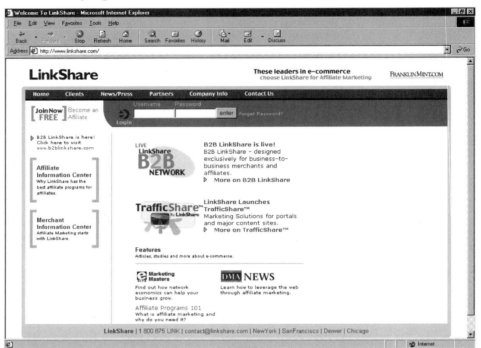

Courtesy of LinkShare Corporation.

tools to offer consumers a small range of carefully selected, branded products. Visitors can purchase without leaving the Web site that prompted them to click through. Virtual stores Nexchange (www .nexchange.com), Affinia (www.affinia.com), and VStore (www .vstore.com) are early examples of this trend.

2. *Big site to big merchant.* When a report or article generates interest, the big site delivers a one-click buying experience from a big merchant that delivers the product. Consumers value the efficiency of researching and purchasing in one session, thus increasing customer loyalty and improving the bottom line for both the big merchant and the big site content owner.

3. *Big merchant to big merchant.* Elastic retailing evolves when big merchants that target similar customer bases and offer complementary

product lines create affiliations among themselves. Big merchants partner with complementary big merchants to meet all their target customers' needs for advice, recommendations, and products, which allows them to stretch their e-corporations into adjacent categories. Overall, these big-merchant-to-big-merchant affiliate relationships allow the participants to spend less per customer for activities to target individuals and integrate marketing and fulfillment efforts.

AUTOMATED SELLING WITH INTERNET PORTALS

Jupiter Communications (www.jupitercomm.com) reports that about 18 percent of all online commerce sales are driven through portals, and the majority of e-commerce players surveyed either already have a portal partnership or are considering entering into one. Consequently, "rent" on high-volume traffic portals such as AOL, Excite, Yahoo!, Disney's Go, and Lycos is in the millions. For example, a $5 million deal with Yahoo! must generate at least $5 million in gross margin. For e-corporations with a 20 percent gross margin, this is $25 million in sales. Figure 9.4 is an abbreviated list of the tenant deals that e-corporations have negotiated with AOL.

As Figure 9.4 indicates, there is no average rental fee for AOL. Overall, e-corporations can expect to pay millions for placement on AOL's portal and potential access to AOL's 23 million subscribers. According to Marc Johnson of Jupiter Communications in a trade press release, with portals so hot and portal placement pricing so high, it's easy to infer that many e-corporations are spending more than a third of their marketing efforts on portal deals. "Commerce players simply have not demanded enough from their portal partners," Johnson says. "While they offer an effective means to drive traffic, primary portals do not help commerce players retain customers. Portals must develop compelling loyalty programs that help deliver repeat purchases for commerce partners, or they will risk losing the ability to garner huge anchor tenancy deals."

Also souring the relationship has been the question of whether portal sites would be better off selling merchandise under their own brand names. This has steered analysts at Jupiter Communications to conclude that your e-commerce corporation needs to develop a diversified distribution strategy that leans less on portals and more on affinity sites (related

FIGURE 9.4   Examples of AOL's Portal Agreements

Merchant	Category	Details
1-800-Flowers	Flowers	Exclusive. Cost: $25 million for four years.
Amazon.com	Books	Exclusive bookseller on AOL.com and integration with NetFind search results. Cost: $19 million for three years.
Americangreetings.com	Books	Anchor tenant in AOL shopping channel and marketing throughout the site. Cost: $3-plus million for three years.
Barnesandnoble.com	Books	Exclusive bookseller on AOL shopping channel and proprietary service. Cost: $40 million for four years.
Beyond.com	Computers	Exclusive electronic software provider; anchor tenant throughout service. Cost: $21 million for three years.
CDNow	Music	Tenant in shopping channel and integration into NetFind search results. Cost: $18 million for three years.
Digital Chef (www.tavolo.com)	Food	Prominent placement in food sections of shopping channel, food channel, influence channel, People Connection, Digital City. Cost: $7.5 million for two years.
eBay	Auctions	Premiere auctioneer; prominent presence on all AOL properties. Expanded from three-year, $12 million deal cut in Sept. 1998. Cost: $75 million for four years.
eToys	Toys	Exclusive on AOL.com. Cost: $3.1 million for two years.
Food.com	Food	Exclusive takeout and restaurant aggregator on AOL.com and on AOL. Cost: $20 million for four years.

FIGURE 9.4   Examples of AOL's Portal Agreements (Continued)

Merchant	Category	Details
Intuit	Financial services	Anchor tenant in the personal finance and workplace channels. Cost: $30 million for three years.
PlanetRx	Health	Premiere pharmacy in health and women's channels; contextual integration in health channel; prominent positioning. Cost: $15 million for three years.
Preview Travel	Travel	Exclusive provider of travel services. Cost: $32 million for five years.
Quicken.com	Financial services	Major anchor tenant in personal finance workplace channels. Cost: $30 million for three years.
Realtor.com	Financial services	Exclusive relationship, providing real estate listings to AOL members. Cost: $14 million for three years.

The following are affiliates for which no numbers were available:

Merchant	Category	Details
Columbia House	Entertainment	Promotion on AOL shopping channel, AOL.com, CompuServe, other AOL media. Term length: three years.
Drugstore.com	Health	Key pharmacy partner on health channel of AOL, CompuServe, AOL.com; contextual placement throughout.
Fidelity Investments	Financial services	Gold placement in brokerage center.

Web sites that provide content, commerce, and marketing with the ability to aggregate potential customers), affiliate programs, and offline marketing. Keep in mind that the portal war has gone wireless. Cellular operators are likely to take advantage of revenue-sharing deals with content providers, but the future may be with independent portals that are smaller and provide a more-qualified audience for greater returns.

REDEFINING SALES FORCE AUTOMATION

Many brick-and-mortar, click-and-mortar and dot-com organizations have sales representatives. Some sales representatives can keep track of their contact information, selling methods, and customer information on electronic notepads or in personal laptop computers. If the sales representative leaves, all this customer knowledge is gone. In the office, quotes can be generated independently, and product and services incorrectly priced or configured incorrectly. If the order is taken over the phone, it can be incorrectly entered into the system. All these errors, omissions, and duplicated efforts are time consuming and run up operating costs.

Today's sales force automation (SFA) allows virtual selling; that is, the field sales force has real-time access to customer databases, product configuration information, and other organization information sources via Internet connections (which can be wireless) or laptop computers. This new technology has moved sales and marketing, often considered stand-alone corporate divisions, towards an integrated function that benefits from the synergistic support of the entire corporation. However, SFA products are not cheap. The Gartner Group (www.gartner.com) reports that the total cost of ownership for SFA products, which can be one component of a customer relationship management (CRM) system, can range from $28,000 to $50,000 per user. The gains in productivity and sales often make up for the financial investment.

Overview of Sales Force Automation Software

CRM enterprise solutions can bring together sales, marketing, and customer service. Sales representatives enter customer information into shared databases called configuration engines and marketing encyclopedias. The technology then provides real-time access to product and competitive information, enabling the sales representative to stay better informed and to complete more profitable sales. Also, the organization does not lose vital customer information when an employee decides to leave. Additionally, automated processes free salespeople from administrative tasks.

In 1999, InfoWorld interviewed several organizations that implemented Onyx, Siebel, and Oracle CRM systems. Each organization came in at or under budget and spent between $150,000 to $900,000 on the implementation, which included software, hardware, and customization. (Due to industry competition, interviewees would not be more specific about how much they spent.)

- Onyx Software Group (www.onyx.com)
  Onyx Customer Center
  Onyx Process Manager
  E-mail Agent
  Sync Assistant

Onyx software combines comprehensive CRM functionality, third-party applications, and Internet content into personalized digital workplaces for marketing, sales, and service employees, business partners, and customers. According to InfoWorld (1999), Onyx's claim to fame is its speedy implementation compared with other vendors. Onyx is specifically suited for offices with Microsoft back-office applications. The Customer Center includes many other features, such as marketing encyclopedias (Onyx Encyc) and configuration engines. The Customer Center's complete CRM solution ships with a Trilogy configuration engine that is integrated into the solution. Onyx also delivers industry-specific sales methodologies and interfaces.

- Siebel Systems Inc. (www.siebel.com)
  Siebel 99
  Siebel Marketing Enterprise
  Siebel Sales Enterprise
  Siebel Service Enterprise
  Siebel Systems, Inc.

Siebel Systems, shown in Figure 9.5, is a supplier of Web-based front-office software systems. Siebel Systems provides an integrated family of sales, marketing, and customer service application software for field sales, customer service, telesales, telemarketing, field service, third-party resellers, and Internet-based e-commerce and self-service. Siebel Systems are designed to meet the needs of small, medium, and large businesses. Siebel Systems offers field-level synchronization, which allows sales representatives to update the information on their laptop computers in real time.

FIGURE 9.5   Siebel Systems eCRM software has a long history of developing sales force automation products.

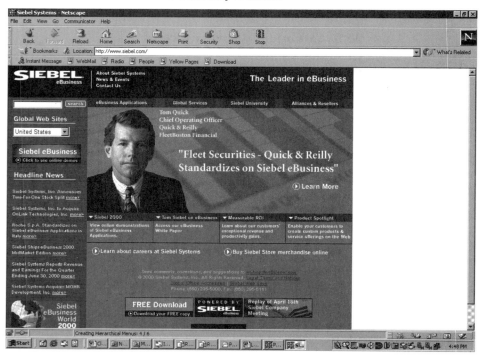

- Oracle Corporation (www.oracle.com)
  Customer Relationship Management Products
  Marketing
  Sales
  Service
  Call Center
  E-commerce

Oracle CRM products are designed to provide a complete view of the impact of customer-related activities throughout the enterprise. In today's market, no company can afford to miss the opportunity of having a complete 360-degree view of its customer relationships, or the opportunity to transform from a traditional business into an e-business. Oracle CRM 3i software combines traditional activities for sales, marketing, customer service, and the call center with e-business applications, allowing companies to create multiple channels for customer interaction. Oracle CRM 3i helps companies manage the entire customer-contact process and feeds into the back-end system for comprehensive customer-interaction analysis. Oracle CRM 3i includes 35 Internet-enabled, integrated modules. Oracle provides out-of-the-box integration between CRM and enterprise resource planning (ERP) applications, which makes it possible for companies to leverage knowledge from customer interactions in order to improve decision making and enhance the management of customer relationship, from marketing execution to sales effectiveness and customer service.

SUMMING IT UP

- E-corporations can virtually sell anything but need the best possible business proposition (or value-added proposition) to keep current customers loyal and to discourage prospects from clicking away to competitors.
- Many e-corporations have increased sales with a point-and-click sales force. You can increase sales almost overnight by implementing your own affiliate program.
- Increasing sales with portals can be a big money game; however, if you are a big merchant, this may be a quick route to increasing sales.
- Automated sales force automation is not contact management software anymore. The latest eCRM software suites make it more powerful and convenient than ever.

ACTION PLAN

EVALUATING YOUR VIRTUAL SELLING COMPETITORS

Studies indicate that e-corporation revenues can increase an average of 30 percent with implementing a virtual sales force of affiliates and portals. As you review your options for virtual selling, you may want to use the following questions and activities to assist you in evaluating your competitors before you implement your point-and-click sales force.

1. Locate online affiliate directories and search by category or keyword to see what types of affiliate programs are offered in your area of business.

2. Review each competitor's program by answering the following questions:
   - Is the competitor's Web site designed to sell products or services? If customers find it difficult to purchase, then affiliates may look for another program.
   - If you are selling the same products, are you competitive? If you are not competitive, can you create a value-added proposition that will attract and keep customers?
   - What does your competitor do to track its affiliate program? For example, does it use an affiliate program network or is the program managed in-house? If the competitor tracks commissions in-house, how does it create trust with affiliates?
   - What commissions does your competitor offer? Does it offer two-tier commissions? Can you offer higher commissions and remain price competitive?
   - What types of affiliate sales tools does your competitor offer? What help and support does your competitor provide to get affiliates started? What benefits or incentives does your competitor offer affiliates?
   - How many affiliates does your competitor have? (Note: You can get a rough idea by using the AltaVista search engine. Just type in <link:your competitorsurl.com>.)
   - Check affiliate discussion boards for any positive or negative comments about your competitor.
   - Check the listings in different affiliate directories to see how well your competitor's program is rated.

3. Use the information you have gathered to make your program more appealing for your affiliate partners.

Source: Adapted from "Review Your Competitors," online publication of Affiliate Marketing,co.uk (www.affiliatemarketing.co.uk), 16 May 2000.

REFERENCES

Berman. Dennis. 1999. Frontier: Digital Manager, a Point-and-Click Sales Force. *Business Week* 3635 (28 June): F14.

Clark, Brian. 1999. Forrester Predicts Future for Affiliates. Online publication of Revenews (www.revenews.com/advice/strategy/predict.html).

Girishankar, Saroja. 1998. E-commerce: Virtual Markets Create New Roles for Distributors. *Internet Week Online*, 6 April (www.internetwk.com).

Heskett, James L., W. Earl Sasser, Jr., and Leonard A. Schlesinger. 1997. *The Service Profit Chain: How Leading Companies Link Profit and Growth to Loyalty, Satisfaction, and Value.* New York: The Free Press.

Newell, Fredrick. 2000. *Loyalty.com.* New York: McGraw-Hill.

Peppers, Don, and Martha Rogers. 1997. *Enterprise One to One: Tools for Competing in the Interactive Age.* New York: Doubleday.

Peppers, Don, Martha Rogers, and Bob Dorf. 1998. *The One to One Field Book: The Complete Toolkit for Implementing a 1 to 1 Marketing Program.* New York: Currency/Doubleday.

Rayport, Jeffery F., and John J. Sviokla. 1995. Exploiting the Virtual Value Chain. *Harvard Business Review* (November-December): 75–85.

Reichheld, Fredrick F. 1996. *The Loyalty Effect: The Hidden Force Behind Growth, Profits, and Lasting Value.* Boston: Harvard Business School Press.

Schreiber, Diane. 1999. Jupiter Communications: Portal Commerce Primacy to Wane. *PressWire*, 6 April.

Siebel, Thomas M., and Pat House. 1999. *Cyber Rules: Strategies for Excelling at E-Business.* New York: Currency/Doubleday.

Siegel, David. 1999. *Futurize Your Enterprise: Business Strategy in the Age of the E-Customer.* New York: John Wiley & Sons.

Anticipating Your Customers' Needs

Customer inquiries are more complex than ever, and customers often expect an instant reply. This chapter explores how online customer service and support have evolved. You'll discover how your Web site design can make customers feel cozy and welcome. See how the value of interactive Web sites increases as they are built into the organization's service channels. Uncover how you can help your customers help themselves and thank you for it. Find out how you can take advantage of the latest technology to help Internet-shy consumers become your best customers. Look into four different types of e-customer software applications to determine which type is best for you. This chapter concludes by pointing out how e-mail response management is an integral part of your e-business and presents several software applications and "rental" solutions that may be just what you need.

DESIGNING YOUR WEB SITE TO PROMOTE CUSTOMER SERVICE AND SUPPORT

In the past, customers were content to make simple requests, such as change of address and loan balance inquiries. Today, customers ask complex questions about how a product or service will benefit them. To fill this need requires Web tools that allow customers access to more online knowledge and information. The Yankee Group, Internet researchers and consultants, forecasts that the Internet customer service market will grow to $1.2 billion by 2003, compared to 2000's estimate of $120 million. Frost and Sullivan project an annual increase of about 18 percent for the help-desk software tools and service market.

Everyone who visits your Web site is a potential customer. Providing only a static online brochure of your company's products or services will lead to lost revenue to competitors who offer better Internet services. This includes the customer service and support function, which can be an opportunity to develop an ongoing relationship with the customer. Your Web site design must facilitate your customer service process and turn it into a revenue generator.

Your Web site's content and design make a comfortable or memorable experience for your online customers. Good online experiences encourage repeat visits, foster relationships, and build loyalty. Keep in mind that customers rely on the presentation of information on your Web site as the primary way to interact with you. Your products or services don't have to be exceptional, but your service and delivery do. Great performing Web sites address the specific needs of your target market. There are many Internet myths about online service. Following are a few suggestions and myth busters:

- *Fast, friendly, and easy-to-use Web site.* Customers can reach what they want within three clicks. Navigation is fast and intuitive. Registration is brief. Customers can view their accounts and purchase histories, find forgotten passwords, and make changes to their profiles. Online capabilities that are worth considering:
  1. Offer customers the ability to organize the home page according to their needs.

2. Offer customers the ability to change the look and feel of the home page. (A good example is My Yahoo!)

   Internet myth: You can't please everyone all the time, so e-customers will just have to "dig" to get the information they need. This isn't true; for example, the *Wall Street Journal* (www.wsj.com) lets subscribers customize the information products they receive. Each customer can select the columns and topics he or she is interested in seeing first.

- *Provide mindless and painless transactions.* Allow customers to apply for and make product or service selections online. Make information easy to find and provide enough for customers to make informed decisions without telephoning for help. Online capabilities that you may want to include are:
  1. Searchable knowledge bases. Consumer time-saving capabilities such as access to databases that customers normally don't have access to can be a terrific value-added feature. A good example is Wells Fargo (www.wellsfargo.com).
  2. Give customers the ability to design their own products.

     Internet myth: My products or services are too complex (or too expensive) to be sold online. This is untrue. If customers are given the ability to properly research, configure, and pay online, you may dramatically increase revenue. At least give customers the option of choosing to purchase on their own. Two good examples are Dell (www.dell.com), which allows customers to design their computer online, and Cisco (www.cisco.com), which offers automated programs that let customers configure their products online.

- *Keep customers informed.* Keep customers up-to-date using e-mail. However, let them tell you what they want to be informed about, how they want to be informed, and how frequently they want to be informed. Make subscribing and unsubscribing easy. Other online capabilities you may want to include are:
  1. Online order tracking: A good example is Federal Express (www.fedexpress.com).
  2. One-click ordering: A good examples is Travelocity (www.travelocity.com).
  3. Personalized billing and shipping methods.

Internet myth: A simple customer service application won't improve online customer service and support. Not true. One of the most popular features of online mortgage lenders is that customers can check the progress of their loan application online. A good example is AppOnline.com (www.apponline.com). When the customer submits his or her online loan application, the customer is assigned a personal identification number. The customer can use this number anytime, anywhere to find out the exact status of his or her loan application. (Note: The loan officer's information and the real-time online information are the same, so there is no need to call.)

- *Be responsive.* Provide toll-free telephone and fax numbers and e-mail contact information for specific questions. Make certain all customer service applications are working (e.g., that customers have access to the amount of their frequent-flyer miles). For complex orders, offer a CD-ROM, Web-based training, or Web-based conferencing. Online capabilities that also are useful include:

  1. Personalized recommendations: A good example is CDNow (www.cdnow.com).
  2. A wish list: A good example is Music Maker (www.musicmaker.com).
  3. Choice of ways to communicate electronically: A good example is Lands' End (www.landsend.com), shown in Figure 10.1.

Internet myth: All Internet customers always want to use the Web to communicate. This is not true. Companies with multichannel communications stand out from the crowd. For example, at Charles Schwab (www.schwab.com) customers can place a trade order via fax, Touch-Tone telephone, wireless palm pilot, or the Internet. Customers can even walk into a branch office to make their trade in person and get an instant trade confirmation. One of the latest in multichannel customer support options is online help buttons. At iGo (www.igo.com), formerly 1-800-Batteries, a customer can start a transaction online and get help by clicking a 24-hour ordering and support button. After reading a few instructions, the customer clicks on the Click Here for Live Help hyperlink and is instantly connected, via the Web, to the company's call center. Using chat technology, the customer asks the question and instantly receives a reply.

FIGURE 10.1   Lands' End lets customers select how they want to electronically communicate.

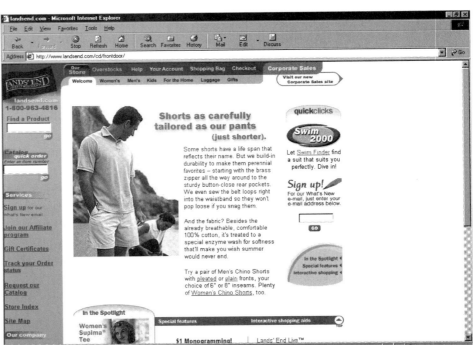

Permission granted by Lands' End, Inc.

HELPING CUSTOMERS HELP THEMSELVES

Customers want what they want, when and how they want it, and don't like to settle for anything less. Frequently, this means giving customers a level of attention that is difficult to deliver and maintain; in other words, instead of continually acquiring new customers, why not pull them in and make them lifetime customers? One way to build customer loyalty is with customer care, which includes aiming for 110 percent customer satisfaction or focusing on one customer group. For many e-corporations, this is the key to success. Outpost.com is geared to computer users, Reel.com targets video buffs, and Expedia.com offers air, hotel, and car deals for price-conscious travelers. These organizations hold onto their customers for dear life, instead of expanding into related areas and trying to please everyone. This doesn't mean that your e-corporation should not expand; at some point, your e-corporation will reach a predetermined goal. If you have a solid foundation on which to diversify, at the time you expand, listen to your customers and they will target your next product or service. Some of the customer-service success metrics you may want to consider include:

1. Customers give your e-corporation high marks for overall customer satisfaction.
2. Customers state they are likely to recommend your products or services to others.
3. Customers believe your selection of products and services is excellent.
4. Customers rank your pricing as outstanding.
5. Customers highly rate your Web site's easy navigation.
6. Customers believe your customer service and support couldn't be better.

Giving Online Customers Personal Care

Anticipating your customers' needs is about personalized care. Personalized care is a value-added service that builds loyalty. All e-corporations that know their customers as individuals will continue to find innovative ways to keep them happy, satisfied, and most importantly, loyal. In other words, if your e-corporation has a lot of information about its customers, it can offer better customer care and treat each customer according to his or her individual needs, characteristics, and expectations. Companies always keep records of customer purchases, complaints, and billing instructions. Using this information for customer service and support was often not cost efficient. As the customer base increased, the problems associated with accessing this information also increased, and customer care frequently seemed impossible. Current technologies make individualized customer care achievable.

Individualized customer care requires zero-loss learning; that is, your company must proactively seek specific information about each customer and determine what makes each customer unique. Every customer interaction (with sales, customer support, and order fulfillment) must yield some insight into the customer relationship that can be stored in a knowledge base that, over time, becomes more comprehensive and accurate. This library of customer information can then be leveraged to provide customers with personalized and consistently excellent service. In addition to transactional data, your company needs to know:

- Is the customer enjoying your product?
- Is the customer getting the most out of your service?
- Is your customer showing productivity increases in their business?
- What features does your customer like or dislike?
- What features does your customer want to see added?
- Has this purchase helped further your customer's goals?

RS Components (www.rswww.com) in the United Kingdom is the next loyalty marketing success story. RS Components uses a consumer-direct strategy to anticipate customer needs and has experienced a tremendous increase in repeat business.

LOYALTY MARKETING SUCCESS STORY

RS Components

▼ **COMPANY:** RS Components (www.rswww.com), a large distributor in the UK, provides electronic, electrical, mechanical components, and related products. The company's six-volume catalog of over 100,000 products makes it difficult for customers to locate the products they need.

▼ **SOLUTION:** RS Components wants to provide personalized services to customers to create greater loyalty. With more satisfied, loyal customers, the firm hopes to generate repeat business, resulting in a rapid return on investment.

FIGURE 10.2   RS Components makes it a habit to anticipate customer needs.

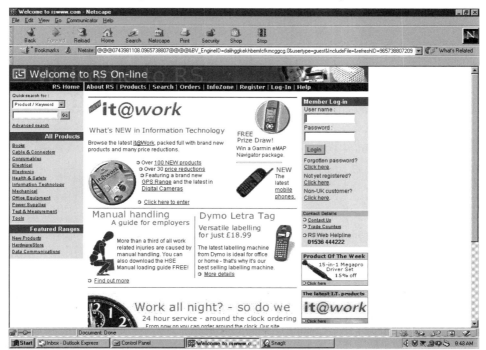

RS Components profiles customers based on their interactions at the Web site. The profiles allow RS Components to personalize its Web site and deliver tailor-made incentives and promotions to individuals to ensure their loyalty.

- Each Web site user is presented with the ten top products that interest him or her. The Web site creates "minicatalogs" based on the individual needs of a customer.
- Each customer has access to a list of regularly ordered products, which can be imported to an order form. Additionally, customers can easily reuse orders for repeat purchases as prices are automatically updated.
- Customers are shown immediate stock availability as well as customer-specific pricing. An automatic save order function saves partially completed orders.

- Customers can access personal technical libraries that show all the technical information linked to their order histories over the past 13 months. Additionally, this order history is an accurate record of past purchases.

▼ **BENEFITS:** RS Components created a Web site that makes it easy for its 150,000 customers to evaluate the company's products.

- Implementation of the Web site reduced the $90 order processing cost to $15.
- RS Components is experiencing a rapid increase in repeat purchases.

Source: Adapted from "RS Success Stories," an online publication of the Peppers and Rogers Group (www .1to1.com), 19 February 2000.

Getting Up Close and Personal

Many consumers find technical help pages overwhelming and confusing. Often, customers who need the most help are the least likely to go to the Internet for help. One way to overcome this information overload is to develop a personalized Web page for the customer. Personalized Web pages allow the customer to select and move content, pick a color scheme, or choose preference settings and layout (two columns or three?). When selecting preferences, users can decide if they want to see what's new by their favorite recording artists, top news stories, their stock portfolios, sports scores, regional weather, TV listings, chat events, reminders, favorite Web links, and so on. The personalized Web page is not designed to replace the call center but to make information more readily available to customers, which in turn can reduce the number of incoming calls. For example, CDW Computer Centers, Inc. (www.cdw.com), of Vernon Hills, Illinois, offers customers personalized Web pages. Place an order with a sales representative, and the order is confirmed via e-mail along with the address of your personalized page.

Software providers for this type of online customer service include Verity Inc.'s (www.verity.com) agent server toolkit. Verity's product monitors external and internal databases, news wires, and indexes and then notifies users by e-mail or personal Web page when new information matches the user's profile. Verity uses Microsoft NT, IBM AIX, HP/UX, Digital Unix, and Sun Solaris operating systems. Pricing is based on specific application requirements and depends on number of users; you can expect to pay approximately $5,000 to $10,000 for medium-sized companies.

In a study completed by Service Industry Research Systems (2000) for Synchrony Communications (www.synchronyinc.com), an eCRM software developer, respondents overwhelming preferred "live" contact with sales and customer service staff while shopping online. More than half of the interviewees stated that having the option of talking with a human would have a lot of influence on which sites they shop, and not having access to a live person contributed to the perception of a "poor" customer experience. Overall, these consumers preferred the option of talking with live customer service personnel on the telephone or by online chat 65 percent to 25 percent. Examples of Web sites that have live contact include Cincinnati Bell Zoom Town (www.zoomtown.com), an online community; Aero Fulfillment for O-Cedar (www.aerofulfillment.com), makers of household products; and Prescriptions.com (www.prescriptions.com). The product has variable pricing based on the number of agent log-ins.

SELECTING THE RIGHT CUSTOMER SUPPORT APPLICATION

Susan Felix (2000), of SCFelix Consulting Services in Saratoga, California, notes that e-corporations usually do not have face-to-face contact with customers, so gauging customer satisfaction is often based on loyalty indicators, including repeat purchases, customer satisfaction surveys, and internal indicators of service responsiveness, such as how long it takes to respond to a question or complaint. Additionally, e-corporations may employ a variety of outside consultants using a variety of media (e-mail, telephone, or face-to-face interviews) to survey customers. The information gathered is often startling. For example, when the makers of Wheaties cereal checked how customers used their product, they were amazed to learn that Wheaties was more than a cold breakfast cereal. Mothers of young children often packed bag lunches with Wheaties in small plastic bags to be used as a healthy replacement for potato chips. Baggies of

Wheaties also were frequently used as after-school snacks and for small children to munch while parents shopped, traveled, or attended sports events.

Many industry experts observe that as the e-corporation becomes more adept at providing the level of care customers require, it may want to communicate its service objectives to its customers. Communicating objectives helps set expectations and provides the metrics for evaluating the e-corporation's quality of online service and support. However, e-corporations must be predictive and reactive to constantly changing customer needs, desires, and requests. Automated tools and tracking methods can assist in leveraging this endeavor.

Martin LaMonica (1999) states that according to Donna Fuss, a consultant for the Gartner Group, it is a difficult task to determine the best computer application for customer service. The interactive Web site brings together sales, customer service, and support, because that's what customers want. Existing businesses must integrate legacy systems with the latest eCRM tools. Web-based start-ups look for flexibility. Not only must the eCRM application expand as the company grows, but it also must be flexible enough to bypass early mistakes and robust enough to support new initiatives. Implementing such systems is often expensive, but the rewards are great. The value of interactive Web sites increases almost exponentially as they are built into service channels. Overall, there are three technology paths you can follow, and each will require some integration:

1. Select a call center, sometimes called a telephony switch solution, that includes Web and e-mail support. Manufacturers include Siemens and Nortel (for details, see Chapter 12).
2. Select a CRM vendor who will revamp and Web-enable its system to meet your needs.
3. Select a stand-alone solution that focuses on e-mail management, collaborative chat, or knowledge management, then consolidate and integrate these systems with other software products.

ORGANIZING CUSTOMER DATA TO IMPROVE ONLINE CUSTOMER SUPPORT AND SERVICE

You can take many approaches to organizing your customer data to improve online customer service. Figure 10.3 shows the data management approach and the software applications used to automate customer service. The first column shows the data management approach of the example computer applications. The software applications are divided into four categories:

1. *Clustering.* Dividing customers into large segments.
2. *Profiling.* Using customer knowledge to segment customers.
3. *Collaborative filtering.* Sorting customers into segments based on their usage of the Web site and compared to a community of Web site users.
4. *Artificial intelligence.* Dividing customers into segments based on predictions of their buying behaviors and needs.

The second column of Figure 10.3 shows examples of the software that is available for each data management approach. Following are short descriptions of each software product.

Figure 10.4 illustrates how you can select the approach that best fits your type of e-corporation. (For more information about types of e-corporation groups, see Chapter 3.) If your customer base is fairly uniform and customer complaints or inquiries can be easily divided into segments, the best software for you may be one that clusters your data. For example, some clustering software allows customers to answer a predetermined set of questions to find solutions to their problems. On the other hand, if your customer base is diverse and customer complaints or inquiries cover a wide range, you may be better off with software that uses collaborative filtering or artificial intelligence, so you can make automatic recommendations. The data management approach you choose is the one that best meets the goals and objectives of your e-corporation. However, be warned, many e-customer software companies are merging with larger or smaller companies, and this may affect ongoing technical support. Additionally, some e-customer software firms are making claims they will find difficult to fulfill at this time. One approach to sifting through e-customer software

FIGURE 10.3   Automated Responses to Customer Questions

Online Customer Support	Software Application
Artificial Intelligence: Loosely describes a range of technologies used to predict user behavior and needs.	eHNC (formerly Aptex) ServiceWare Brightware
Collaborative Filtering: Uses algorithmic techniques to infer what may be of interest to users based on a comparison of their preferences.	Quintus eContact Suite Kana Communications Net Perceptions
Profiling: Divides visitors into categories based on how they use the Web site.	MatchLogic True Select Ask Jeeves Personal Service Suite Engage Profile Server
Clustering: Divides Web site visitors into large categories.	Inference k-Commerce Personify Essentials Cognos e-Applications

Source: Adapted from Seamus McAteer, Lucas Graves, Marissa Gluck, Michael May, and Ken Allard, "Proactive Personalization: Learning to Swim, Not Drown in Customer Data," Jupiter Communications, 19 August 1999.

candidates is to discover which software package your industry leader or chief competitor is using.

The following four sections show a few examples of online applications that manage customer data by clustering, profiling, collaborative filtering, or artificial intelligence. Examples in each of the four sections describe the software, and when possible, indicate the type of operating platform used and identify several customers and the price you can expect to pay. Please keep in mind that prices are often based on the number of modules purchased in a software product and the size of the Web site installation or call center.

Figure 10.4   What type of customer data management approach is best for you?

Online Capability Option	Category of Loyalty	Industry Examples	
		Uniform Customer Needs	Diverse Customer Needs

Artificial intelligence	Premium loyalty	Group VII
		Airlines
		Manufactured
		   packaged goods **
			Group VIII
			Computer systems **
			High-end hotel chains
			Legal and professional
			   services**
			Auto manufacturers
			Large department stores

Profiling	Convenience loyalty	Group V Commoditylike services ** Book publishers Travel agents	Group VI Pharmacies Small retailers Tax return preparation

Collaborative filtering	Latent loyalty	Group III
		Niche goods
		Exercise equipment
			Group IV
			High-end industrial
			   equipment*
			Information &
			   entertainment **
			Apparel for consumers

Clustering	No loyalty	Group I Gas stations Dry cleaners Mass-marketed items	Group II Mortgages Digital publishers Janitorial services *

* Business-to-business enterprises
** Either business-to-business enterprises or business-to-consumer enterprises

---

Clustering Software

- *Inference* (www.inference.com). k-Commerce support applications use rule-based and case-based technologies. The software runs on Windows NT and Solaris platforms. Examples of clients include America Online, LucasArt Entertainment LLC, PeopleSoft (www.people

soft.com), Sun Microsystems (www.sunmicrosystems.com), British Telecommunications, and Bank America (www.bankofamerica.com). Cost: $70,000 plus and $25,000 per year for support.

- *Personify* (www.personify.com). Personify Essentials collects and combines information from logfiles, as well as from transactions, user registrations, and offline databases. The software uses NT and Solaris platforms. Examples of customers include eToys (www.etoys.com), Volvo (www.volvo.com), and Blue Shield of California (www.blue shieldca.com). Personify Essentials 2.0 incorporates server software, add-on modules for specific functionality, and a suite of professional services. Pricing is based on an annual subscription, starting at $5,500 per month.

- *Cognos* (www.cognos.com). Cognos e-Applications allows you to examine or customize the packaged reports included in the data marts. This can assist you in staying on top of the metrics you require to improve business performance. Examples of customers include Allegheny Power (www.alleghenypower.com), BMG Entertainment (www.bmg.com), and Dr. Pepper (www.drpepper.com). The software runs on NT and Unix operating platforms.

Profiling Software

- *Match Logic* (www.matchlogic.com). Match Logic True Select segments customers based on how they interact with the Web site. Various Web site elements are tagged and associated with different attributes. Examples of customers include Ancestry.com (www.ancestry.com), World Wrestling Federation (www.wwf.com), and Hard Rock Café (www.hardrockcafe.com).

- *Ask Jeeves* (www.askjeeves.com). Ask Jeeves Personal Service Suite delivers customer conversion and retention services by connecting you to answers through a combination of automated technology and human intelligence. Examples of customers are Nike (www.nike.com), Dell (www.dell.com), and Office Depot (www.officedepot.com). Pricing varies depending on the number of Ask Jeeves Personal Service Suite modules purchased.

- *Engage Technologies* (www.engage.com). Engage Profile Server's anonymous Web visitor profiling technology helps corporations increase the relevance of their Web site's advertising, editorial, and commercial content for both first-time and repeat visitors. Engage Technologies is also the creator of EngageKnowledge, a database of anonymous Web visitor profiles for use in real-time marketing and sales applications on the Internet. Examples of customers include AltaVista (www.altavista.com), FastTV (www.fasttv.com), and CyBuy (www.cybuy.com).

Collaborative Filtering Software

- *Quintus* (www.quintus.com). The Quintus eContact Suite enables companies to personalize, route, manage, and report customer interactions over the Internet and telephone. The suite is a set of integrated software products that allows businesses to operate as "contact centers" and that works across a variety of communications media with equal ease and effectiveness. Pricing for WebCenter 2.4 begins at $40,000 and varies according to the number of licensed modules and number of agent seats. Examples of customers include Bigvine.com (www.bigvine.com) and Coldwater Creek (www.coldwatercreek.com).
- *Kana* (www.kana.com). Kana provides an eCRM suite that includes Kana 5, which enables selective escalation across multiple contact channels, including e-mail, Web self-help, real-time messaging, and voice over the Internet. This software allows companies to provide the appropriate level of support to each customer, depending on contextual information, such as the value of the customer and the value of the related transaction. Examples of Kana's customers include eBay (www.ebay.com), The Gap (www.gap.com), and Northwest Airlines (www.nwa.com). Pricing depends on the number of Kana 5 software modules purchased.
- *Net perceptions* (www.netperceptions.com). Net Perceptions offers collaborative filtering software, so that big corporations can tailor their services to meet individual customer needs better than small competitors. Net Perceptions harnesses a "community of knowledge," which is the combined needs and preferences of all the members of the corporation's customer base. Net Perceptions runs on Windows NT or

Sun Solaris platforms. A few examples of companies that use Net Perceptions include: CDnow (www.cdnow.com), Living.com (www.living.com), Egghead.com (www.egghead.com), and HomeGrocer (www.homegrocer.com).

Artificial Intelligence Software

- *eHNC Inc., formerly Aptex* (www.ehnc.com). The eHNC software uses neural network technology to provide e-commerce value-added services that are designed to boost sales and minimize risks through customer interaction management. These services should result in increased buy-through, reduced fraud, and improved customer satisfaction. The software runs on Windows NT, NT 4.0, and Solaris 2.5.1 operating platforms. Examples of customers include Amazon.com (www.amazon.com), Circuit City (www.circuitcity.com), and Suretrade, Inc. (www.suretrade.com).
- *ServiceWare Inc.* (www.serviceware.com). ServiceWare delivers a comprehensive, integrated family of e-service solutions that enable organizations to provide customers with accurate answers to free-form inquiries across all touch points. The software runs on Windows NT 4.0 and SP 5 or 6 operating platforms. Examples of customers include AT&T (ww.att.com), Compaq (www.compaq.com), and ESPN (www.espn.com).
- *Brightware* (www.brightware.com). The Brightware 2000 Web customer-assistance software suite includes the Concierge and Converse components. Concierge includes four modules that perform a variety of customer service tasks, such as dynamically composing Web pages that answer a customer's inquiry when there is no existing page that addresses it.

  Brightware's 3.5 software application manages e-mail traffic and automatically responds to customers' questions based on technology that determines the message's context and an appropriate answer. Brightware 3.5 includes a function called Assisted Answer, which generates a response and routes it to a representative before mailing to make sure the response is correct. The starting price for Brightware 3.5 is $50,000.

The Brightware Advice Agent is a turnkey application for interacting with customers, organizing and accessing relevant content, and guiding customers to execute the sales or service transactions that best meet their needs. Brightware license fees start at $95,000 annually, or $190,000 for a perpetual license. This price includes a choice of either the Brightware Answer Agent or the Brightware Advice Agent. If a second agent is purchased at the same time, license fees for this agent start at $47,500 annually, or $95,000 for a perpetual license. Brightware runs on Windows NT. Examples of customers include eMusic (www.emusic.com), Neiman Marcus (www.neiman marcus.com), and Trip.com (www.trip.com).

GETTING THE MESSAGE TO YOUR E-CORPORATION

Debbie Bauer (1999) notes that a Harris Survey Poll discovered that 25 percent of all Americans use e-mail on a daily basis. Internet experts expect consumers to send *50 million product-information or service inquiries per day.* Forrester Research predicts that 20 to 30 percent of customer contacts will move from telephone and fax to Internet sites. Even with the best-designed Web site, your e-corporation may receive hundreds or even thousands of customer e-mail messages and telephone calls per day.

Internet users expect to have a response to their e-mail messages within 24 hours, if not sooner. Forrester Research analyst Bruce Kasrel notes that Internet users have not only become accustomed to submitting support requests at the drop of a hat, they also expect a nearly immediate answer. This places huge demands on e-corporations to be responsive. Web sites must prepare for user feedback by automating transaction-tracking systems and answering questions on the spot. Web sites can dramatically increase the odds of a completed transaction if the user can get an answer to a question and immediately act on the information.

Heavily trafficked Web sites find it useful to provide more than one e-mail address. With more than one address, the e-corporation can direct customer inquiries or requests to the right department. For example, Geico Direct (www.geico.com) offers specific e-mail addresses for consumers who have questions about its automobile or homeowner policies, and for other policyholder correspondence. Providing specific e-mail addresses automatically routes inquiries to the right departments. At the Geico Direct Web site, if you want to be contacted by a salesperson, there are e-mail addresses for auto insurance, homeowners insurance, motor-cycle insurance, and boat insurance. Again, customers use self-direction to contact the right sales personnel.

The following loyalty marketing success story of Bose (www.bose.com) shows the importance of managing e-mail responses.

LOYALTY MARKETING SUCCESS STORY
Bose Corporation

▼ **COMPANY:** Bose carefully planned a Web site to build brand awareness and improve its ability to deliver sound equipment and information about its products. The name Bose is a well-known brand name that is associated with fine sound. Building and enhancing the Bose brand is a primary concern for the Bose Corporation.

With the release of its first Web site, Bose quickly realized it had underestimated the importance of managing e-mail. Bose did not anticipate the depth and breadth of e-mail questions and requests. There was no system in place to ensure that customers received informative and timely replies. The company did not want a temporary solution, so it removed all the Web site's e-mail tags and replaced them with a hyperlink to a page that offered an apology for not being able to accept e-mail and a toll-free telephone number for customers.

▼ **SOLUTION:** Bose made e-mail management part of their e-commerce strategy. In planning its solution, Bose recognized that managing customer e-mail was an organizational and technical issue.

- Bose surveyed call center, sales, and marketing personnel to develop a response library for standard questions. This library is categorized so support personnel can give consistent answers. However, the company expects and is prepared for 20 percent of customer questions to be nonstandard.
- The e-mail management system selected makes each customer's correspondence history and information file available to personnel. This allows Bose support personnel to know the context of the question, so they can create a more personalized response.

FIGURE 10.5   Bose uses e-mail to deliver its message.

▼ **BENEFITS:** After selecting the e-mail management application, implementing the software, and training personnel, Bose deployed its new e-mail support capability. Now Bose is able to respond to customer e-mail in a fashion that is consistent with their corporate objectives. Benefits include:

- Establishing e-mail communications as the primary interface with customers
- Increasing communications by asking customers what they want at every opportunity
- Using the Web site to reflect the company's core business principles

Source: Adapted from Charles R. Rider, "Bose Gets the Message," *Best Practices in Electronic Commerce,* an online publication of the Patricia Seybold Group, November 1998.

Anticipating the Unexpected

The best e-mail management program cannot accommodate volumes of e-mail created by an uncontrollable event, such as an overwhelming response to a promotional campaign or media coverage. The result is a slowdown in the e-corporation's response to its current customers and damage to customer loyalty. This is where advanced Web-based technology comes to the rescue. For example, artificial intelligence software programs like Brightware allow e-corporations to single out sales leads and respond instantly, while also referring messages to the appropriate humans for follow-up. If the software cannot understand the customer's free-form e-mail message, it will send the customer an e-mail message with specific questions that will enable the software to better handle the customer's message. All of this happens instantly and without human intervention. Following are a few examples of software applications for e-mail response management:

- *eGain Communications Corporation* (www.egain.com). eGain is a provider of integrated, multichannel e-customer communications solutions. eGain offers licensed and hosted applications for e-mail management, interactive Web and voice collaboration, intelligent self-help agents, and proactive online marketing. The solutions are built using a Web-native architecture; the eGain platform provides scalability, global access, diverse integration, and rapid deployment. The software runs on the Windows NT 4.0 operating platform. Examples of customers include Monster.com (www.monster.com), mp3.com (www.mp3.com), and WebMD (www.webmd.com).
- *Mustang.com Inc.* (www.mustang.com). The Mustang Message Center 3.0 automatically answers e-mail and faxes or routes messages to employees who can. The Mustang Message Center uses keyword searches and provides automated responses and basic audit trails. The software runs on Windows NT 4.0 or Workstation operating systems. Examples of customers include Andersen Consulting (www.ac.com), United States Mint (www.usmint.gov), Nordstrom (www.nordstrom.com), and Victoria's Secret (www.victoriassecret.com).
- *Right Now Technologies* (www.rightnow.com). Right Now Web 3.1 builds on the systems FAQ and self-help functions by adding an automated e-mail response and a live text chat with customer-care

representatives. It also opens up the system's knowledge base to let representatives better answer customer questions. Right Now Web 3.1 runs on Windows NT, Solaris, and Linux operating platforms. A sampling of customers includes Ben & Jerry's (www.benjerry.com), Ford Motor Company (www.ford.com), McKesson Corporation (www.mckesson.com), John Deere (www.deere.com), and the Chicago Stock Exchange (www.chicagostockex.com). Starting price is $29,995 for a two-year license.

Many Web sites do not have the resources to build the infrastructure needed to respond to the large numbers of e-mail messages their Web sites generate. For example, 10thAvenue.com, which offers a unique collection of art, gifts, and home accents, received about 200 telephone calls per day and 300 e-mail messages. Nine employees could respond within four hours. According to Jeff Sweat (2000), 10thAvenue.com decided they needed the customer service capabilities similar to a large, traditional retailer but didn't have the resources for a full-blown CRM suite or to staff a 24-hour-a-day call center. The company tapped TouchScape (www .touchscape.com) and rented services for about $1,000 a month. With TouchScape, 10thAvenue.com now has virtual agents, e-mail marketing capabilities, and e-mail sorting and response functions. The goal of Touch-Scape is to help subscribers increase sales velocity, create market opportunities, and improve customer satisfaction and loyalty. The pricing model is $1,000 a month for 1,000 transactions. This is often an affordable way to increase online customer care and relationship marketing for emerging and midsize companies that previously couldn't afford traditional relationship management (CRM) solutions.

SUMMING IT UP

- Everyone who visits your Web site is a potential customer (even if you are offering a complex or expensive product or service). Give customers enough information to be able to make a purchase decision. Let customers decide if they want to purchase online or contact a sales representative.

- E-corporations must be predictive and responsive to the ever-changing needs of their customers. The e-customer software you purchase must be flexible enough to cover your early mistakes and robust enough to support your new initiatives.

- Regardless of the type of e-customer software you purchase (a Web-enabled CRM suite, call center–based software, or a stand-alone product), you'll have to budget time and money for integration.
- Your successful Web site will generate a large volume of e-mail. All e-mail messages are sales leads and should be classified, sorted, tracked, and responded to as quickly as possible. Your automated responses can be a boilerplate message, an artificial-intelligence-generated response, or a custom-made message based on your company's lexicon.

ANTICIPATING CUSTOMER NEEDS CHECKLIST

ACTION PLAN

Ensuring that customers receive what they want, when they want it, and how they want it is a sure way to succeed in e-business. This means gathering as much information as possible about your customers, so you can anticipate their needs and forecast their questions. This, in turn, can assist you in predicting what will motivate a midtier customer to purchase and opens untapped marketing opportunities targeted to a segment of customers rather than mass markets. Sometimes, it is difficult to determine a starting place. The following checklist can assist you in anticipating your customers' needs.

Anticipating Customer Needs Checklist

✓ Define who your customers are.
Knowing who your customers are can assist you in developing the next product or service your customers will need or require. This information can also be used to differentiate your e-corporation from competitors with similar products.

✓ Clearly present your products and services.
Avoid ambiguity and unclear product or service descriptions. Clearly state features, benefits, content, size, color, and so on.

Anticipating Customer Needs Checklist (continued)

✓ Provide enough information so customers can make a buying decision.
Give customers the option of buying your products or services online. Provide a "buying path" so customers who want to help themselves can travel through your Web site to a purchase point.

✓ Gather as much information about your customers as possible.
As users travel around your Web site, you can gain information about their characteristics from their interactions with Web site elements. Learn as much as possible about each customer, so you can anticipate his or her needs and next question.

✓ Make purchasing easy for customers.
Provide billing, invoicing, and shipping information. Once a transaction is complete, e-mail an order confirmation to the customer.

✓ Maintain competence at all times.
Deliver what you promised, when you promised, and at the price the customer expects. Make certain your e-corporation has the ability and capacity required to complete tasks and supply products and services.

✓ Define your service standards.
Reliability is defined as having minimum standards that are consistently exceeded. Encourage personnel to identify closely with customers. This can allow your organization to understand customer expectations and requirements.

✓ Provide many customer communication channels.
Give customers peace of mind. For example, allow customers to start a transaction online and complete it with a telephone call or other type of communication. This shows that you are in control of their business.

✓ Be courteous and friendly at all times.
Review standard e-mail responses and make certain they reflect your company's mission, goals, and objectives. Customer service is based on relationships between people and requires courtesy and honesty at all times.

Source: Adapted from Paul Grainger, "Customer Service Review, Under Promise and Over-Fulfill," an online publication of the Ferrar Grainger Group, 1997.

REFERENCES

Bauer, Debbie. 1999. How to Manage E-Mail Effectively. *Customer Relationship Magazine* 1, No. 1 (5 December).

Felix, Susan. 2000. Customer Relationship Management: The Road to E-Service Excellence. *What's New Article.* Online publication of SCFelix Consulting Services (www.felixconsulting.com/crm0006.html), 16 April.

Kasanoff, Bruce, Toria Thomson, and Kimberly Hill (ed.). 1999. Advanced Strategies for Differentiating Customers and Partners: Software That Enables 1 to 1 Relationships. Online publication of Accelerating 1 to 1 (www.accelerating.com), October.

LaMonica, Martin. 1999. Top of the News: Putting Together the Interactive Puzzle. *InfoWorld* 21 (1 November).

McNabb, Paul, and Michel Steinbaum. 1996. Reclaiming Customer Care: The Milkman Returns. *Topics for a Knowledge Economy.* Online publication of Cambridge Information Network, a division of Cambridge Technology Partners (www.cin.ctp.com).

Riehle, Kathleen. 2000. Online Retailers Find Bad Service Experience More Destructive, Synchrony Study Shows: E-Tailers Lose Customers Twice as Fast as Brick-and-Mortar Businesses When Service Is a Problem. *BusinessWire,* 25 January.

Seybold, Patricia B., and Ronni R. Markshak. 1998. *Customers.com: How to Create a Profitable Business Strategy for the Internet and Beyond.* New York: Random House.

Sterne, Jim. 2000. *Customer Service on the Internet: Building Relationships, Increasing Loyalty, and Staying Competitive.* 2nd ed. New York: John Wiley & Sons.

Sweat, Jeff. 2000. Fast Focus on Web CRM—Businesses Find that Customer Services Is as Vital to Success Online as It Is in the Brick-and-Mortar World. *Information Week* 786 (15 May).

Online Lead Generation Management, Security, and Privacy

▼ Discovering how lead-generation-management solutions vary

▼ Providing security for your online customers

▼ Protecting your online customers' privacy

▼ Overcoming privacy concerns

Electronic customer relationship management (eCRM) is a combination of technology, process, and organization; it is not any of these three in isolation. If you can integrate these three elements in your e-business, you will be targeted for success. In this chapter, you'll see how e-corporations can use these elements and a variety of technological approaches to develop lead generation programs. Having an interactive lead management program that assists you in acquiring, qualifying, and tracking leads can expand your customer reach by keeping your e-corporation ahead of the customer and by turning interactions into customer relationships and customer loyalty. This chapter covers e-corporation security and shows you exactly how online merchants receive payment for online credit card purchases. The chapter concludes by discussing privacy issues and provides suggestions about how you can assuage customer privacy concerns without placing limits on your e-business.

DATA, DATA EVERYWHERE

Product awareness is just the beginning; the next step is lead generation. Lead generation management can be handled a number of ways. Many e-corporations use large eCRM suites, sales force automation packages, contact management, data-mining tools, and Web site analysis software. Most e-corporations have various forms of "homegrown" lead-generation management solutions. In this fragmented market, no single product, technology, or customer tracking solution seems to have captured the "mind share" of e-corporations.

The sales and marketing departments of your e-business place a high priority on acquiring sales leads. For e-corporations, getting leads to produce the desired results cannot be accomplished without technology and management oversight. Figure 11.1 shows the online lead generating process. Lead generation management is divided into four steps: The first step is the generation of legitimate sales opportunities. The second step is qualifying leads, because all leads are not created equal. The third step is tracking leads, so that you know the status of each lead. The last step is measuring and analyzing the effectiveness of your lead generation management program.

Generating E-corporation Leads

What most e-corporations want is a way to extend the performance and functionality of their existing systems. Once again, integration becomes tricky when implementing a sales lead generation management program; however, the effort is worthwhile. Having a lead management program in place can assist you in acquiring leads, which become prospects and then customers. The program can expand your customer reach by converting episodic interactions into ongoing customer dialogues, which build customer loyalty.

Figure 11.1   Online Lead Generation Management

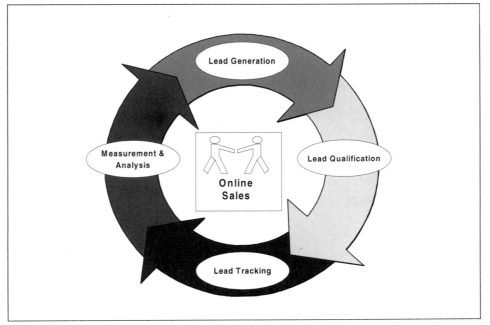

The management cycle begins with marketing efforts designed to generate a list of potential customers. These lists of potential customers can come from either inbound or outbound sources:

- *Inbound leads.* Inbound leads are generated by a Web site that provides a toll-free telephone number, contact information in the form of e-mail addresses, and fax numbers. You can even generate leads by using registrations, guest books, and inquiry forms. Offline leads can come from advertising on television, radio, magazines and newspapers, direct mail, product brochures, and business reply cards.
- *Outbound leads.* Outbound leads are generated by using in-house databases or outside lists. Outbound lead generation can be accomplished by following up on e-mail, print, or Web site requests for additional information. Additionally, online network-based loyalty programs can be used for outside lists. However, participation in online network

loyalty programs is not the total loyalty strategy for the company, because consumers frequently develop primary loyalty to the online network loyalty program and not the e-corporation participating in the program.

Qualifying E-corporation Leads

Anyone who contacts the e-corporation is a lead; however, not all leads are alike or equal. Generating real sales opportunities starts with a clear understanding of what is a lead and what isn't. Next, the challenge is to present the best offer to the right audience in the most effective way. You will have to determine the criteria for qualifying a lead as a prospect. There are three steps to qualifying leads:

1. Select a technological solution that can assist you in sorting all leads based on your preset criteria. Your technological solution may be a Web-based program, sales force automation software, a contact management application, or a large eCRM suite. (For information about these solutions, see the Resource Center at the end of this book.) Additionally, many e-corporations use a technological approach based on its own expertise and knowledge of its customer base. Keep in mind that wireless communications may be a necessary part of your lead generation program strategy.
2. Determine the nature and extent of potential customer needs and the ability of the e-corporation to meet those needs.
3. Rank leads into three or more categories, making certain that leads with serious sales potential receive the attention they deserve. To do this, figure out the characteristics of prospects and determine which are the most able, willing, and ready to buy (often by using online forms that gather this information). For example, Class A leads are hot prospects and should be immediately sent to sales personnel who may send the prospect special Web page content. High-quality leads often provide new sales opportunities that result in closing the sale. Class B leads may be sent e-mail responses, paper-based media, or a targeted newsletter, and may be placed on a list for subsequent follow-up. (If the prospect's level of interest increases, he or she is moved to Class A.) Class C prospects are sent periodic e-mail mes-

sages or print media and contacted within six months. Class C prospects should be removed from this list if they do not respond to the e-corporation's marketing attempts. Working with these leads can be a waste of time and money.

Timeliness is an important issue in lead management. Prospective customers can be quickly lost if they are not moved to the next phase of the lead management program. Keep in mind that prospects have a short attention span, and their interest in the e-corporation's products or services decreases over time.

Tracking E-corporation Leads

Keeping track of leads as they proceed through the lead management process is often time consuming. However, using a simple system of accountability, each lead can be assigned to a salesperson with follow-up procedures, so that everyone in the organization knows the status of each lead.

Management decides how leads are distributed to sales personnel. Some sales representatives work in specific geographic areas, and others only sell specific products or services. Keep in mind that the marketing program must work with the sales force to make certain that marketing campaigns do not raise more leads than can be effectively handled by the sales personnel.

Measuring and Analyzing Your Success

A successful lead management program must be coordinated with every step. Each step must complement the next, so that the entire process is measurable. The lead-generation-management program should be able to measure:

1. The productivity of the marketing campaign in terms of new customers or increased sales
2. What market segments have the greatest potential
3. Which offers or presentations work best for each of the e-corporation's products or services

Sales personnel have to work with marketing to provide feedback about the success in converting leads to customers. A poor conversion ratio may be due to poorly targeted marketing. Timely feedback can assist marketing in taking immediate corrective actions.

CommVault (www.commvault.com), a provider of high-end, enterprise-class storage management solutions, is the next loyalty marketing success story. The release of a new product, Galaxy, forced CommVault to develop new ways to broaden its markets. This meant developing an effective interactive lead-generation-management program.

LOYALTY MARKETING SUCCESS STORY

CommVault

▼ **COMPANY:** CommVault Systems, Inc., in Oceanport, New Jersey, is a provider of enterprise-class storage management solutions that ensure the reliability and availability of business data. CommVault offers a complete application-integrated suite of network-aware storage management solutions and provides users with a comprehensive file system, database backup and recovery, and disaster recovery. In addition to its hierarchical storage management, archiving, and data migration software, CommVault released a new product called Galaxy and needed to broaden its customer base. This meant changing the firm's marketing intelligence and material to target the right individuals at the right time.

▼ **SOLUTION:** CommVault implemented technology that allows them to offer interactive e-mail campaigns and database management and that can be tightly segmented between types of prospects, channels, and partners. CommVault also built a lead qualification system to feed high-quality new prospects straight to the sales force.

▼ **BENEFITS:** In the past, many tasks were not automated. Now, CommVault has the tools to automate many of the things it did manually.

- CommVault implemented the tools for targeted e-mail and streamlined video marketing campaigns. Response rates are about 8 percent, which is more than double the response rate of previous direct mail promotions.

FIGURE 11.2   CommVault broadened its customer base by using new interactive lead management tools.

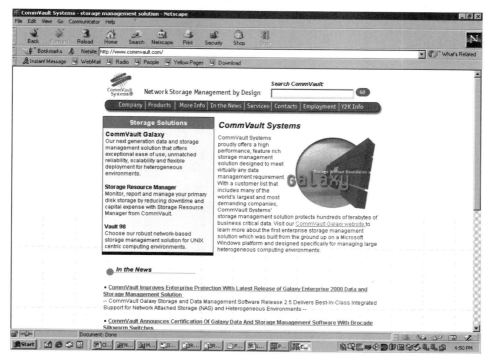

- Prospects are automatically cultivated until they are ready to be handed off to the sales force. Additionally, the software solution sends e-mail messages reminding the sales department to contact prospects and customers.
- Leads are now automatically tracked through various media, such as direct mail, e-mail, and Web banner ads. Automated reports on results, such as the marketing cost for each response to the Web banner advertisement are now available.

▼ **TECHNOLOGY:** CommVault selected MarketFirst software (www.market soft.com), a Java-based client. The MarketFirst Software Developer Kit (SDK) allows CommVault to exchange information with its other enterprise systems in real time.

LEAD-GENERATION-MANAGEMENT SOLUTIONS

There are many technological products that can assist you in developing your e-corporation's lead management program. Following are a few examples:

- Entice 1.5 (www.multiactive.com) is a storefront and a customer-management system. For midsize companies that want to go online to sell their products or services and manage customer relationships, Entice 1.5 is a good first step. (For e-corporations that already have online stores, it's not appropriate unless you want to start all over again.) Entice 1.5 includes 13 modules that are neatly integrated. One of the best features of Entice 1.5 is that it allows sales representatives to build simple customer interaction sites on their own. The program operates on a Windows NT platform. Prices start at $25,000 for the Entice server and ten user licenses.

- GoldMine (www.goldmine.com), shown in Figure 11.3, reads e-mail, checks for duplicate contacts, creates new contact records, alerts the appropriate people within the organization, and provides different responses and follow-ups based on different requests. Users can route sales leads for a product to the sales representative for that product. Sales leads for another product can be routed to another part of the organization and processed in a different way. GoldMine 5.0 runs on Windows 95/98 and NT platforms. Single-user licenses are $295 and $995 for a five-user network license.

- MarketFirst 2.3 (www.marketfirst.com) includes a contact manager that oversees data-management tasks, such as list management, deleting duplicates, and merging and purging. MarketFirst automates survey response gathering and analysis, and combines multiple lists with multiple media. The marketing campaign management features let users take several programs (which support a key initiative or an entire function, such as direct marketing) and rolls them up into the campaign manager (the campaign manager allows e-corporations to determine if a certain marketing effort is successful). MarketFirst 2.3 provides reports about lead-generation effectiveness, the lead cost-to-revenue ratio, program and media effectiveness, survey response

FIGURE 11.3   GoldMine is a low-cost approach to managing online leads.

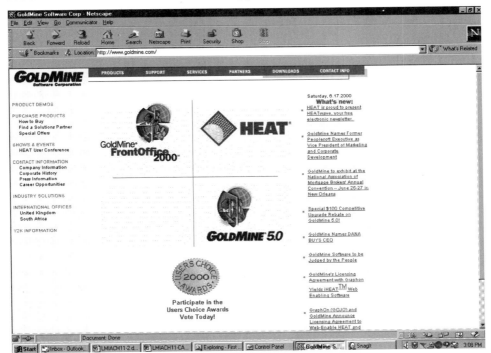

results, profiles, and other metrics, all in real time. MarketFirst 2.3 operates on Solaris and Windows NT platforms. Average price is $150,000 to $200,000.

• UpShot (www.upshotonline.com) is a Web-based solution that helps individuals track the activities of sales teams and assists sales representatives in communicating with customers and prospects. It is designed to provide access to fresh leads, deliver the news from the Web or your company's intranet, provide a comprehensive history of interactions with any prospect, allow communication with contacts, let individuals assign and track to-dos and follow-up tasks, and provide analyses of potential bottlenecks in the sales process. The first five UpShot users are free; then it's $29.95 per month per additional user. The Intellisync user license is $7.95 per month (this feature can synchronize sales data), and the data delivery service (a backup of your data) is $24.95 per month.

PROVIDING SECURITY FOR YOUR ONLINE CUSTOMERS

Security issues for e-corporations cover two areas: The first area is the reliability of the company's server. The second area of concern is customer security. According to Bill Machrone (2000), a writer for *PC Magazine,* Web servers are an inviting target for Internet hackers. Hackers often take pride in disrupting, bringing down, or defacing Web sites. For consumers, the reliability of your Web site is vital. Recourse Technologies (www .recourse.com) offers ManHunt and ManTrap to assist your e-corporation in avoiding "denial of service" problems by backtracking and diverting attacks to dummy machines. Often, isolating host servers from each other can lower the likelihood of service disruptions. In situations where internal and external servers must communicate with each other, you can set up sub-LAN networks with nonroutable addresses for the sole purpose of interserver communication. If you are sharing data with a partner, make certain that all communications are encrypted.

One way to dispel consumers' security fears is to employ server security software that uses a security alert message (shown in Figure 11.4) and an indicator, which appears in a consumer's browser, to indicate the transaction is being processed on a secure server. Netscape browser users who are accessing a secured Web page get a security alert message and see a closed lock highlighted in the bottom left corner of the screen. When using a secured Web page on an Explorer browser, users get a security alert message and see a closed lock in the bottom right corner of the screen.

Following is a list of a few of the secure Web server products that include this feature:

- Netscape Communications Enterprise or Commerce (www.netscape .com) operates on a Unix (in various flavors) and Microsoft NT.
- Microsoft Corporation IIS (www.Microsoft.com) operates on NT and Windows 95 platforms.
- C2Net Stronghold (www.c2.net) is based on the Apache Web server (www.apache.org) and operates on a Unix platform.

FIGURE 11.4   Example of a Security Alert Message

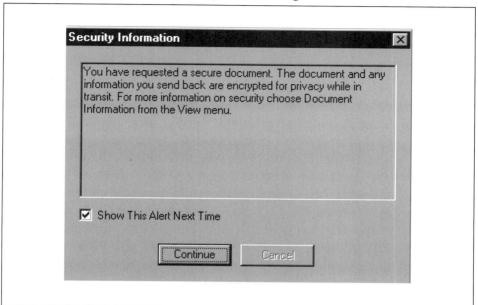

Security for Customer Transactions

A fundamental problem for e-corporations is customer transaction security. The dilemma is only allowing authorized users data access and keeping private data away from prying eyes. One technique for keeping customer and corporate data secure is using encryption. Encryption is defined as scrambling characters, so that if data are intercepted they are unintelligible. When the encrypted data are received by the correct entities, the encryption is reversed so the data are readable. Overall, there are four types of security used on the Internet:

1. SSL (Secure Sockets Layer) is a security protocol developed by Netscape Communications (www.netscape.com) for a variety of Internet applications, including Netscape's Web server and browser products.

2. RSA (RSA Data Security, Inc) is a patented encryption process developed by RSA Data Security, Inc. (www.rsa.com). Standards organizations have been reluctant to include this approach as an official standard but may once the patent expires and the methodology becomes part of the public domain.

3. SET (Secure Electronic Transactions) architecture was developed in 1997 and is used by credit card moguls Visa and MasterCard for online consumer credit card approval. This standard provides software specifications for the three entities generally involved in an online credit card transaction: the cardholder, the merchant bank, and the acquisition processor. SET defines the certification process and certificate formats for each of these entities. This specification includes the encryption and authentication methodology for financial transactions. One of the drawbacks of the approach is that authorizations generally take longer than other methodologies.

4. ECC (Elliptic Curve Cryptosystem) is a public key cryptosystem developed by Certicom Corporation (www.certi-com.com). It is useful for low-memory or wireless devices, such as smart cards, cellular phones, and television set-top boxes.

How Would You Like to Pay for That?

As electronic commerce takes off, transaction security will become increasingly important. Today individuals can pay for purchases with e-cash, e-check, debits, micropayments, or credit cards. (Some auction sites provide consumers with escrow services or PayPal (www.paypal.com) or Billpoint (www.billpoint.com) services that process credit card payments for small businesses, auction sellers, and wireless transactions.) The majority of consumers prefer to pay by credit card; however, a recent survey highlighted an important fact: While survey respondents said they were concerned about Internet security, nearly 60 percent had already made an online purchase using a credit card. Additionally, most consumers know that in cases of credit card fraud, credit card companies will only hold them liable for the first $50 of purchases. Processing credit card payments on the Internet involves following five steps:

1. The consumer (usually the credit card holder) visits a Web site that allows credit card purchases. The customer provides the vendor with his or her credit card information, which is supplied by the issuing bank. (This is usually the cardholder's name, credit card number, credit card expiration date, and credit card billing address, which may be different than the shipping address.)

2. The merchant or vendor offers products or services by using a payment-enabling merchant Web server software. The payment information is secured by one of the four security protocols mentioned earlier (SSL, RSA, SET, and ECC). With the secured form payment information shielded, if anyone intercepts the transmission to the vendor, all the interceptor will receive is an unreadable, jumbled message. The secured form is the vendor's credit card sales slip. To accept credit cards, the vendor must have an account with a merchant bank that offers Internet credit card processing.

3. The merchant bank accepts credit cards via the Internet. The vendor sends the encrypted credit card slip to his merchant bank. The merchant bank may process the vendor's credit transactions or may outsource them to a third party (an acquiring processor).

4. The transaction processor processes the merchant's credit card transactions through the financial network. The acquiring processor authorizes the credit card transaction and issues an authorization code or declines the transaction. The acquiring processor reduces the limit on the credit card but does not charge the customer or credit the vendor.

    Vendors do not charge a customer's credit card until the product or service has been sent or rendered (as required by the rules of Visa and MasterCard). Once the transaction is complete (and the product shipped), the vendor can capture the transaction and charge the credit card. If the customer cancels an order before it is captured, the transaction is void. If the customer returns the goods after the transaction has been captured, then a credit is created.

5. The acquiring processor settles with the vendor's merchant bank. Captures and credit card credits are usually processed in groups called batches. When a batch is processed, the acquiring processor finalizes transactions by transferring monies to the vendor's merchant bank account.

PROTECTING YOUR ONLINE CUSTOMERS' PRIVACY

Due to public relations campaigns and the online shopping experiences, consumers are less concerned about security than privacy. However, a Jupiter Communications (www.jup.com) research report warns e-corporations about failing to address consumer privacy concerns. The Jupiter report cautions e-corporations about their lack of focus and predicts that if e-corporations do not shape up, by 2002 they are likely to lose $18 billion of a potential $42 billion market. That is 42 percent (almost half) of the potential market. As consumers become more educated about the technologies that can invade their privacy, their concerns will rise and are likely to become an ongoing problem online and offline. Following are three examples of what happens when e-corporations don't tell online customers they are collecting or passing along their personal information:

- In February 2000, the federal and New York state authorities launched separate inquiries into how online advertising firm Double-Click uses personal information from its Internet customers. According to authorities, DoubleClick misled Internet users by collecting confidential information on their habits and identities with the intent to sell the information to advertisers. According to SEC documents, DoubleClick is also involved in six private lawsuits over its Web privacy practices.
- RealNetworks was the subject of a consumer outcry when it disclosed that it was monitoring users of its RealJukebox (www.realjuke box.com) Web site. The e-corporation used a unique identification number assigned to the software that tracked personal data and the music-listening habits of users. Due to the number of complaints, RealNetworks was forced to release a patch that allows its 12 million

customers to block the transmission of personal information. The company publicly apologized for invading the privacy of users.

- Amazon.com (www.amazon.com) faces similar public relations problems due to privacy issues. Amazon.com is fighting two lawsuits alleging that its Alexa subsidiary, which collects Web surfing data, secretly captured personal data about Web users and gave it to Amazon.com and third parties. Despite Amazon.com's promise that it would not capture such data when it purchased Alexa in 1999, it denies having captured and correlated the personal information without permission.

Shopping in cyberspace is fundamentally different than going to the mall. When you shop in a traditional store, you are anonymous until you pay for an item with your debit or credit card or write a check. Today when you shop in cyberspace, you can be monitored the moment you log on. In the future, it is likely that e-corporations will take profile targeting to levels that are difficult to imagine. New technology will support loyalty programs that can't be ignored, affinity programs will become must-haves, and cross-selling will become so directed and subtle that consumers will almost unknowingly buy more products and services than ever before. In addition, automated advertising campaigns and sales programs will be so finely tuned they will be aimed at the almost unstated needs of each individual in the e-corporation's customer base. E-corporations in the new economy will be extremely effective in targeting a desirable product at a customer who is ready to buy. Consequently, consumers will be more concerned about privacy than security. Today, there are a variety of privacy intrusions:

- Cookies, used for easy Internet navigation, can be used to profile customer preferences and activities.
- Program coding (Java, JavaScript, and Active X) can be embedded in Web pages, so companies have full access to a consumer's history file and to the consumer's file system. Referrer codes can notify third parties by e-mail that customers have been to a particular Web site. Small programs called Trojan horses can give remote users full access

to customers' desktop computers, allow password stealing, and computer rebooting.

- Intercepting customer e-mail messages is another abuse of customer privacy. Copies of e-mail messages are at the sender and receiver locations, in addition to any servers or backup machines that pass along the message. This means that e-mail messages can be read or stolen at the server.
- Keystroke monitoring can record everything customers type, even when they are not connected to the Internet. These programs can send the information to a remote site or save the information on the user's computer to be retrieved later, when the customer is away from his or her computer.
- Spam (unsolicited e-mail) is often considered the vilest invasion of privacy. No one likes spam; it clogs servers and fills in-boxes with junk mail. Additionally, unwanted spam that uses HTML coding may be used for profiling and identifying users.

The Worst Kind of Privacy Violation

Tom Siebel and Pat House (1999) observe that every time consumers use a credit card, they leave a trace of their activities. Over time, these "traces" can be strung together to form a powerful purchase history that can be used to predict buyer behavior. If a consumer uses a credit card for any length of time, the credit card number is probably stored on hundreds of computer systems around the world. Paper-based histories are often difficult to access, degradable, and slow to use. Electronic-based histories that record your online credit card purchases are quick, open, and durable. For consumers, the benefits are instant information exactly how and when they want it. The disadvantage is that consumer information may be available to government entities, unauthorized third parties, and, of course, e-corporations. This can result in "stolen identities," such as the following:

- *Using your e-mail accounts for illicit activities.* There are many ways to gain access to someone's e-mail address; for example, fraudsters can use AOL's Instant Messenger service to pose as AOL employees who claim they are having recordkeeping difficulties and need your password for verification. If you comply, you may get an unpleasant surprise the next time you log on to AOL. Imagine discovering a warning and a statement from AOL that your e-mail account was involved in criminal activity. Proving that someone else was using your personal e-mail account is extremely difficult.

- *Using your Social Security number to steal your identity.* Financial companies identify individuals by using a name and Social Security number. With this information, someone can steal your identify. Social Security numbers are used as account identifiers by financial service firms, health care companies, and motor vehicle departments, all of which are either online or going online. If your identity is stolen, you can count on endless telephone calls and letter writing as you try to reclaim your true identity.

Self-Regulation and Your Online Customers' Privacy

In congressional testimony in 1998, Robert Pitofsky, chairman of the Federal Trade Commission, addressed online privacy issues and stated that online consumers are concerned about the collection of personal data, which in turn appears to be affecting their participation in the online marketplace. In his statement, Pitofsky cited the following examples of the types of data collected online and noted that *none* of the Web sites listed below posted a privacy statement:

- A medical clinic's online doctor-referral service invites the consumer to submit his or her name, postal address, e-mail address, insurance company, and any comments concerning medical problems, and to indicate the wish to receive information on any of a number of topics including: urinary incontinence, hypertension, cholesterol, prostate cancer, and diabetes. The online application for the clinic's health education membership program asks the consumer to submit name, address, telephone number, date of birth, marital status, gender, insurance company, and the date and location of his or her last hospitalization.

- An automobile dealership's Web site offers consumers help in rebuilding their credit ratings. To take advantage of this offer, the consumer is urged to provide name, address, Social Security number, and telephone number through the Web site's online information form.

- A mortgage company operates an online prequalification service for home loans. The online application form requires that each potential borrower provide his or her name, Social Security number, home and business telephone numbers, e-mail address, previous address, type of loan sought, current and former employer's name and address, length of employment, income, sources of funds to be applied to closing, and approximate total in savings. The online form also requires the borrower to provide information about his or her credit history, including credit cards, car loans, child support, and other indebtedness, and to state whether he or she has ever filed for bankruptcy.

- A child-directed site collects personal information, such as a child's full name, postal address, e-mail address, gender, and age. The Web site also asks a child extensive personal finance questions, such as whether a child has received gifts in the form of stocks, cash, savings bonds, mutual funds, or certificates of deposit; who has given a child these gifts; whether a child puts monetary gifts into mutual funds, stocks, or bonds; and whether a child's parents own mutual funds. Elsewhere on the Web site, each contest winner's full name, age, city, state, and zip code are posted.

- Another child-directed site collects personal information to register for a chat room, including a child's full name, e-mail address, city, state, gender, age, and hobbies. The Web site has a lotto contest that asks for a child's full name and e-mail address. Lotto contest winners' full names are posted on the site. For children who wish to find an electronic pen pal, the site offers a bulletin board service that posts messages, including children's e-mail addresses. Keep in mind that the Web site asks children to post messages if they are looking for a pen pal, and anyone of any age can visit this bulletin board and contact a child directly.

In his testimony, Chairman Pitofsky recommended that Congress enact legislation that sets standards for collecting online information from children. The Commission deferred its recommendation for the collection of information from general online consumers and is evaluating the efficacy of self-regulation.

OVERCOMING CUSTOMER PRIVACY CONCERNS

With regard to privacy issues, e-corporations are caught in the middle. Consumers will be more and more concerned about the invasion of their privacy, and e-corporations will be pressured to make better use of online information. Your e-corporation can overcome customer privacy concerns by implementing the following:

- *Provide an understandable, easily accessible privacy policy statement.* Prominently display the firm's commitment to privacy, whether the Web site collects customer information or not.
- *Assure customers that privacy policies are binding, even through mergers and acquisitions.* Additionally, assure them that purchasing information will not be sold to third parties, where it can result in unwanted e-mail solicitations, telemarketing calls, or stolen identities.
- *Allow customers to voice their privacy concerns.* Web sites can provide users with e-mail contact information and can provide individual feedback on customer privacy issues.
- *Educate consumers about privacy.* Allay vague privacy issues and show consumers where they should focus their online privacy concerns. In other words, help consumers define their privacy fears.
- *Promote your e-corporation's privacy efforts.* Letting customers know how you protect their privacy will help you build trust and loyalty.
- *Overcomply with regulations.* Show customers that you are willing to go the extra mile on their behalf. You can serve your customers (and build long-term relationships) by helping them protect their own privacy; for example, remind them how to avoid invasions of privacy and security on their own computers. Suggest running the latest version of their virus software and give warnings about providing extra information to others and keeping passwords in their desks or on their computers.

The Internet provides many privacy sites that are worth your time. These privacy sites can be used to assist you in developing your approach to consumer privacy issues. Following is a sampling of what you'll find online:

- The Better Business Bureau (www.bbb.org) offers a voluntary certification and assessment program that evaluates and rates online vendor privacy policies. If your e-corporation meets the Better Business Bureau's requirements, you can display its certification logo. Prices for this service vary from $150 for small firms to $3,000 for large companies.
- TRUSTe (www.truste.org), shown in Figure 11.5, is an independent, nonprofit privacy initiative dedicated to building users' trust and confidence on the Internet, and to accelerating growth of the Internet industry. TRUSTe has developed a third party oversight "seal" program that is designed to alleviate users' concerns about online privacy.
- Privacy's (www.privacy.org) goals are to raise consumers' awareness of how technology affects personal privacy. Privacy empowers consumers to take action to control their own personal information by providing practical tips on privacy protection, responding to specific privacy-related complaints from consumers, and, when appropriate, referring consumers to the proper organizations for further assistance. It helps document the nature of consumers' concerns about privacy in reports and makes those reports available to policymakers, industry representatives, and consumer advocates.
- Privacy Alliance (www.privacyalliance.com) believes those businesses and other entities that operate in the online or electronic commerce environment should take steps to ensure the privacy of personally identifiable information collected from consumers. Privacy Alliance provides links to guides for assisting businesses in building effective privacy policies, guidelines for the effective enforcement of self-regulation, an online brochure about creating consumer confidence online, principles of children's online activities, and a legal framework white paper.

FIGURE 11.5   TRUSTe can assist you in showing customers that you are serious about protecting their privacy.

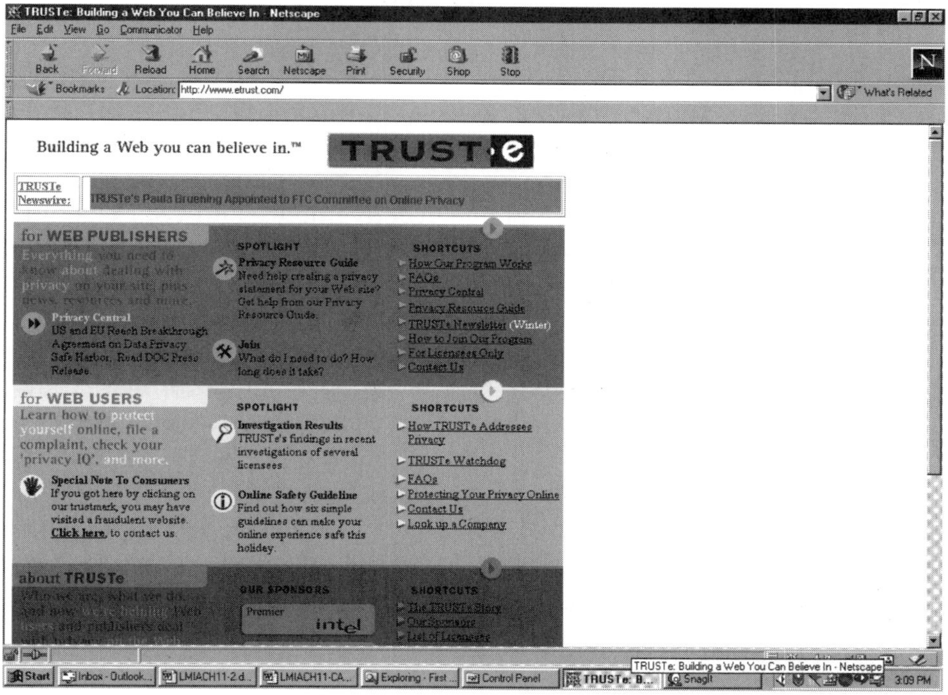

SUMMING IT UP

- All e-corporations need an interactive approach to capture leads that are generated online and offline. Technological solutions can vary, but all successful e-corporations need a lead management program that measures the success of generating, qualifying, and tracking leads.
- Security for your e-corporation's server and customer transactions is a priority. Online customers want reliability and safety.
- If your e-corporation can't protect customer privacy, your customers will go to another online business that can. Make certain you post a privacy policy statement, even if you're not collecting personal information.

DEVELOPING THE FRAMEWORK FOR YOUR E-BUSINESS PRIVACY STATEMENT

Privacy guidelines should educate and meet the needs of online customers. Communicate that your company's highest priority is the preservation of consumer privacy. The worksheet below provides a starting point for the development of your e-corporation's privacy policy. Remember, privacy is a tradeoff between convenience and your customer's right to confidentiality and security. Assure your online customer that the data you collect is not being misused or mismanaged.

1. **Identify the purposes of personal information.** How will you inform the customer about what data you are or are not collecting?

   _____

   _____

   _____

2. **Get the customer's consent.** How will you entice customers to leave personal information?

   _____

   _____

   _____

3. **Set limits for collecting personal information.** Collecting customer data is not a "fishing expedition"—keep your requirements simple.

   _____

   _____

   _____

4. **Keep personal information accurate.** How will you give customers the opportunity to update their personal profiles?

   _____

   _____

   _____

5. **Safeguard personal information.** What sort of security does your e-corporation require?

   _____

   _____

   _____

6. **Legal issues.** Are there any new laws that require you to disclose or make customer data available to government entities?

   _____

   _____

   _____

7. **How can you give customers the opportunity to opt out?** In other words, how can you let customers decide if you can collect personal information?

   _____

   _____

   _____

REFERENCES

Allen, Cliff, Deborah Kania, and Beth Yaeckel. _Internet World: Guide to One-to-One Web Marketing._ New York: John Wiley & Sons.

Keen, Peter. 2000. Designing Privacy for Your E-Business. _PC Magazine,_ 6 June, 132–36.

Machrone, Bill. 2000. Protect & Defend. _PC Magazine,_ 27 June, 168–200.

Privacy in Cyberspace: Robert Pitofsky. 1998. Congressional testimony. Federal Document Clearing House, 21 July.

Sandberg, Jared. 1999. Losing Your Good Name Online. _Newsweek,_ 20 September, 56–57.

Seiler, Marianne, and Jody Martinez. 1998. Leads on the Line: Using Inbound/Outbound Telemarketing to Manage the Leads-to-Prospects Customer Cycle. _Marketing Tools,_ 1 July, 20–25.

Siebel, Thomas M., and Pat House. 1999. _Cyber Rules._ New York: Currency/Doubleday.

12

Reducing Costs and Increasing Customer Loyalty at the Interaction Center

Customer service is likely to be the key differentiator in your market. New technologies have made the Web an intensely interactive medium. Web sites that offer "brochureware" of their products and services are yesterday's Web sites. In this chapter, you'll discover how Web-based customer service can increase customer retention and loyalty. You'll discover how Web-enabled call centers are less costly than traditional call centers and can be a central depository of the "customer's memory," which can be accessed by individuals throughout the organization. Find out how you can have Internet interactions that are so seamless that customers don't have to leave their computers to talk to a live customer service representative. You'll uncover how call centers have "morphed" into new entities that are contact centers or interaction centers with five functions:

1. Customer interaction
2. Interaction with company divisions
3. The ability to contact others
4. Support of constituencies
5. The management of data

This chapter concludes with a discussion of how business leaders plan an active commitment to Web-based customer service and support, but only about half can even guess an appropriate budget amount.

ZEROING IN ON CALL CENTERS

Call centers often represent the largest customer touch point, improving access to information and support services that enhance each customer's experience, reduce defections, and build customer loyalty. The term call center covers reservation centers, help desks, information lines, or customer service. The Gartner Group, a research firm in Stamford, Connecticut, estimates that there are 60,000 to 100,000 call centers in the United States. Frost & Sullivan, Inc., a Cambridge, Massachusetts, research group, predicts the U.S. Web-enabled call center market will increase at a compound annual growth rate of 110.4 percent between 1997 and 2004. Call centers are organized so they can accommodate many types of customer communications (telephone, fax, the Web, e-mail, and interactive video kiosk). Traditional self-service call center technology for inbound calls includes:

- Automatic Call Distributor (ACD) is a specialized telephone system that automatically answers, queues, and routes incoming calls to customer service agents; plays announcements; and provides analytic reports about caller activities. "Jumping the queue" is an ACD feature that allows a caller on hold to be plucked from the queue and immediately redirected—a good way to treat different customers differently.

- Interactive voice response (IVR) is a computerized telephone system that responds to caller-entered digits or speech and provides a computer-generated voice. When linked to the firm's database, IVRs allow callers to check current information, such as account balances, or complete transactions, such as transfers. IVR can be used to monitor the health of diabetes, asthma, or heart patients; for example, a patient calls and supplies the company with information about how he or she is managing his or her diabetes. (Many patients feel more comfortable talking about the intimate details of their diseases to a computer-generated voice asking questions.)

    IVR technology is a form of self-service and is built on the customer's comfort level with Touch-Tone phones. It can improve the routing of telephone calls, shorten call times, and differentiate the level of service needed to provide top-flight service. A benefit of IVR is that it is available 24/7 without staffing costs. A good example of IVR technology is telephone requests for refills of drug prescriptions. In contrast, the disadvantage of IVR is that names and addresses are difficult to spell out using a Touch-Tone phone. Speech recognition helps in this area, but accents and limited vocabulary hinder the technology. For example, imagine ordering a man's light blue long-sleeve shirt by listening to a menu of options or entering numbers via the phone keypad. On the other hand, calling for your bank balance can be relatively simple.

- Computer telephony integration (CTI) is the software, hardware, and programming used to allow computers and telephones to work together; in other words, with CTI the telephone is connected to the company's database. For example, the diabetic patient's information is directly entered into the firm's database.

- On-demand publishing is the creation of customized personalized reports, which are the feedback of "conversations." For example, the diabetic patient's information is used to generate an individualized report, which can then be sent to the patient and the doctor via fax or U.S. mail.

AVOIDING HIGH CUSTOMER SERVICE COSTS WITH WEB-BASED CUSTOMER SUPPORT

In 1998, Justin Hubbard, Gregory Dalton, and Mary E. Thyfault stated that traditional call centers are often costly. These individuals interviewed Jeff Rumburg of Meta Group, Inc. (www.metagroup.com), who observed that every time a customer can get support through a Web-based system, the cost is minuscule compared to the cost of a typical customer service transaction. For example, it costs $5 for a live agent call or $0.50 for an IVR transaction. At the Web site, the cost is a few cents. Hubbard notes that, according to Forrester Research, many e-corporations believe they can move customers from the call center and support half of their customers, service needs online. Many firms believe that this will cut their call center costs by 43 percent. In contrast, without Internet solutions for customer service and support, the same labor costs are likely to rise 3 percent in the near future.

A big part of the Web's fundamental appeal is instant gratification. Users want to quickly find the information they need, so they can make a buying decision or solve a problem. In other words, delays cost sales. If users can't find the answer in a matter of seconds, they often click away to another Web site. This means that Web sites need ease of navigation and e-corporations must accurately anticipate the needs of all types of users, which can be nearly impossible. Users range from seasoned Internet customers to inexperienced newcomers. Also, the variety of requests can be staggering and constantly changing due to breaking news, successful marketing campaigns, or other uncontrollable factors.

Often, e-corporations try to solve this problem by providing a low-cost solution called a "contact us" button. This is similar to an IVR system that requires your Touch-Tone response to a menu of questions. When clicked, a "contact us" button activates a generic e-mail query. The user types in his or her contact information and checks off the type and nature of his or her query (complaint, question, concern, etc.). However, this is often the source of more frustration. Users have no idea where the e-mail message is going or when they will receive an answer. Consequently, the Internet user will use the Web site's toll-free telephone number and call the e-corporation.

The Yankee Group (www.yankeegroup.com), a Boston think tank, in an April 2000 report, states that Web-based customer care has gone from being a "fanciful future consideration" to a high-priority item for e-corporation customer care. At this time, online customer care is a hodgepodge of internal development, customer touch-point solutions, emerging suites from a large number of start-ups, and superficial changes to many standard call center applications. Companies with less than $1 billion in revenues and e-corporations that have been online for two years are moving aggressively toward online customer support. Companies with less than $1 billion in revenue handle 33 percent of their support requests online. Companies with over $1 billion in revenue handle about 10 percent of their support requests through the Web. Both types of companies plan to give online customers a number of options for support. The most popular options include Web site icons to request customer service agent callbacks, requests for e-mail responses, and Web-enabled self-help via a problem resolution knowledge database.

RINGING IN THE WEB

The Gartner Group reports that 70 percent of all customer interactions occur through the call center. In the past, the call center was the center of customer service, but in the e-commerce environment, a more appropriate name for a call center is the interaction center or contact center. The interaction center is responsible for customer service and the collecting and dissemination of customer data throughout the organization. With new eCRM technology, the interaction center works not only with customers but also with the e-corporation's sales, marketing, project development (which includes quality assurance), and fulfillment divisions. An enterprise can maximize customer service and provide primary research about customer perceptions of the e-corporation's products and services. This, in turn, enables the e-corporation to increase customer service and retention while simultaneously (and potentially) increasing revenue. For example:

- *Sales personnel* use customer profiles to qualify prospects and to upsell and cross-sell customers, which reduces the cost of sales and the need to acquire new customers with discounts or special offers.

- *Customer service representatives* use customer data to support complex or expensive products or services. This type of effective customer service and support can reduce costs, because customers don't have to make a second call.
- *Marketers* use customer service records to fine-tune their marketing campaigns, which reduces the need to purchase the services of focus groups or secondary marketing information. In addition, targeting ancillary services can increase customer loyalty.
- *Project management* uses customer information as a source for ideas about how to modify, mass-customize, and develop new products and services.
- *Fulfillment and distribution* use customer data to assist the e-corporation in resolving customer complaints, shipping, and inventory control.

Storing the "Customer Memory" in the Interaction Center

One of the advantages of the interaction center is caller ID or ANI technology, which allows the e-corporation to look up the caller's history and customer profile while the telephone is ringing. This allows the call to be routed to the appropriate individual. For example, high-value customers may be routed to account specialists who are knowledgeable about certain high-volume (or frequent purchasers) and the customer support they require. Additionally, this feature allows you to identify many of the anonymous individuals who call or choose to identify themselves on your Web site. Dell Computer, shown in Figure 12.1, routes corporate customers calling its toll-free telephone number to a corporate account manager who is familiar with the corporate policies, specifications, and ordering requirements of frequent or high-revenue corporate purchasers.

In general, if the e-corporation places a priority on customer loyalty, the interaction center will naturally become the hub for ensuring customer satisfaction and retention. Customers expect support, integration of the organization's resources, and a satisfying experience. In addition, customers have the ability to contact the e-corporation 24/7 in any manner they select (and more and more frequently in any language they choose). If

FIGURE 12.1   Dell Computer automatically reroutes high-value customer calls.

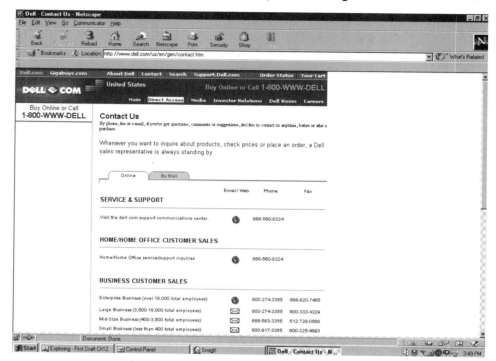

Screen shot courtesy of Dell Computer Corporation. © 2000 by Dell Computer Corporation.

customers can't get an answer online, they want immediate answers via telephone, fax, video, e-mail, or even face-to-face contact. Ideally, the interaction center will capture the customers' contact history and integrate sales and marketing databases. This way, the interaction center becomes the organization's "customer memory" and is one consistent database that can be accessed by individuals throughout the organization.

The loyalty marketing success story of Thomas Cook (www.thomas cook.com) shows how the organization integrated all their services into one call center to get closer to customers and maximize the value of every customer.

LOYALTY MARKETING SUCCESS STORY

Thomas Cook Global Services

▼ **COMPANY:** Thomas Cook Global Services is a prestigious financial and travel service company. Until recently, Thomas Cook handled financial and travel services as two separate operations. This arrangement was not the seamless customer experience many customers expected and led to frustration, problems, and additional costs.

▼ **SOLUTION:** Thomas Cook decided to integrate all its services into one call center to get closer to the 75,000 customers who call each day and maximize the value of every customer.

▼ **BENEFITS:** Using new call center technology, Thomas Cook now offers personalized features such as agent access to the entire range of products and services from a single application; caller ID recognition before the call is answered; agent access to all customer preferences, across all Thomas Cook business units; and intelligent capturing of all relevant personalized data as it is presented by the customer. Other benefits include:

- Matching the phone number dialed with the caller's profile to route the call to an operator who can speak the customer's language—a very important feature, because Thomas Cook customers speak more than 30 languages.
- Reduction in multiple phone-call handoffs and customer wait times.
- Customer information and preferences are now recorded, so Thomas Cook can provide more personalized services when a customer calls again.

▼ **TECHNOLOGY:** Thomas Cook Global Services selected Chordiant software. The implementation time of other products was three years. Using Chordiant software, Thomas Cook's new system was up and running in eight months and with an investment of $39 million.

Source: Adapted from "Success Stories: Thomas Cook Global Services," *Peppers and Rogers Group, Marketing 1 to 1 Success Stories* (www.1to1.com), 21 June 2000.

FIGURE 12.2   The Thomas Cook organization uses its customer service center as the hub of its customer retention program.

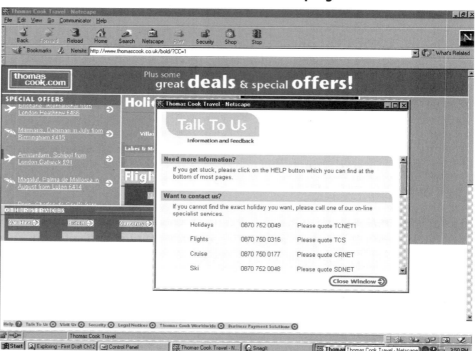

Figure 12.3 shows the new role of the interaction center. In this new role, the interaction center has five primary functions. The first function is the ability to accept almost any type of inbound communication. The second function is the ability to interact with all major divisions within the e-corporation. The third role is how the interaction center will contact others, via assisted-live communication, assisted-virtual communication, or self-service for both inbound and outbound interactions. The fourth function is how the interaction center supports constituencies such as prospects, customers, suppliers, fulfillment and distribution channels, employees, and partners or outsourcers. The fifth job of the interaction center is the management of data for billing, ordering, shipping, customers, and inventory.

FIGURE 12.3   Five Functions of the E-corporation's Interaction Center

---

Means of Communications

1. Telephone
2. Fax
3. Face-to-face
4. Interactive voice response
5. U.S. mail
6. Voice recognition
7. Internet
8. Video

Support of Organizational Functions

1. Customer service
2. Marketing
3. Sales
4. Fulfillment
5. Distribution
6. Project management

Method of Inbound and Outbound Interactions

1. Assisted-live
2. Assisted-virtual
3. Self-service

Constituencies

1. Prospects
2. Customers
3. Suppliers
4. Distribution
5. Fulfillment
6. Partners
7. Outsourcers

Data (Facts, Statistics, Information, and Records)

1. Billing
2. Open orders
3. Shipping
4. Customer profiles
5. Inventory
6. Other data

Source: Adapted from Cater J. Lusher, Colleen McCormick Amuso, Donna Fluss, and Scott Nelson, The Gartner Group (www.ncr.com/publications), 16 November 1998.

CHECKING OUT THE CAPABILITIES OF INTERACTION CENTERS

Many individuals feel overwhelmed by the Web or believe that it is impersonal. The interaction center must provide customers with a choice of how they want to interact with your e-corporation. Keep in mind that each type of interaction channel must provide the same level of access to information. Following is a list of the options you may want to consider:

- Self-service or self-help by providing online white papers, specifications, answers to product or service FAQs, troubleshooting guides, a technical library, configuration data, downloadable software product patches, video clips that show how to use the product, and so on. (This option usually needs a toll-free telephone number or call-me button for live support if online self-service isn't sufficient.)
- Automated e-mail customer responses using predetermined templates or artificial intelligence based on the e-corporation's database and lexicon. In the e-mail message, it is often wise to include an e-mail link or telephone number to a human being (usually the e-corporation's expert for this product, service, or geographical area) for additional information.
- Talk over the Internet using free downloadable software that connects the customer to a customer support representative. If the customer has the correct equipment, he or she can talk over the Internet (at no charge and from anywhere in the world) via his or her computer's microphone and can listen to the customer service agent's advice with their computer's speakers.
- Live or Web-based interactions using text-chat software. The customer clicks on an icon at the Web site and a chat box appears. The customer service representative sends a typed greeting and asks how he or she can be of service. The customer responds by typing his or her inquiry, comment, or complaint in an online text box. The customer service representative continues the "conversation" until the matter is resolved. If the matter can't be resolved in this manner, a manager immediately contacts the customer by telephone.

- "Call me now" buttons, where the customer clicks on a button icon, enters his or her phone number, and then receives a phone call from the customer service agent. A variation of this is the callback button, where the customer schedules a convenient time for the customer service representative to call.

- Sharing the customer's browser. When the customer service agent calls the customer, both agent and customer share a browser "sync session" while talking on the telephone. The customer service representative also can create special content on a Web page and send the Web page to the customer.

- Traditional call center interaction where the customer service agent receives the incoming call, identifies the customer, routes him or her to the appropriate agent, and views a record of the customer's Web session. If the customer has identified himself or herself, the agent can see the customer's profiles and purchase history on one screen.

EXAMPLES OF WEB SITES WITH INTERACTIVE CALL CENTERS

Giving online customers access to live customer support representatives is important, because it avoids dehumanizing customer contact on the Internet. Rakesh Kaul, chief executive of Hanover Direct, a catalog retailer, in an interview with David M. Rappaport (1998) states: "You have to have that link between the salesman and the customer, not just the computer and the customer. In the catalog world, we have up-selling, where a good representative can offer enough suggestions that 30 percent of the time the customer will buy 30 percent more than intended—a 9 percent average increase in the sale, and just about all of that drops to the bottom line." Following are a few examples of how e-corporations provide live customer interactions via the Web:

- To get shopping help at Lands' End (www.Landsend.com), at the home page, look for Interactive Shopping Aids. From your choice of options, click on Lands' End Live. If you can't find an item, need suggestions, or just get lost on the Web site, you can click on the Lands'

FIGURE 12.4   Geico uses a "call me" button to provide Internet users with almost instant insurance quotes.

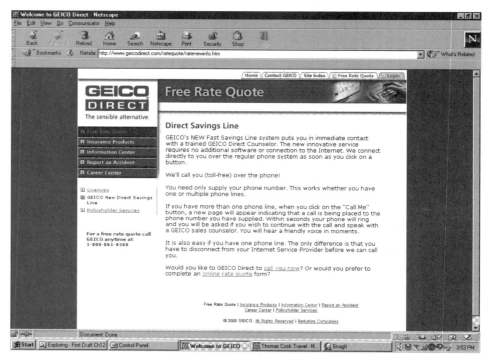

Free Rate Quote screen courtesy of GEICO Direct.

End Live button. Users have their choice of being contacted by telephone (if they have a second phone line or direct connection to the Internet) or by live text-chat.

- To get insurance quotes from Geico Direct (www.geicodirect.com), customers can receive immediate rate quotes for insurance using Web Callback (see Figure 12.4). At the home page, click on Geico New Direct Savings Line to request an instantaneous call from a Geico sales counselor. Key in the telephone number where you can be reached and indicate if you have one or two phone lines. (Web users with one line have to disconnect from the Internet to receive the Geico call.) You can also use the Web Callback option to schedule the agent's call back.

- To get voice help at FTD.com (www.ftd.com), at the home page, click on Help. The Help page allows you to place a free call to FTD over the Internet by using Net2Phone. To place the call, download the free Net2Phone software. Users can place a call to FTD.com from anywhere in the world. After you download the software, click on the Click2Talk icon. At the other end of the line, an FTD agent receives the call as if it were placed by telephone. Talk into your PC's microphone and listen to the customer service agent with your computer's speakers.
- To get help for complex financial transactions at Barclays (www.barclays.co.uk), Barclays has relaunched its personal banking Internet site with an integrated call button facility on the Barclays mortgages pages and new pages for Barclays premier banking and Barclays life.

BUDGETING AND PLANNING YOUR INTERACTION CENTER

At this time, no one Web-based customer support methodology or product is an industry leader. Many large e-corporations plan to develop their own customer interaction centers using in-house sources. Other e-corporations that don't have access to this type of in-house talent plan to purchase software products from several vendors. A primary concern of all e-corporations is cost and the ability to integrate new technologies with existing systems. According to a Yankee Group (2000) survey, nearly three-quarters of companies surveyed plan an active commitment to Web-based customer support in the next 18 months. About a quarter of the respondents felt the cost should be under $100,000. About 20 percent expect costs to be from $100,000 to $1,000,000. Nearly half of the respondents were not sure what a reasonable budget would be.

When planning your Web-based customer support effort, you may want to consider starting with just one page of your Web site or one aspect of Web-based customer service. Continue to include additional Web-based customer service and support features. Keep in mind the customer service and support that exceed customer expectations build customer loyalty. Following are a few examples of the types of technological solutions that may meet your needs. When possible, prices for these products are included; however, all prices listed are subject to change and vary because they are often based on the number of "seats" for customer service personnel in the interaction center and the overall size of the organization.

- Chordiant (www.chordiant.com) is a flexible customer service system that allows live and self-service interactions. Individuals who call more than three times receive priority routing to senior personnel, and screens are created that show the customer's entire history. Chordiant is an eCRM suite that allows, among other things, special shipping opportunities, product mixing, individual pricing, promotions, and changes in customer service options.
- CyberCall (www.atio.com) offers users a callback button that displays a form asking for the user's name and telephone number. The user types in the information, and the Web server sends it to the company's telephone system, which places the message in a queue for the next available agent to put up on his or her screen. A callback tag travels with the user's name and number. The agent also receives a screen pop (computerized customer history or product information that pops up on an agent's screen at the time of the call) of the Web page the customer is viewing, so he or she is ready with information about what is or isn't on the Web page. CyberCall costs $4,995 for ten agents and around $110,000 for call centers with 100 seats.
- Efusion (www.efusion.com) provides e-Bridge, shown in Figure 12.5, which offers voice-enabled Web pages. Users have direct and immediate contact with customer service representatives without having to turn off their computers to use the telephone. The call center can mix Web interactions with calls routed through a traditional ACD. This methodology does not require users to wait for an agent callback. Expect to pay about $50,000 for ten ports.
- eFrontOffice from Clarify (www.clarify.com) provides an integrated call center solution that allows one customer service agent to handle a customer from start to finish with the information at hand. For example, in the past, customer support representatives had to hang up, research company records, and call the customer back. The program routes the customer to the appropriate agent and creates a screen with the right information.

FIGURE 12.5 Efusion offers VoIP (voice over the Internet) technology for instant customer care.

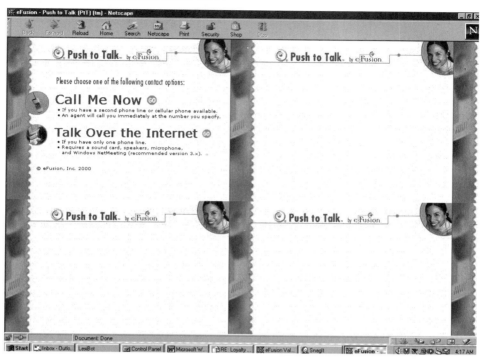

Reproduced with permission from eFusion, Inc.

- Enterprise Interaction Center from Interactive Intelligence (www.in ter-intelli.com) allows agents to view a listing of all the customers' contacts (faxes, phone calls, e-mail, and Internet telephony calls) on one screen. When the agent clicks on the phone icon, his or her telephone rings and he or she can speak to the caller; a click on the fax icon allows the agent to view the fax on-screen.

- Remedy (www.remedy.com) offers a Web-enabled CRM suite that automates sales, marketing, customer support, and quality assurance processes across the organization. Remedy also provides Action Request System 4.0, which consolidates the management of internal operations, and Remedy HelpDesk 4.0, which includes a mail server and integrates problem management, resolution, and other tasks. All products can support multiple media channels. Prices vary, but you can expect to pay at least $10,000 for HelpDesk 4.0.

- Siebel Systems (www.siebel.com) provides a large family of Web-based eCRM enterprise products, including sales, marketing, call centers, field service, and e-commerce. Siebel also makes a point to offer products tailored to small and medium-sized businesses, as well as very large businesses. For example, the Siebel Call Center integrates Siebel Sales Enterprise and Service Enterprise products into one application. Siebel Sales Enterprise is an information system designed to make sales personnel more effective and to shorten the sales cycle. Siebel Service Enterprise assists customer service representatives by providing tools and information for multiple methods of problem resolution. A base version of Siebel Sales Enterprise and Service Enterprise can cost $1,350 per named user.

- SomeOne service (www.netcallplc.com) allows the agent to embed a tag on the Web site that the customer can use to establish voice communication. The customer clicks on the tag, sending a message through the Internet to any telephone system, telling it to set up a call between the agent and the customer. Within several minutes, phones on both sides ring.

- Vantive (www.peoplesoft.com) estimates that 80 to 90 percent of inbound customer service calls involve a type of problem that has been solved before. Knowing the roster of the e-corporation's most common problems, a call center operator can design self-service solutions delivered to the customer via the Web. Vantive is a large CRM suite that runs throughout the enterprise and organizes everything from sales and support to order processing and distribution. The enterprise suite includes five integrated modules. Costs are $30,000 to $50,000 per server, and $2,500 to $3,500 per concurrent user.

- WebCall from Spanlink (www.spanlink.com) offers a "Talk to a Person" button. Users are prompted to enter the telephone number where they can be reached and up to 15 additional pieces of information. The system gives the user an estimated wait time for the callback and queues a virtual request for a customer service representative. WebCall assigns an agent, and the software retrieves the Web page the user was viewing. The price is $15,000. Similar software programs are provided by Answersoft (www.answersoft.com) and Versatility (www.versatility.com).

SUMMING IT UP

- Outstanding customer service is one of the keys to customer loyalty. If you don't provide Web-based customer support and service, you are probably spending too much money, losing prospective customers, and weakening the bonds of customer loyalty.
- You can spend as much as you can or as little as you want for Web-based customer support. You may want to start with just one page of your Web site. Over time, you can expand and fine-tune your support services as you get a better grasp of customer needs.
- Many e-corporations plan to build their own Web-based customer interaction centers; others plan to purchase products from a variety of vendors. Whichever way you go, one thing is certain, a key differentiator between you and your competitors is customer service. It is important now and will become even more important in the next two years.

ACTION PLAN

EVALUATING YOUR WEB-BASED CUSTOMER SERVICE OPTIONS

Assessing your Web-based customer service needs is a qualitative process. There are many technological solutions available, but not all of them are right for your market and e-corporation. To get started in the right direction, complete the following Web-based customer service questionnaire. Read the description of the communication tool. If there is a market need, mark an "X" in the box provided. If implementation for your e-corporation is easy, mark an "X" in the box provided. If purchase and operating costs are within your budgetary guidelines or cost-effective, mark an "X" in the box provided. If the communication tool required is within four training limits, mark an "X" in the box provided. Communication tools with four Xs are must-haves for your organization. Those with three Xs should be thoroughly investigated. And, those with two or fewer Xs have a lower priority but require additional research.

Communication Tool	Market Need	Easy to Implement	Purchase & Operating Costs within Limits	Required Training within Limits
Toll-Free Customer Service Numbers Are familiar to customers but may be costly if your Web site is not designed correctly.	_____	_____	_____	_____
FAQ List Use the most popular questions asked of your customer service agents and sales personnel as the basis for your FAQ list.	_____	_____	_____	_____
Product or Service Information Provide detailed descriptions of your products or services, so that customers do not have to go anywhere else to get the information they need to make a buying decision. Product information can include color photos, manufacturer information, and availability. Include benefits, performance, price, and features.	_____	_____	_____	_____
Web Site Search Engine Discover the keywords customers use to navigate your Web site. Select a Web site search engine that's right for you.	_____	_____	_____	_____
Automatic E-Mail Responses Use an automated e-mail message response program to track and route customer e-mail inquiries to the appropriate individuals. Create instant responses from artificial intelligence or custom-made templates.	_____	_____	_____	_____
Community Building Tools Encourage your customers to talk to one another about your products or services using chat rooms, bulletin boards, or interactive e-mail lists. Make certain these are moderated to reduce confusion and misinformation. (This can reduce customer service costs but can be very labor intensive.)	_____	_____	_____	_____

Communication Tool	Market Need	Easy to Implement	Purchase & Operating Costs within Limits	Required Training within Limits
Live Agent Customer Service Tools Provide live text chat, telephone callbacks, or scheduled chat sessions for customers who use your "call me" icon.	___	___	___	___
Voice over the Internet Customer service agents can talk to Internet users immediately with VoIP (voice over the Internet technology). However, customers must have computers with a sound card, microphone, and speakers.	___	___	___	___
Create a Customer Service Center Dedicate a section of your Web site to customer service and support. Here, customers can ask questions, air concerns, and request help. Include live chat, "call me," or VoIP technology, so customers can ask questions of live agents, view order status, order histories, profiles, and other secure account information.	___	___	___	___

REFERENCES

Bianchi, Alessandra. 1998. Lines of Fire. *Inc.com* (www.inc.com), 15 June.

Customer Relationship Strategies. 1999. *The Yankee Group Report* 1, no. 1 (April): 1–13.

Hubbard, Justin, Gregory Dalton, and Mary E. Thyfault. 1998. Top of the Week: Cover Story—Web-Based Customer Care—Businesses Turn to the Internet to Improve Customer Service and Lower Costs. *Information Week,* 1 June, 18.

Lusher, Carter J., Colleen McCormick Amuso, Donna Fluss, and Scott Nelson. 1997. Technology-Enabled Relationship Management (TERM)—Possibility or Pipedream? *The Journal of Customer Relationships* 5 (www.bentleygroup.com/journal/index.htm), Winter.

McNab, Leslie. 1998. Web-Based Support Leaves the Thinking to the Customer (Online Problem Solving Services on the Internet). *Computer Dealer News,* 1 September, 25–27.

Rappaport, David M. 1998. The Next Wave in Do-It-Yourself Customer Service. *Business Communications Review,* 1 June, 37–42.

Increasing Customer Loyalty with Data Mining

Hidden in your data you may discover benefits that are greater than brand awareness or new products or services. Data mining is the search for *actionable patterns* in customer data. Actionable patterns are those patterns that have a measurable effect on the business. Data mining has been around for a long time, but with today's new technologies and the Internet, information is easier to gather and use to increase the value of your customer base. Paper-based direct mail firms and catalog retailers frequently use data mining for target marketing. Their direct marketing campaigns often use large, cumbersome software applications that require highly trained technicians to distribute coded catalogs or coupons to track repeat purchases. Today, e-corporation customer service representatives, marketing managers, or technology personnel can easily use sophisticated data mining technology with their desktop computers.

Data mining products range from complete inventory management suites to targeted communications with customers using wireless hand-held devices. Winterthur has over one million customers in Spain; more than 130,000 of these customers cancel their automobile insurance policies each year. Winterthur wanted to identify customers who were at risk and keep them. (Retaining customers can significantly lessen operating costs by reducing the cost of underwriting policies for new customers.) Winterthur invited several data mining software companies to produce predictive models from a large data set and tested the predictive models on real, unseen data. The initial data set detailed each car insurance policyholder with a record containing 250 fields. The successful predictive model used only 30 variables and consisted of a combination of neural networks. The model correctly predicted who would cancel their policies for 90 percent of the blind test data. Each customer was given a "likely cancellation" score and ranked. Winterthur found this type of ranking valuable for building customer loyalty and focusing their efforts on retaining customers.

Is using customer information in this fashion an invasion of privacy? Privacy is an unavoidable issue that companies who use data mining have to address. Fair information guidelines suggest giving customers access to information about themselves and allowing them to update and modify their personal profiles. Additionally, the information your e-corporation gathers should be secured from unauthorized access and only be used for the purposes you specify in your privacy statement (for more information about privacy considerations, see Chapter 11).

Kayte VanScoy (2000) points out that despite privacy controversies, business success often depends on data mining. It is likely that in the future all businesses will come to resemble the Web, and data mining will apply to television, cell phones, kiosks, direct advertising, and so on. In this futuristic world, when customers visit your Web site, a real person will appear in a pop-up window. Instead of asking "Where do you want to go today?," the live service representative will ask, "Can I help you select the best product for you?" The service agent will have access to your buying history and personal preferences. The customer service agent will know the scope and context of what you're interested in or what you are researching.

PUTTING YOUR CUSTOMER INFORMATION TO WORK

Data mining uses computerization to discover patterns that reveal insights into your e-corporation's business and customers; in other words, data mining is the process of sifting through large amounts of data to discover actionable patterns in the data. For e-corporations, data mining assists in determining the right message to send to the right customer at the right time. For example, a cellular company was surprised to learn that their best and most valuable customers were often the ones who made the most complaints to customer service representatives.

Matt Cutler and Jim Sterne (2000) point out that e-business is real-time business, and using your Web site data can assist you in seeing marketplace trends as they happen. For example, a banner ad placed on a portal site generates click-through statistics almost immediately; improved Web site navigation changes shopping cart activity; and the impact of breaking news or press releases on the company's brand or bottom line can be measured within hours. The business world is shifting its focus from production, distribution, and gaining market share to focusing on customer needs and gaining "wallet share." For example, one of the traditional ways of measuring increases was to compare last year's sales to the current year. Today, success is measured by determining if the business increased its share of a certain customer's potential buying capacity; in other words, did the e-corporation gain a bigger part of the customer's budget or wallet share?

The challenge today is to enrich the customer's online buying experience and build intelligence into Web sites, making them "stickier." Developing Web site stickiness and customer loyalty is important to your overall strategy. Figure 13.1 shows why and how measuring hits or page views on your Web site is not a good metric for forecasting revenue. In general, this illustration shows why gross Web site statistics do not indicate customer behavior.

Figure 13.1 is an example of data volume measured in Web site hits. The example company has 100,000,000 hits. A high or low number of Web site hits may be due to Web site design; yet this number is often used to form a broad foundation for more complex measurements. Your e-corporation's data on page views, visits, and users are valuable in a general sense but don't provide any insight into common customer characteristics or

FIGURE 13.1   Determining What Web Site Data to Measure

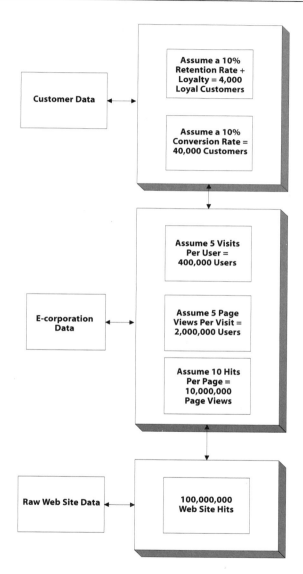

Source: Adapted from Matt Cutler and Jim Sterne, "E-Metrics: Business Metrics for the New Economy," Net Genesis and Target Marketing of Santa Barbara, Net Genesis Corporation (www.net-gen.com/emetrics), 3 July 2000.

unique customer needs. According to e-corporation information, the example company has 400,000 users. Your e-corporation's data increase in value as the data are managed and focused on customer activities. Focusing on customer data and using the knowledge of the e-corporation, the conversion rate and retention rate of customers can be determined. In the example, out of 10,000,000 Web site hits the Company estimates there are 4,000 loyal customers.

Today's technology takes this information one step further. Data analysis software integrates and analyzes purchase transactions, page-viewing patterns, declared interests, and other external data down to the smallest detail. This information is used for the "individualization" of your Web site; in other words, you can deliver highly individualized content to each individual user, prospect, or customer. Today's data mining technologies provide you with insights about:

- *Customer targeting.* Directing promotions, messages, and content to each unique user
- *Product affinity analysis.* Discovering the best cross-selling and up-selling opportunities for each customer
- *Price optimization.* Targeting price points for each product and customer
- *Market basket analysis.* Identifying the products to promote to each customer in order to maximize transaction size

With this technology, it is easy to see how the bonds of customer loyalty can be strengthened, especially when customer loyalty is defined as "a state of mind that occurs in a customer when a company fully delivers and often exceeds on its promise to the customers." Therefore you'll find it useful to:

- Identify case examples of loyalty customers.
- Determine the metrics that reflect loyalty based on the cases you have identified.
- Discover if these metrics of customer loyalty are being captured in your company's databases.
- Evaluate meaningful units of comparison by customer segments (discussed later in this chapter).

CAPTURING THE RIGHT DATA

Capturing data and using it in the right way is often more difficult than it sounds. Kayte VanScoy provides a few examples of how companies can get lost in the maze of data terabytes:

- *Some companies ignore or abandon their most useful data.* For example, a catalog company only held six months of data so they were missing all of their seasonal information.
- *Many corporations just need to look at their data in a different way.* For example, Victoria's Secret had an ongoing inventory shortage problem with underwear. Using MicroStrategy software (www.micro strategy.com), the firm soon discovered that customers in the Northeast like brightly colored underwear, and individuals from the Southwest preferred neutral colors.

The story of HomeRuns.com (www.homeruns.com) shows how data mining builds customer loyalty. HomeRuns.com provides Internet grocery shopping to thousands of time-starved families. The firm is committed to providing busy wage earners with the right products and services at the right price and to delivering at the right time. With new data mining tools, HomeRuns.com can now transform volumes of day-to-day customer data into information that allows the e-corporation to fine-tune their customer online shopping experience, build customer loyalty, and ultimately increase company profits.

LOYALTY MARKETING SUCCESS STORY

HomeRuns.com

▼ **COMPANY:** HomeRuns.com was one of the first Internet grocers serving the Boston market. When HomeRuns.com began its e-corporation in 1996, customer acquisition was their top priority. Acquiring customers costs five times as much as retaining its 40,000 current customers; therefore, maintaining or increasing market share by increasing customer satisfaction and building customer loyalty is the firm's key to business success.

▼ **SOLUTION:** HomeRuns.com had five years of customer and order information available to begin building its customer loyalty approach and increasing its value proposition to the customer. Over a six-month period, the firm selected and implemented all of the components of an eCRM system aimed at this effort.

▼ **BENEFITS:** Using data mining tools, HomeRuns.com can now boost satisfaction, improve its customers' shopping experience, and strengthen the bonds of customer loyalty. The advantages of its data mining solution include:

- Allowing the firm to identify affinities between products and purchasers, so the firm can optimize customer satisfaction
- Enabling HomeRuns.com to study customer purchase patterns, so it can offer faster service
- Letting the firm suggest products that the customer hadn't purchased lately to personalize the buying experience and build customer loyalty
- Enabling the firm to increase customer convenience by suggesting substitutions for products that are not available, based on past purchase information

▼ **TECHNOLOGY:** HomeRuns.com wanted software tools that were consistent with its existing systems. The firm chose Microsoft NT hardware and Microsoft SQL Server 7.0 as its target warehouse. Business Objects was selected for reporting and ad hoc analysis. The firm selected Data Stage, because it "off-loaded" the analysis of purchase behavior from the operational systems. The e-corporation managers were able to run potentially large queries at the data warehouse without impacting customers using the online production environment.

Source: Adapted from "HomeRuns.com Takes Internet Grocery Shopping to the Next Level with a Data Warehouse to Understand, Fine-Tune, and Personalize the Online Experience." *Data Warehousing What Works?* 9 (2000) 28–29.

FIGURE 13.2   HomeRuns.com shows that building customer loyalty can reduce operating costs.

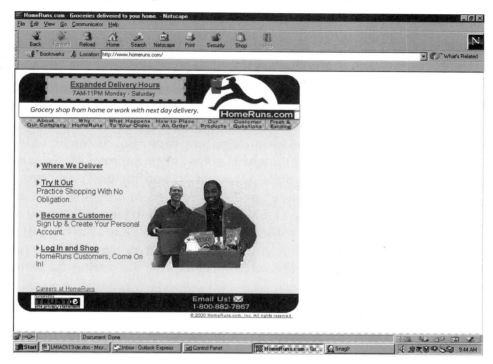

BUILDING YOUR DATA MINING APPROACH

VanScoy (2000) notes that while customer information is a valuable resource, most e-corporations quickly discover that it isn't easy to use this resource for sales opportunities. For example, by using drip irrigation questioning you know the birthday of each of your online customers. To strengthen the bonds of customer loyalty and to encourage return visits to your Web site, you send a birthday greeting that includes a special offer. This sounds like a straightforward proposition, but execution of your sales promotion isn't easy. Figure 13.3 shows how executing this sales plan requires several types of data mining technological solutions (details of the software solutions example are discussed later in this chapter):

- *Information capture and data routing.* Information can be captured by requesting users to complete surveys or participate in contests, or by requiring Web site registration. This information is stored using database software such as Oracle, IBM, MicroStrategy, and Infomix. Selected database information is then tagged and routed to data analysis. Figure 13.3 shows how the raw customer information is now routed to data analysis. This example points out that management must make some decision regarding capturing customer information.
- *Data analysis.* Data analysis software programs look for actionable patterns and statistical information and include programs such as SAS Enterprise Miner, eHNC's Content Mining software, and Net-Genesis NetAnalysis. Using the example in Figure 13.3, you may discover that 20 percent of your customer base has a birthday in January. Using data analysis, you may also discover that for three years in a row a spouse purchased flowers for his wife during the week of her birthday.
- *Rules creation.* Data then go to customer relationship programs, which create rules that apply to the customer base. Customer relationship management programs include Siebel, E.piphany E.4, Personify, and Pivotal. Using the example in Figure 13.3, the rule could be "Send a discount coupon in December for customers who buy flowers in January."
- *Rules application.* Your e-corporation's market analyst then puts rules in a content management program, such as Vignette's StoryServer or Art Technology Group Dynamo Personalization Server. The system creates a 10 percent discount offer for floral arrangements and sends it to the customer.
- *Greeting card and sales promotion launched.* The customer receives a greeting card and sales promotion by e-mail; on his wireless pager, cell phone, or other handheld device; by U.S. mail; or as a personalized greeting when he logs on to your Web site.

FIGURE 13.3   The Process of Turning Data Mining into Sales

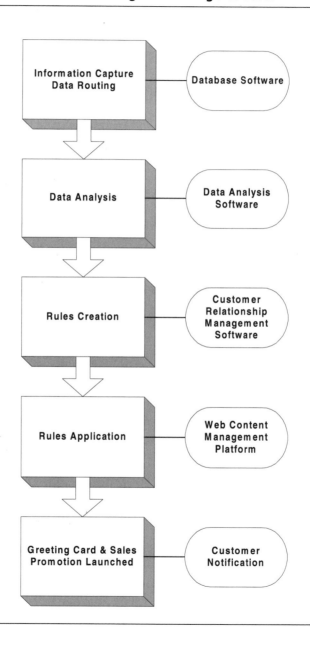

VanScoy observes that data mining software comes in all sorts of combinations, often with promises that just one product will meet all your needs. Consequently, you may find it helpful to select the right type of technological solution by looking at the software vendor's success stories. Locate a company that has goals similar to yours and discover how the software application assisted that e-corporation in achieving its objectives. Prices can start at $50,000, and the average price for complete systems is around $500,000. Keep in mind that inexpensive technological solutions may have hidden costs. For example, a top-notch data mining solution may look inexpensive until you have to upgrade all your computers and other software. (For more about data mining applications, see the end of this chapter.)

SEGMENTING YOUR CUSTOMER BASE FOR FUN AND PROFIT

Knowing which customers are your best and worst can assist you in focusing your efforts where they will count the most. Even if you sell only one product, it is likely that you do not have a homogeneous customer base. Segmenting your customer base attempts to identify distinct subgroups in your audience and to assess their unique needs and desires. Knowing your best customers can assist your e-corporation in focusing on the Web site features and content that will serve your high-value customers.

Loyal customers with the most value are not only bound to your products or services but also to your company. (Think about all the Harley-Davidson tattoos you've seen. A tattoo of a company logo shows real company loyalty.) These are the customers who are willing to recommend your products or services to other individuals. In the virtual world, loyalty can also mean high dollar purchases and recent and frequent visits to your Web site. For example, a customer who visits an automobile Web site once a day for a month is more likely to purchase a car than a customer who makes less frequent visits. Consequently, it is reasonable to divide your online customer base into 125 cells, using the three dimensions of recency, frequency, and monetary value, or RFM. (You can still add other dimensions you feel are important.)

According to Matt Cutler and Jim Sterne, segmenting your customer base in this manner can assist you in identifying your very best customers:

- *Recency.* Statistical analysis indicates that customers who recently made a purchase are likely to make a repeat purchase. Recency is a measure of how long it has been since the user last visited the Web site or made a purchase. In comparison to frequency and monetary value, recency is considered the strongest indicator of future behavior.
- *Frequency.* Repeat purchasers are likely to continue purchasing in the future. Frequency may mean different things to different Web sites. For retail Web sites, a customer who buys flowers four times a year may be considered a loyal customer when compared to other customers who only make two purchases per year. For Web sites with big-ticket items, a few visits that increase in frequency indicate the customer is getting ready to make a purchase.
- *Monetary value.* Customers who are big spenders are likely to make more high-volume purchases. A customer is considered high value even if he or she makes large purchases infrequently. Monetary value indicates your customer's total spending and the e-corporation's profitability. Another way to describe this dimension is "yield."

Figure 13.4 shows a visualization of customer segmentation. In this example, customers are given a score of 1 to 5 with 5 having the highest value for recency, frequency, and monetary value. The math works this way: in RFM Cell 111 the recency score is 1, the frequency score is 1, and the monetary value score is 1, for an overall score of 3. These are your worst customers, who haven't been to your Web site recently, are not frequent visitors, and don't make a lot of purchases. In contrast, customers in RFM Cell 555 are your best customers. They are recent visitors and score 5; they also score 5 for coming to your Web site often, and another 5 for buying your products or services. The total score for a best customer is 15.

With the customer base divided in this manner, you can see how you need to provide different levels of customer service to different customers. Additionally, you can now work on ways to sell and support customers in, say, RFM Cell 255 or RFM Cell 511. Keep in mind that your Web site may use different indexes, such as duration, to predict the likelihood of repeat purchases.

FIGURE 13.4   Visualizing How to Segment Your Customer Base

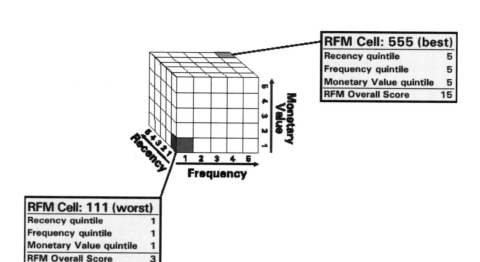

Matt Cutler and Jim Sterne point out that in combination, recency, frequency, monetary value, and duration show a detailed picture of how an individual customer interacts with the Web site. However, duration is a two-edged sword. Customers who spend a lot of time at your Web site are likely to make more purchases. Or customers may spend a lot of time at your Web site due to poor Web site design and navigation difficulties. In addition, the duration of the average customer's visit often varies by type of Web site. Following are a few examples:

- *Duration and technology Web sites.* Customers tell technology e-corporations over and over again that they only want product information and not entertainment or community. Online customers want fast-loading pages, so they can make a decision and move on.
- *Duration and consumer Web sites.* Customers at consumer Web sites want good online search capabilities and are often willing to spend time looking for the right CD, book, or piece of apparel. However, once they make their purchase decisions, they want to leave quickly, making express checkout a market requirement.

- *Duration and Web sites with high-ticket items.* Longer stays often indicate that the user has a high interest in purchasing the automobile or other pricey item. In contrast, users that only stay for a few minutes are just browsing.

Customer segmentation allows you to identify each customer, so you can see what *influences* that customer and so you can *profile* the potential value of the customer. Additionally, you can develop customer classifications and target what is unique about a customer. Next, you can design relationship rules for different customer segments to optimize the value of that uniqueness. When you implement these rules, at different points of customer interaction, you can analyze the outcomes. Based on this analysis you can adjust your assessment of the potential value of the customer. For example, let's say your latest analysis indicates that a customer was incorrectly categorized in the first customer segmentation analysis and doesn't belong in the best customer classification. This second analysis also may indicate that a customer who was ranked as low value deserves to be reclassified as a high-value customer.

DESIGNING YOUR DATA MINING REQUIREMENTS

There is a general sequence to developing an understanding of your e-corporation's data mining requirements. The following seven steps shows how you can focus on the customer information that matters to your e-corporation:

1. Establish the goals and requirements of your e-corporation's data mining initiative. Define what functionalities, benefits, and performance standards you *require.* Make another list of the functionalities, benefits, and performance standards you *desire.*
2. Define the scope, boundaries, and limits of your data mining initiative. For example, you may not need to analyze your entire customer base every time you make a decision.
3. Prioritize your key elements and performance requirements. Rank your priorities on a scale of one to five. For example, five is a need,

four is high desire, three is a want, two is acceptable in the background, and one is dispensable, if required.

4. Define what interrelationships you want to analyze, such as recency, frequency, and monetary value. Determine what's essential or what's desirable.

5. In laying out your data mining initiative, define your constraints, which may include operating platforms, network designs, costs, timing, and so on.

6. Break the total data mining initiative into smaller independent subsystems, such as those used in this chapter (database, knowledge management tools, eCRM software, and Web site content management).

7. For each independent subsystem, determine your performance targets and decide how you'll monitor performance. In addition, establish data mining interface standards and timing–cost limits. (Software vendors can often provide you with the type of technical documentation you'll need for decision making.)

CHOOSING THE RIGHT DATA MINING SOLUTION

Your data mining solution may require the integration of several software products. Clinton Wilder (1999), a writer for *Information Week*, provides this information about MatchLogic, a good example of a company that has successfully completed its data mining initiative. MatchLogic of Westminster, Colorado (www.matchlogic.com), provides integrated marketing services to help advertisers such as Charles Schwab, Dell Computers, General Motors, and Proctor & Gamble orchestrate online advertising campaigns. MatchLogic maintains three primary databases of information gathered through Web sites:

1. One database consists of anonymous data about an Internet user's computer. (These data are collected as visitors click through your Web sites, click on ads, ask for a brochure, or purchase goods, etc.) The MatchLogic research and analysis database currently collects data on 160 million users per day.

2. The second database includes these data in summarized (or aggregated) form and are used for reporting purposes, such as judging the effectiveness of a particular ad campaign for a client.
3. The third database has "self-reported" data, information freely supplied by about 6 million people through Web-site registrations, sweepstakes entry forms, and responses to e-mail campaigns. MatchLogic uses this information to build 57 million demographic profiles for its clients to use for advertising campaigns that target specific individuals with common characteristics, such as age, geography, and income.

MatchLogic uses an Oracle database to store the data and DataStage for knowledge management processes (extraction, transformation, and loading) and for directing the data from collection points to the databases. MatchLogic also uses data analysis software from SAS Institute Inc. and Oracle Discoverer for ad hoc queries and to generate internally developed reports. The company uses Sun Enterprise 4000 and 6000 servers to support its efforts.

Figure 13.5 provides an overview of the types of software applications and a few examples of solutions that are available for data mining.

Below you'll find more information about the computer applications listed in Figure 13.5. You may find these technological solutions useful for turning your Web site into a channel for sales, customer service, and information gathering. These products can assist you in understanding customer behaviors, preferences, and how your customers perceive the products or services you offer. Prices listed vary by number of users and size of the organization. Prices can start at $50,000, and the average price for a complete system is around $500,000. Any listed prices are subject to change.

Databases

Oracle 8i (www.oracle.com). Oracle 8i allows traditional files to be stored and managed by the database. It also removes the need for operating systems, such as Windows 2000, by joining with Sun Microsystems to create an Intel-based server, called the Oracle 8i appliance, which includes an Oracle database and its own simple operating system. Some claim that

FIGURE 13.5   Classifications and Examples of Data Mining Solutions

Online Project Development

Data Mining Category	Examples of a Technological Solution
Database	• Oracle 8i
	• IBM DB2 Version 7
	• MicroStrategy 7
	• Infomix Internet Foundation 2000
	• Microsoft SQL Server 7
Knowledge Management Tool	• SAS Enterprise Miner
	• eHNC Content Mining™
	• NetGenesis NetAnalysis
Customer Relationship Management	• Siebel .COM
	• E.piphany E.4
	• Personify Essentials
	• Pivotal eRelationship 2000
Web Content Management	• Vignette StoryServer
	• Art Technology Group Dynamo Personalization Server

the Oracle 8i appliance is a less-expensive and less-complex alternative to a database that runs on NT, because it minimizes the cost and complication of the operating system. Pricing starts at around $18,000.

IBM DB2 Version 7 (www.ibm.com). DB2 Version 7 Universal Database Enterprise Edition is a multiuser, object-relational database for complex configurations and large database needs for Intel Unix platforms. It is designed for midsize to large businesses. Version 7 includes Object-Relational Database engine (multiple users), Multimedia Support–DB2 Extenders (runtime), Replication Support–DataPropagator, Relational

Extended GUI Administration Tools, Client Pack (all supported platforms), NetData, Lotus Domino Go Webserver, and Host Connectivity–
DB2 Connect (for multiple connections). Pricing is about $5,000 for five
users.

MicroStrategy 7 (www.microstrategy.com). MicroStrategy 7 uses collaborative analytics by a built-in analytical engine working with a data-
warehouse-processing capability to speed queries and get more accurate
answers. The software also performs advanced data-set analysis within its
core analytical engine for such applications as customer segmentation. The
new version is more scalable and provides new caching, personalization,
and security features. Pricing begins at $30,000 per server CPU and $15,000
per Web server CPU.

Infomix Internet Foundation 2000 (www.infomix.com). Infomix Internet Foundation 2000 provides a complete and extensible data management platform that enables organizations to manage their data while
providing the ability to quickly publish business data to the Internet and
support Internet-based applications or services.

Microsoft SQL Server 7 (www.microsoft.com). Microsoft SQL Server
Version 7.0 is a database built on the foundation established by SQL Server
Version 6.5 Relational Database Management System (RDBMS). According
to the manufacturer, customer needs and requirements have driven significant product innovations in ease of use, reliability, and scalability and data
warehousing. Pricing starts at around $1,399 for five users.

Knowledge Management Tools

SAS Enterprise Miner (www.sas.com). SAS Enterprise Miner is a
graphical data mining solution that operates on Windows 95, Windows
NT, AIX, HP-UX, Digital Unix, and Sun Solaris platforms. Enterprise
Miner includes integrated data mining and warehousing capabilities that
can create data mining data marts for direct input into the software.

eHNC Content Mining (www.ehnc.com). The eHNC Content Mining software uses SelectProfile, a marketing automation product able to segment so finely that it makes one-to-one marketing practical. The use of eHNC's real-time profiling in concert with Content Mining™—the ability to read, understand, and make decisions from unstructured text data—enables SelectProfile's precision and insight.

NetGenesis (www.netgen.com). NetGenesis NetAnalysis software is a Web site usage analysis package that reports useful facts and statistics about those accessing a Web site. It can tell you how many individual users have visited, whether changes to the site are affecting usage positively or negatively, which advertising links are working most effectively for you, and which parts of the site are most visited by overseas users.

Customer Relationship Management Software

Siebel .COM (www.siebel.com). Siebel .COM Applications enable organizations to leverage the Internet to acquire new customers and enhance customer relationships. By implementing Siebel .COM Applications, companies can create and execute Internet-based marketing campaigns to identify and acquire new customers; develop customized product and service offerings that meet customers' unique requirements and expectations; facilitate unassisted selling over the Internet; and provide effective customer service and support. Siebel .COM Applications include six modules that use dynamic rules-based personalization engines, enabling organizations to display targeted content based on customer profiles.

E.piphany E4 (www.epiphany.com). E.piphany E.4 for e-commerce captures and analyzes customer information from internal and external systems. For example, it integrates customer data captured on a Web site with financial data that resides within an internal enterprise resource planning system. According to company officials, by combining this critical information, companies can better measure online campaign effectiveness, identify what content converts prospects into buyers, and segment customers based on online behavior. E.piphany E.4 for e-commerce consists of

16 Web-analytic applications for reporting and analysis, distributed data-base marketing, and Web commerce. Pricing begins at $250,000.

Personify Essentials (www.personify.com). Personify Essentials was designed for the Web as a profiling and analytical platform. The software transforms clickstream data (the path of pages and links followed by a user during a Web site visit), online transactions and registrations, and offline data into unique, comprehensive profiles for your e-corporation's entire Web audience. These visitor profiles can assist you in developing statistical analysis and reports.

Pivotal eRelationship 2000 (www.pivotal.com). Pivotal eRelation-ship 2000 is a way for companies to extend their customer knowledge base to their entire enterprise and to unite sales, marketing, and service with external customers, partners, and suppliers. Pivotal eRelationship 2000 includes three modules (employees, sales and service partners, and cus-tomers). Changes made to the enterprise database through Pivotal's Web Client are available to LAN-based users and are automatically sent to mobile users through the relationship data synchronization process. Sim-ilarly, changes made by enterprise users are available to Pivotal's Web Cli-ent users. The virtual customer knowledge base that Web Client creates provides everyone in the organization with access to up-to-the-minute information. Companies have the option of purchasing Relationship LAN, Mobile, or Web Client licenses, each priced separately.

Web Site Content Management

Vignette StoryServer (www.vignette.com). Vignette's StoryServer is a database-driven, template-based Web site publishing system. StorySer-ver stores content and graphic elements in a database, and as visitors re-quest a page, the content is "poured" on the fly into design templates. Prices begin at $40,000 for the basic installation.

Art Technology Group Dynamo Personalization Server (www.atg .com). Dynamo Personalization Server is a rule-driven personalization platform. The Personalization Server is designed to target specific content to a particular user (or group of users) based on business rules created by the e-corporation. It combines explicit user data from existing marketing databases with implicit information gathered on user behavior, technical platform information, and other sources of data to adjust every element of content seen by an end-user at the time of the request.

SUMMING IT UP

- Keeping track of Web site statistics is not very valuable for predicting customer behavior. If you want to know who your best customers are, you'll have to do a little data mining.
- If you want to use customer information to create sales opportunities, you may have to purchase as many as four different types of data mining solutions (database, data analysis, rules creation, and rule application).
- The best way to know your customers individually is to sort them into customer segments. If you use just three dimensions (recency, frequency, and monetary value), with each dimension having a score of one to five, you'll have 125 categories of customers.
- Designing your mining requirements can assist you in making the best decisions for technological solutions. Be wary of vendors who provide blurry definitions; you may not receive what you expected. Ask software vendors for success stories and see how they solved the problems of an e-corporation that is similar to yours.

FOCUSING ON THE ISSUES OF DATA MINING IN YOUR E-CORPORATION

Implementing an eCRM data mining project is time consuming and expensive, and requires a commitment from all personnel. The following questions are designed to assist you in focusing on the issues, hurdles, and metrics of data mining in your e-corporation and can help you understand if your eCRM data mining initiatives are "working."

1. What are four reasons to implement data mining in your e-corporation?

2. Who are your chief competitors using data mining?

3. How are these e-corporations using data mining?

4. How do you plan to reach customers on the Web who are constantly changing?

5. What technologies will you use to identify your customers' buying patterns?

6. How will you gain an understanding of your customers' preferences?

7. What proportion of customers in each segment have purchased within each product or service category?

8. What are the biggest obstacles to data mining your customer data?

9. Do you have to consolidate the information in several types of databases?

10. How can you make certain that information in your database is correct?

11. What percentage of high-value customers has been acquired compared to the potential prospect population?

12. How can data mining help you retain customers and improve customer loyalty?

13. How many previously inactive customers have been enticed to purchase again?

14. How can you track your improvements over time?

REFERENCES

Conway, Kelly D., Julie M. Fitzpatrick, and Ellice D. Uffer. 1999. Building Customer Loyalty: Letter from the Editors. *Journal of Customer Relationships* 10 (Spring) (www.eloyalty co.com/journal/body.htm).

Cutler, Matt, and Jim Sterne. 2000. E-Metrics: Business Metrics for the New Economy. NetGenesis and Target Marketing of Santa Barbara, NetGenesis Corporation (www.net gen.com/emetrics), 3 July.

IntelliQuest World Wide Internet/Online Tracking Study Q3, 1998. 1999. Online publication of IntelliQuest (www.intelliquest.com).

Quinn, James Brian, Jordan J. Baruch, and Karen Anne Zien. 1996. Software-Based Innovation. *Sloan Management Review,* 22 June, 11–35.

Sweat, Jeff, 2000. Customer Knowledge: The Well-Rounded Consumer—Companies Must Strive for a Complete View of Their Customers as the Relationship Shifts from Commerce to Collaboration. *Information Week,* 10 April, 44–52.

VanScoy, Kayte. 2000. Get Inside Your Customer's Heads (and Their Wallets Too). *Smart Money* (www.zdnet.com/ecommerce/stories/), 16 May.

Whiting, Rick, and Jeff Sweat. 1999. Trends: Business Intelligence—Profitable Customers—Businesses Are Using IT to Identify High-Yield Clients and Formulating New Strategies for Dealing with Those That Aren't. *Information Week,* 29 March, 44–50.

Wilder, Clinton. 1999. Trends: Web Data—Tapping the Pipeline—Web Sites Can Offer a Wealth of Customer Data; Smart Companies Are Mining, Analyzing, and Acting on It for Competitive Advantage. *Information Week,* 15 March, 38–53.

14

Developing eCRM Projects

Established less than five years ago, Amazon.com is considered a mature business. The innovative company shattered all the business models and put other online booksellers on the defensive. The same can be said of Dell to Compaq, Charles Schwab to Merrill Lynch, and Cisco to its industry. These e-corporations are built on customer relationships and loyalty. Companies of all sizes want to move forward in this direction and use the Internet to extend their customer relationships; however, most companies have customer-related information scattered throughout their organizations. Incomplete customer knowledge can cost you opportunities, sales, or the loyalty of your customers. Having a blurry picture of customer preferences and purchasing histories makes marketing ineffective with the Internet's savvy customers who have many choices and are demanding better, more personalized products and services.

For companies with a Web presence, the back-office infrastructure is often not in place to accommodate a high level of online demand. The goal of all e-corporations is to achieve a "holistic" view of the customer and an integrated interaction that includes all the company's major divisions (sales, marketing, customer service, project management, and distribution). Most corporations have customer information scattered throughout the organization in three, four, five, or even ten different databases. Each database captures different aspects of the customer's relationship with the organization. This isolated information prevents companies from having a real-time, accurate, single view of the customer, so personnel are equipped to respond appropriately and can offer personalized service. Consolidating your information in a way that allows access by all parts of your e-corporation facilitates a 360-degree view of the consumer that can result in a satisfied customer. It will also create a positive attitude toward the corporation, encourage repeat purchases, generate greater-than-average transaction values, stimulate higher rates of customer retention, lengthen and increase customer lifetime values, and build customer loyalty.

Many companies believe that nonquantitative results, such as improved customer relationships, create strong bonds with customers. Customer loyalty increases as the consumer begins to feel that the company knows him or her and values his or her individual business. Companies that implement eCRM solutions are frequently seeking opportunities for an immediate return on investment. This return on investment can come in the form of cost savings, shorter customer buying cycle times, mass-customized products and services, and automated fulfillment. The real benefits of eCRM and customer loyalty over the long term are the increased value of the customer base.

IDENTIFYING THE ELEMENTS OF YOUR INTERNET TRANSITION

As we begin the new millennium, it seems nearly impossible to discern exactly what customers want from one day to the next, and e-corporations aren't exactly certain about what they will be creating. Under these circumstances, it is difficult to tell what market opportunity windows will open.

Consequently, in the e-commerce environment it is difficult to develop a long-term strategy. In this market, e-corporations founded only five years ago are considered mature, online veterans. What e-corporations do know is that customers want the "Five As":

1. Any volume
2. Anytime
3. Anybody
4. Anywhere
5. Anything

In the e-commerce marketplace, companies have to deliver a wide array of new products and services in unlimited combinations to capture and satisfy the needs and desires of smaller and smaller market niches. This requires flexible, responsive, and rapid-learning strategies. E-corporations also will need to facilitate customer relationships and experiment with new products and processes.

Using the elements of the Strategic Service Vision can assist you in completing a smooth, or at least a less-disruptive, transition to the Internet (see Chapter 3). The Strategic Service Vision, when adapted to e-corporations, can combine both marketing and operating functions and assist in a value-cost leveraging situation—and bigger profits. The four relationships of the Strategic Service Vision can be adapted for the e-commerce environment in the following manner:

1. *The e-service delivery system.* Envision what features are important to your e-business in terms of the organization, capacity, technology, and competitive strategy.
2. *The e-operating strategy.* Determine what elements of the strategy are important, so the company can focus its efforts and measure its success.
3. *The eCRM service concept.* Gain an understanding of what the customer perceives as a good online buying experience and determine how the organization can provide that experience.

4. *Targeting e-market segments.* Identify the various segments of the customer base, determine the importance of each segment, and single out each customer's unique needs.

These four steps of the e-commerce approach to the Strategic Service Vision are straightforward and easy to understand. Each step is detailed in this chapter and can assist you in navigating the transition to an e-corporation.

CREATING YOUR E-CORPORATION'S SERVICE DELIVERY SYSTEM

The Yankee Group (1999) points out that e-commerce is not just for Web-based newcomers. The Internet has matured beyond the early adopter stage, and large corporations are going online, building their e-businesses and "returning fire" against dot-com start-ups that pose a threat to their enterprises. Most companies define e-commerce as the redesign of processes spanning the entire organization. This is a lot more than just using the Internet as one way to approach markets and customers. The Internet is not just another way to sell products or services; it is a profoundly different experience. The Internet is about customer choice, freedom, and control. In other words, e-corporations must reinvent their businesses in a manner that produces positive results by blending marketing skills, technology, and business know-how.

In this stage of developing your Internet transition strategy, you'll need to define the vision, initiatives, and intended results of your e-corporation. Keep in mind your business goals, environment, and market position. Figure 14.1 is a list of 16 questions designed to help stimulate discussion. At this early stage, you will not have nearly the information you need to answer most of the questions; therefore, it's OK to make your best guess. If any of these questions opens a significant gap in your understanding of the e-corporation's Service Delivery System Vision, make note of it and research the topic.

FIGURE 14.1   E-strategic Service Vision Delivery System Questionnaire

---

Questions for Discussion

1. What are the key business drivers or competitive advantages to going online? Briefly summarize.

2. What are the key cultural issues that are not apparent on the proposed Web site that may affect your organization? (Outline them in a few words.)

3. What are your e-corporation's key success criteria for the next three years? (Think in terms of your ability to innovate your e-corporation's product or service, increase sales growth, and provide better customer service.)

4. What are your high-level business problems and how will you address them with your e-corporation? (Concisely describe.)

5. What are the opportunities you hope to take advantage of with your e-corporation? (Describe in a few words.)

6. What makes you want to take your business online?

7. What are the primary benefits of taking your business online?

8. What does your ideal e-corporation look like?

9. In your organization, who are the key people and what is their stake in taking the company online?

10. What is the availability of the individuals listed in Question #9 to contribute to the transition process?

11. Has anyone in your organization even been involved in implementing an e-corporation before?

12. What corporate computer infrastructure is in place? (Include networking, remote access, e-mail, and other major applications.)

13. How much will it cost and how long will it take to bring your company online? (Quickly estimate.)

14. How will you evaluate different vendors?

15. What are some of the key criteria that you will use to make your technology selections?

16. Do you have a schedule for your evaluation and implementation? What are the key milestones that will drive the overall schedule?

ORGANIZING YOUR E-OPERATING STRATEGY

Your e-corporation needs to align its business strategy, corporate culture and organization, customer data, and supporting information technologies, so that each time a customer visits your Web site, you can promote a mutually beneficial relationship. This, in turn, builds customer loyalty, reduces customer acquisition costs, and provides cross-selling and up-selling opportunities. Your Strategic Service Delivery Vision (discussed earlier) brings all these factions together through diligence and consensus building.

Once you have developed your Service Delivery System Vision, you'll need to focus on an operating strategy and support system. Here, you'll have to address work flow, process, and operations in the different functional areas of your e-corporation. For example, is one of the following five elements more important than the others in your vision of your new e-corporation?

1. *Online sales.* Increase sales revenue.
2. *Online marketing.* Acquire profitable customers.
3. *Online customer service.* Increase customer retention.
4. *Online project management.* Increase cross-selling and up-selling.
5. *Online distribution and suppliers.* Reduce operating costs.

The five elements listed are just a few examples of the elements that can be important to your e-corporation's operating strategy. Other elements, such as financing, human resources, control, and organization, may be at the top of your list.

Deciding Where to Concentrate Your Efforts

When determining your operating strategy, it is important to consider what online capabilities you'll need to support the level of customer loyalty you are seeking (see Chapter 3). You'll also need to pay attention to how you can differentiate your e-corporation's customer service and support from others, and how you can provide barriers to entry by competitors and manage intangibles, such as brand management, content, trust, reliability, security, and privacy, in an e-commerce environment.

At this point, you'll want to determine where you should concentrate your efforts. You may want to begin by gaining an understanding of your current technological infrastructure and evaluating what is needed to make the company e-customer centric. For example, you can evaluate each of the five functional areas in terms of what type of technological support is required for your e-corporation:

1. *Online sales.* Do you need to manage groups of contacts or companies? Do sales personnel use wireless devices that need to be synchronized with a central database or integrated with your contact center?

2. *Online marketing.* How are you managing your opportunities? Do you need better integration with the sales department? How can you tell if your online marketing campaigns are working? What marketing functions need to be automated?

3. *Online customer service.* Do you have or need a shared corporate knowledge base? What are the key reports you require? What fax and e-mail management do you need? How are you going to manage call avoidance or eliminate unnecessary service calls?

4. *Online project development.* How are projects being managed? Do you need real-time access to statistics? What type of data do you need to gather? How are you going to personalize your interactions with customers?

5. *Online distribution and suppliers.* What quality assurance, inventory control, and order management do you need to support online sales? What is the order fulfillment process?

Developing a good support system is important or even critical in your e-operating strategy. Be wary of independently developed eCRM capabilities that focus on the short-term needs of different divisions within your organization. To be successful, you'll need end-to-end eCRM that integrates all your corporate functions; however, this doesn't mean you can't start in one department and work out from there. When deciding where to make capital investments, remember that you want to support your company's transition to a customer-centric way of doing business. Individuals throughout your organization must have access to a set of capabilities necessary to plan and manage customer interactions or customer touch points.

Identifying Likely Technological Solutions

In the past, you may have evaluated each of your company's major divisions in terms of staffing requirements, profitability, or capital expenditures. In planning your e-operating strategy, the next step is focusing on where you'll make capital investments. Think in terms of work flow, processes, and management. What are the limitations of your current system and what do you need for your e-corporation? Figure 14.2 provides a few examples of the types of eCRM solutions that are available for each of the corporation's major functional areas.

When looking over the examples in Figure 14.2, keep in mind that you may already have some of this infrastructure in place. The question to ask is, What are the specific requirements for your new system? When acquiring eCRM technological solutions, you have several alternatives:

- Custom-build applications in-house using the skills and talent of hired staff (frequently the most time-consuming and expensive choice).
- Rent a solution from an application service provider or vendor (often a good choice for companies in markets that are rapidly changing, but it can lead to "customer ownership" difficulties).
- Purchase an eCRM solution that supports one functional area or an eCRM suite that covers the entire organization (sometimes an eCRM solution looks cost efficient until you add integration and computer upgrade costs).

Three or four years ago, much of the technology we now take for granted was not available or was just being introduced. Online customers were fascinated and flattered that they were greeted by name when they returned to a Web site. This assisted e-corporations in building customer loyalty. Today, this personalization feature is almost taken for granted and

FIGURE 14.2   Examples of Technological Solutions for Each Functional Area

| **Major Corporate Divisions** | **eCRM Solutions** |

Online Sales

Examples of Applications:
- Sales Force Automation
- Sales Management Services
- Lead Generation Management
- Contact/Case Management
- eCRM Suite

Online Marketing

Examples of Applications:
- Marketing Automation
- Marketing Campaign Management
- Personalization Software
- Content Management
- eCRM Suite

Online Customer Support

Examples of Applications:
- Search Capabilities
- CTI Computer Integration
- Telephony (Voice over the Internet and Call-Back Buttons)
- Fax Management
- E-mail Management
- Text Chat/Live Agent Chat
- Contact/Case Management/Problem Resolution
- Knowledge Management/Database Management
- Help Desk Software
- Reporting and Document Management
- eCRM Suite

Online Project Development

Examples of Applications:
- Data Mining Management
- Data Warehouse Management
- Customer Segmentation
- Customer Profiling
- Configuration Management
- Application/Systems Integration
- eCRM Suite

Online Distribution

Examples of Applications:
- Order Management/Distribution
- Partner Relationship Management
- eCRM Suite

is often a market need that your e-corporation must include in order to compete.

There are a number of e-operating strategy options and online business models available that can assist you in building customer loyalty (see Chapter 5). Knowing which customer loyalty mechanisms work for your type of e-corporation is critical; however, the best customer loyalty strategy is the one that anticipates the evolution of customer advantage. If your e-operating strategy does not provide the online customer with some distinct advantage, someone else will.

Show Them the Money?

J. William Gurley in *Fortune* magazine (1998) noted that at first glance it looked like the Internet would be a cheap place to reach more customers with little risk. He reminded us of the AT&T television commercial for a company called Rubbereyes (www.rubbereyes.com), where two entrepreneurial young women get an idea for a business after breaking several pairs of sunglasses. The duo design and manufacture innovative rubber sunglasses and run into trouble with distribution. Merchants were not buying their product, so they gleefully turn to the Web, bypassing retailers, and become an instant success. The commercial did a good job of illustrating the advantages of doing business online, but it never addressed the cost.

It's true that it takes money to make money. Developing a profit-making Web site can be a major capital investment. Figure 14.2 showed the types of technological solutions that are available for each of the five major functional areas of the e-corporation (sales, marketing, customer service, project management, and distribution). Figure 14.3 shows how the Net may not be a relatively inexpensive way to reach more customers. It details a relatively small 15-seat Web-based contact center with an average initial cost of $1,853,000 and a 75-search contact center with average initial costs of $2,877,000.

The contact center shown includes telephony (interactive voice response, computer and telephone integration, and a "Call Me" button); fax and e-mail management, which includes a fax server, fax-to-e-mail feature, automated e-mail response, and routing; Web-based interactive chat,

FIGURE 14.3   Examples of the Cost for One Functional Area of the E-corporation

Online Customer Support	Average Total Cost 15-Seat Contact Center	Average Total Cost 75-Seat Contact Center
SOFTWARE		
Telephony	$ 176,000	$ 323,000
Fax	137,000	141,000
E-mail	129,000	137,000
Chat	83,000	200,000
Contact/Case Management	162,000	517,000
Knowledge Management	218,000	543,000
Reporting	59,000	109,000
Solution Subtotal	$ 964,000	$1,970,000
INTEGRATION	683,000	683,000
Total Solution Costs	$1,647,000	$2,653,000
HARDWARE	206,000	224,000
Total One-Time Costs	$1,853,000	$2,877,000
Average Total Initial Cost per Contact Center Seat	$ 124,000	$ 38,000

MAINTENANCE

Annual Maintenance Cost	$ 309,000	$ 478,000
Three-Year Total Investment	927,000	1,434,000
	$2,780,000	$4,311,000
Five-Year Total Investment	618,000	956,000
	$3,398,000	$5,267,000

Source: Adapted from "Cost Research Report: Cost of Buying, Building, and Maintaining a Multi-Channel On-Site Customer Service and Support Contact Center," prepared by Deloitte & Touche for Synchrony Communications, Inc. (www.synchrony.com), 1 November 1999.

document management, and control systems; knowledge management authoring and management tools; a knowledge management server; and a report writer and query tool.

Figure 14.3 illustrates how larger e-corporations have an advantage in cyberspace. The average total initial cost per Web-based contact center seat in a 15-seat contact center is $124,000. In contrast, the cost of one seat in a Web-based contact center with 75 seats is $38,000. This indicates how economies of scale affect e-corporations. The small company pays three times the amount paid by a large company for one seat in the Web-based contact center, effectively dispelling the notion that the Internet provides a level playing field. When it comes to technology costs, large corporations definitely have the upper hand.

Furthermore, Figure 14.3 shows how e-corporations can spend millions of dollars on Web-based technology. The large initial capital outlay for a Web-based contact center may lead you to believe that e-corporations are spending huge amounts of money on their infrastructures. Recent studies indicate that this may not be true. A 1999 study of almost 400 organizations by MetaGroup (www.metagroup.com) revealed that corporations are not spending as much for their e-business initiatives as the media and software developers would like us to believe. For example, of the surveyed companies, 65 percent are spending less than $1 million annually on e-business, and fewer than 10 percent spend more than $5 million annually.

Measuring and Monitoring Your Success

If your company is going to focus on developing customer loyalty using eCRM techniques, you'll need a way to measure your success. Your organization will need a new way to measure the increased value of its customer base. Corporations have no lack of customer data, but it is usually divided into different databases that are not integrated. This means that customers can be double-counted; related transactions may appear to have no connection; and customers who stop buying and resume buying in another city may be erroneously counted as defectors and new customers. Making your e-corporation customer centric means you'll need a customer knowledge base that all departments can access. When you want to track customers and customer value, this is often the best approach.

Additionally, your e-corporation will need to develop a way to measure the long-term benefits of customer loyalty and profit. Figure 14.4 provides an example of a way to forecast and measure the customer loyalty results of your e-corporation. Let's assume your company has a customer base of 100,000 individuals. You sell product XYZ for $200. Every two years, you release an upgrade of product XYZ for $100. When consumers purchase additional products, the average price is $200. The average lifetime of a customer is ten years, and your required rate of return is 12 percent.

Based on your customer knowledge, you expect an *additional* 15 percent of existing customers to purchase upgrades because of your eCRM customer loyalty efforts. To calculate the sales revenue, multiply your customer base number by the price of the upgrade and then by the percentage of customers you expect to purchase the upgrade (100,000 × $100 × .15 = $1,500,000). Customers will purchase upgrades in year two and year four (that's once every two years). To arrive at the discounted sales amount, multiply $1,500,000 by 0.797 (the present value interest factor for discounting the revenue 12 percent in year two). Next, multiply $1,500,000 by 0.636 (the present value interest factor for discounting the revenue 12 percent in year four). Add the amounts for the net present value of five-year revenues ($1,195,500 + $954,000 = $2,149,500). The total discounted revenue for five years is $2,149,500. This is additional revenue you would not have realized without your eCRM customer loyalty efforts.

Based on your customer knowledge and expectations of your eCRM customer loyalty efforts, you expect 5 percent of your current loyal customers to purchase one additional product each year (100,000 × $200 × .05 = $1,000,000). The present value interest factor for an annuity with a discount rate of 12 percent for five years is 3.605. To find the net present value of revenue of loyal customers purchasing additional products, multiply $1,000,000 by 3.605. The total discounted revenue for five years is $3,605,000.

Based on your customer knowledge and expectations of your eCRM customer loyalty efforts, you expect 3,000 new customers will feel less risk with your e-corporation and will purchase one new product each year (3,000 × $200 = $600,000). The present value interest factor for an annuity with a discount rate of 12 percent for five years is 3.605. To discover the net present value of revenue of new customers purchasing more products as a result of your eCRM efforts, multiply $600,000 by 3.605. The total discounted revenue for five years is $2,163,000.

Loyal customers make customer recommendations that increase sales. You expect 8 percent of existing customers to make one referral per year (100,000 × .08 = 8,000). You expect these referral customers to purchase one product (8,000 × $200 = $1,600,000). The present value interest factor for an annuity with a discount rate of 12 percent for five years is 3.605. To find the net present value of revenue of referral customers purchasing a product as a result of your eCRM efforts, multiply $1,600,000 by 3.605. The total discounted revenue for five years is $5,768,000.

The grand total of the net present value of five years of revenues from eCRM customer loyalty efforts is the total of additional upgrades purchased ($2,149,500), the additional products purchased by current loyal customers ($3,605,000), new customers purchasing more because they feel less risk ($2,163,000), and revenue from referral customers ($5,768,000). The net present value of five years of additional revenues is $13,685,500. This is additional revenue the company would not have realized if the firm did not implement an eCRM customer loyalty program.

Figure 14.4 shows the importance of setting up your e-corporation's information system and metrics to measure the impact customers have on the bottom line. It illustrates how building customer loyalty can be a key to increased profits.

DEVELOPING YOUR ECRM SERVICE CONCEPT

In cyberspace, business models can move faster than technology. The fundamentals of your e-corporation and the technology you employ are useful, but the ability to determine how to use the Web to acquire and retain customers is the key to success. Therefore, it is constructive to evaluate your e-Strategic Service Vision Plan by looking at your capabilities from the customer's point of view:

- How will your e-corporation acquire the initial customer relationship? (This includes needs development, product or service awareness, customer learning, the e-corporation learning about the customer, etc.)

FIGURE 14.4 Calculating the Monetary Benefits of Customer Loyalty

---

Assumptions:

Initial size of customer base	100,000
Product XYZ list price	$ 200
New release of Product XYZ	$ 100
Average price of additional products	$ 200
Number of years between upgrades	2
Life of customer in years	10
Required rate of return on investments	12%

Upgrades Purchased by Current Customers as a Result of eCRM Customer Loyalty:

Increase in the percentage of customers purchasing upgrade	15%
Product revenue increase from greater upgrades every two years	$ 1,500,000
Net Present Value of Five-Year Revenues	$ 2,149,500

Additional Products Purchased by Current Loyal Customers:

Number of additional products purchased per year	1
Portion of current customers purchasing additional products	5%
Additional product revenue from current customers per year	$ 1,000,000
Net Present Value of Five-Year Revenues	$ 3,605,000

New Customers Purchase More as a Result of eCRM Customer Loyalty Efforts:

Number of new customers per year purchasing additional products	3,000
Number of additional products purchased	1
Additional product revenue from new customers per year	$ 600,000
Net Present Value of Five-Year Revenues	$ 2,163,000

Customer Recommendations Bring New Product Sales from Referral Customers:

Percentage of existing customer base making one referral per year	8%
Number of additional new referral sales per year	8,000
Additional product revenue from referrals per year	$ 1,600,000
Net Present Value of Five-Year Revenues	$ 5,768,000

Grand Total

(Forecast of the Net Present Value of Five-Year Revenues from eCRM Customer Loyalty Efforts)	$13,685,500

- How will your e-corporation work to earn the customers' ongoing loyalty?
- How will your e-corporation expand the customer relationship to gain a greater share of each customer's purchasing capacity?

Before purchasing online, consumers expect to receive a certain level of service. They also have a *minimum* level of service they will accept. Between these two is the e-customer's tolerance and the expected or predicted level of service he or she anticipates. To build customer loyalty, e-corporations must consistently perform at or near the consumer's *desired* level of service and at or above the *anticipated* level of service.

To discover how your target audience perceives your e-corporation, you'll need listening posts, which can assist you in determining the important elements of your e-corporation strategy in terms of results produced for your online customers. Listening posts can be as simple as reading e-mail complaints, analyzing reports from sales and service personnel, or checking the interaction logs of the Web-based contact center. Often, little things that annoy e-customers can radically reduce sales. Jonathan Gaw (1999), a writer for the *Los Angeles Times,* provides these examples:

- MotherNature.com (www.mothernature.com), in a focus group, observed how Internet newcomers interacted with their Web site. To their surprise, the focus group members had a hard time filling in the shipping labels. When it was time to click on the two-letter abbreviation for a state nam+e in the drop-down dialogue box, the Internet newcomers didn't know what to do. Users clicked on the first state that had the beginning letter they desired and then typed in the second letter of the abbreviated state's name. Somehow "MN" for Minnesota became "N" for Nebraska.
- Proflowers Inc. (www.proflowers.com) was swamped with abandoned transactions and long transaction times during the holidays. Their credit card verification vendor was too slow, and customers would abandon their transactions. Users will tolerate a five- or ten-second wait at the most. Proflowers has now learned their lesson and hired a speedier credit card transaction vendor.

- Amazon.com (www.amazon.com) did away with requiring repeat customers to click through eight or nine Web pages to find or order their items. (Often, three to five clicks are the optimal number for first-time customers, because the next click is to another Web site.) Amazon.com's one-click ordering is now an innovation that many e-corporations are using.

Jonathan Gaw points out that these examples show how difficult it is for e-corporations to understand how customers perceive their Web sites. Also, many e-corporations do not use the tons of data they collect about their customers in a way that increases personalized selling and customer service. For example, most online businesses know which products customers looked at and passed up, which products they put in their virtual shopping carts and later decided not to buy, and what products or services customers eventually bought. However, this information is almost never used to promote targeted sales on the second visit. Let's say a current customer passed on the five CDs offered on the Web site's front page. When he or she logs on again, the e-corporation should use their customer knowledge to present five different CDs on the front page.

TARGETING E-MARKET SEGMENTS

Your e-Strategic Service Vision Plan should be designed in such a way that it positions your e-corporation to meet customer needs (the results sought by customers) and enjoy a competitive online advantage. The key is interacting with each customer in a way that's valued by the customer. Developing needs-based customer segments and creating business rules for each segment are important to building online customer relationships. As contrary as it sounds, dividing customers into market segments allows you to serve individual customer needs.

According to William H. Davidow and Bro Uttal (1989), the essence of any customer service strategy is to divide customers into families of homogeneous sets that can be profitably served. In general, service customer segments are narrower than product customer segments. The reason for this is simple: Products are what individuals *need* and services are what individuals *expect.* Additionally, many companies use demographic data (age, sex, income, geographic location, education, and so on) to create segments and understand their e-customers.

An eCRM customer loyalty approach to identifying characteristics of important market segments, such as "fashion conscious consumers," is important. Segmenting customers in this way lets you develop needs-based segments. One of the best ways for your e-corporation to make intelligent decisions about the capabilities and content you offer is to use the following six-step approach:

1. Define high-value customers based on each customer's unique needs. Determine common characteristics of this customer segment.
2. Create test areas online for each customer segment and offer tailored content and capabilities.
3. Identify which customers belong to each customer segment (see Chapter 13). Determine what dimensions can be used to segment your customer base.
4. Offer members of each customer segment individualized or tailored content.
5. Measure their behavior against a control group. Determine the importance of various customer segments and pinpoint their needs.
6. Build additional approaches based on segments, content, and business rules that produce measurable positive results. Determine how well customer needs are being served and in what way customer needs are being served and by whom. For example, does online self-service work for your e-corporation or do you need a Web-based contact center?

SUMMING IT UP

- Transforming your company into an e-corporation focuses management thinking on what is necessary to detect the needs and ensure the satisfaction and loyalty of targeted customers. It requires an investment in effort to identify customers and to understand their unique needs, as well as investing in online capabilities to meet those customer needs.

- Developing a strategic plan for your proposed e-corporation can assist you in navigating a smooth, or at least a less-disruptive, transition to the Internet.
- In your e-delivery system, you'll need to address the important issues about capacity, how to differentiate your company from other e-corporations, and how to create barriers to entry by competitors.
- In your e-operating strategy, you'll have to decide where you'll concentrate your efforts, what type of technological support you'll need, and how to measure the results of your eCRM customer loyalty efforts.
- In your service strategy, you have to put yourself in your customers' shoes and see how your e-corporation is perceived by them.
- In creating segmenting strategies, you'll have to determine the common characteristics of important segments and how vital these segments are, so that you can target individual customer needs.

REFERENCES

Daly, Cindy, and James S. Harrison (ed.). 2000. e-Customer: Revolutionizing Relationships Through the Web Produced in Association with AMR Research, Inc. Fortune Custom Projects, *Fortune Sections* (www.fortunesections.com), 3 April.

Davidow, William H., and Bro Uttal. 1989. Service Companies: Focus or Falter. *Harvard Business Review* (July–August): 77–89.

E-Reality Sets In: Separating E-Fact from Fiction for the Second Phase of Business. 1999. *INforum Business Driven Publications* by MetaGroup (www.metagroup.com), November.

Gaw, Jonathan. 1999. Online Retailers Not Yet Adept at Art of the Sale. *Los Angeles Times* (www.scient.com/ebusiness/external_articles/latimes.htm), 15 February.

Hamel, Gary, Jeff Sampler, Patty deLosa, Jane Hodges, and Len A. Costa. 1998. The e-Corporation, More than Just Web-Based, It's Building a New Industrial Order. *Fortune,* 7 December, 80–90.

Heskett, James L. 1986. Managing in the Service Economy. *Harvard Business Review* (November).

Heskett, James L., W. Earl Sasser, Jr., and Leonard A. Schlesinger. 1997. *The Service Profit Chain: How Leading Companies Link Profit and Growth to Loyalty, Satisfaction, and Value.* New York: Free Press.

Justifying the Web for Your Business. 2000. Online publication of Dynamicnet (www
.dynamicnet.com), 13 June.

Peppers, Don, and Martha Rogers. 1997. *Enterprise One to One: Tools for Competing in the
Interactive Age.* New York: Currency/Doubleday.

Reichheld, Fredrick F., 1996. *The Loyalty Effect.* Boston: Harvard Business School Press.

Slocum, Jr., John W., Michael McGill, and David T. Lei. 1994. The New Learning Strategy:
Anytime, Anything, Anywhere. *Organizational Dynamics* 23 (22 September): 33–48.

Systems Innovation. 1999. *Internet Computing Strategies Report* 4, no. 9 (August), The Yankee Group (www.yankeegroup.com).

Wang, Gigi, and Carol Glasheen. 2000. Ten Things You Need to Know About Successful
eCommerce Strategy. *Bulletin,* a publication of IDC (www.idc.com), 27 June.

Resource Center

Through the pages of *Loyalty Marketing for the Internet Age,* I describe dozens of Internet resources that can assist you in reaching your goals. These selected Web sites provide excellent examples of the latest and greatest customer loyalty initiatives available. In the Resource Center, I provide you with a listing of Web sites that you are likely to use for additional information, including a sampling of the great resources for eCRM information and tools available online.

The Resource Center has a special section for technological solutions. These software applications are divided into major categories and indexed, allowing you to do two things:

1. See which technological solutions have modules, because you may want to reduce integration problems and costs by adding new modules to your current technological solutions.
2. Determine if the software products you currently own are part of an eCRM suite. If so, you may be able to easily add online capabilities to your existing technological infrastructure.

BEST PRACTICES

Don't reinvent the wheel! Best practices are the identification and exchanges of successful solutions. These Web sites can show you what works and what to avoid.

APQC Best Practices Page <www.apqc.org/best/>
Learn from the best and benefit from the power of best practices. Find content, products, and services that will help you identify and understand the processes used by world class organizations.

The Benchmarking Exchange and Best Practices Homepage
<www.benchnet.com>
The Benchmarking Exchange is an electronic benchmarking network comprising thousands of business professionals and managers who collaborate on business excellence, best practices, performance, and so on.

Best Economic Value Added (EVA) Business Practices, Strategies, Tactics, and Actions <biz.onramp.net/valuinfo/>
Any enterprise can now directly compute their competitive edge or best practices positioning. Publications from Valuable Information Ltd. describe the hows and whys.

Best Practices in Corporate Communications
<www.tpag.com/BestPractices/index.shtml>
Best Practices in Corporate Communications provides a series of reports and consulting services on superior business communications methods that are guaranteed to substantially improve your corporate communications department and allow your company to excel in a highly competitive business arena.

CONFERENCES AND EVENT ORGANIZERS

Conferences are often useful for discovering the latest in technological solutions, or how old technology can be used in new ways. Learn the latest eCRM trends and see how other firms are grappling with their successes or failures.

Business Intelligence <www.business-intelligence.co.uk>
Business-focused reports, conferences, and exhibitions, in addition to a discussion board, press centers, and search capabilities.

CRMSS: Customer Relationship Management/Support Services Conference & Expo <www.zdevents.com/crmss/index.html>
ZD's CRM/Support Services Conference & Expo is designed to teach an organization how to manage its people, process, and technology issues in order to effectively support and service its internal and external customers.

DCI <www.dci.com>
Educational events for the corporate IT community, with focus on computer hardware, software, and communications, including the Internet and intranets.

E-COMMERCE CONSULTANTS

E-commerce consultants offer a wide range of services that include improving business processes, software integration, and facilitating the exchange of business information electronically to help you communicate better with your online customers.

Agency.com <www.agency.com>
Agency.com is a global Internet solutions provider offering integrated strategic, creative, technology, and media services to businesses seeking to grow interactive relationships through branding, content management, and e-commerce.

Andersen Consulting <www.ac.com>
An international consulting firm devoted to business and technology consulting.

AppNet <www.appnet.com/>
AppNet was created to help companies meet the challenge of redefining their businesses, creating new strategies, and building new technology capabilities by combining Internet strategy, marketing, and technology into a single solution.

Ascendant Solutions <www.asdsystems.com/>
Ascendant Solutions is an e-solutions company providing and managing the infrastructure behind e-commerce, using systems to integrate and manage clients' Web sites, call centers, fulfillment centers, and drop-ship vendors.

Braun Consulting <www.braunconsulting.com>
Braun Consulting is a professional services firm focused on advancing customer loyalty in the Internet economy with strategy and information technology solutions.

Cambient <www.cambient.com>
Cambient is a business and technology consulting firm focused on providing solutions that help companies develop long-term, profitable relationships with their customers.

Channell Communications Inc. <www.channell.com>
Channell offers a variety of e-business services, including consulting, software, and hardware, to help you make the most of your site as a way to build relationships with customers and prospects.

Cognizant Technology Solutions <www.cognizant.com>
Cognizant is a provider of e-business solutions and application management services to Fortune 500 and blue chip companies in the U.S. and Europe. The company has more than 2,000 technical professionals, extending across a wide range

of technologies encompassing the Internet, data warehousing, and object-oriented software development, as well as legacy and client-server applications.

Globeset, Inc. <www.globeset.com>
Globeset is a supplier of secure e-payments infrastructure services and products for buyers, sellers, and financial service providers.

iMediation <www.imediation.com/>
iMediation develops a business-to-business platform for e-commerce that enables companies to build and manage effective, collaborative commerce marketplaces.

Informatica <www.informatica.com>
Informatica develops and markets analytic applications, infrastructure software, and related services that give e-businesses the ability to evaluate the performance of their entire e-business value chain of customer, partner, and supplier relationships.

Infosys <www.inf.com>
Infosys solutions cover a wide range of business areas, including e-commerce and e-business enabling, warehouse and inventory management, and customer management for vertical industries such as financial services, insurance, retail, telecommunication, utilities, and manufacturing.

Management Information Consulting, Inc. <www.micinc.com>
MIC is an e-business, IT consulting, and systems-integration firm specializing in the implementation of e-business systems, including e-commerce, e-custom development, and e-enabled enterprise resource planning (ERP).

NetMarketing™ Brand Internet Marketing Services <www.netmarketing.com>
NetMarketing analyzes your business inside and out to help construct a comprehensive online marketing plan to serve as the foundation for all online marketing initiatives.

The NetSys Group, Inc.—Computer Networking Solutions
<www.netsysgroup.com>
The NetSys Group provides systems and network integration and engineering services. Services include the planning, design, implementation, operation, optimization, and maintenance of computer networking products and solutions.

Networld Exchange WorldCommerce <www.networldexchange.com/>
Networld provides e-commerce service for foodservice and hospitality suppliers. A system designed with industry-specific features, it also provides suppliers and distributors a rapid and reliable entry into doing business online.

Origin <www.origin-it.com/>
   Origin's services include consulting, enterprise solutions, application and infrastructure management, and data processing, together with systems development, implementation, integration, and management.

SOFTWARE SOLUTIONS

   Technological solutions are what make eCRM work. Having the right solution for the right need is critical to your success. Following is a list of many popular technological solutions, with each type of application divided by category. With eCRM software, there are a lot of modular crossovers. To assist you, the following have been categorized and cross-referenced. The indexing key is as follows:

   CIC   = Customer interaction center software
   CRM = Customer relationship management software
   CSA = Customer service automation software
   eCUS = E-customer software
   MA   = Marketing automation software
   PRM = Partner relationship management software
   SA   = Sales automation software

Customer Interaction Center Software (CIC)

Artificial Life, Inc. (CIC, eCUS)
<www.artificial-life.com>

Aspect Communications (CIC, eCUS)
<www.aspect.com>

Call Center University (CIC, CRM, PRM)
<www.callcenteru.com>

CCNG (CIC, CRM)
<www.ccng.com>

Chordiant
<www.chordiant.com>

Clarify
<www.clarify.com>

Cybercall
<www.atio.com>

Efusion
<www.efusion.com>

Enterprise Interaction Center
<www.inter-intelli.com>

Envision Telephony (CIC, CRM)
<www.envisiontelephony.com>

e-solutions Software, Inc. (CIC, CRM, MA, PRM, SA)
<www.e-solutions.com>

ichat, Inc. (eCUS)
<www.ichat.com>

iLux (CIC, CRM, eCUS)
<www.ilux.com>

Infotech Research International, Inc. (CIC, CRM, eCUS, MA, PRM, SA)
<www.infotechRI.com>

NetMoves (CIC, CRM, eCUS, MA)
<www.netmoves.com>

Norkom Technologies (CIC, CRM, eCUS)
<www.norkom.com>

On!contact Software Corporation (CIC, CRM, MA, PRM, SA)
<www.oncontact.com>

Onyx Software (CIC, CRM, eCUS, MA, PRM, SA)
<www.onyx.com>

Pivotal Corporation (CIC, CRM, eCUS, PRM, SA)
<www.pivotal.com>

Remedy (CIC, eCRM, eCUS)
<www.remedy.com>

Sales Authority, Inc. (CIC, CRM, eCUS, MA, PRM, SA)
<www.salesauthority.com>

SalesLogix Corporation (CIC, eCUS, MA, PRM, SA)
<www.saleslogix.com>

Saratoga Systems, Inc. (CIC, eCUS, MA, SA)
<www.saratogasystems.com>

Siebel Systems, Inc. (CIC, CRM, CSA, MA, PRM, SA)
<www.siebel.com>

SomeOne Service
<www.netcallplc.com>

Spanlink
<www.spanlink.com>

SPLASH-NET (CIC, CRM, eCUS, PRM, SA)
<www.splash-net.com>

Unisys Corp. Worldwide Telesales Services (CIC)
<www.unisys.com>

Vantive
<www.peoplesoft.com>

Worldtrak Corporation (CIC)
<www.worldtrak.com>

Customer Relationship Management Software (CRM)

Accrue Software, Inc. (CRM)
<www.accrue.com>

AIT—Advanced Information Technologies (CRM, SA)
<www.advaninfo.com>

Allegis Corporation (CRM, eCUS, PRM)
<www.allegis.com>

APAC Customer Services (CRM)
<www.apacteleservices.com>

Applix, Inc. (CRM, MA)
<www.applix.com>

Aprimo, Inc. (CRM)
<www.aprimo.com>

Baan Company
(CRM, CSA, MA, SA)
<www.baan.com>

Business Objects—Customer Intelligence Applications (CRM)
<www.businessobjects.com>

Call Center University
(CIC, CRM, PRM)
<www.callcenteru.com>

Cambient (CRM, eCUS)
<www.cambient.com>

CCNG (CIC, CRM)
<www.ccng.com>

ClickAction, Inc. (CRM, eCUS)
<www.clickaction.com>

Computer Horizons Corp. (CRM)
<www.computerhorizons.com>

Conita Technologies (CRM)
<www.conita.com>

Consumer Goods Magazine (CRM)
<www.consumergoods.com>

Eastman Software (CRM, eCUS)
<www.eastmansoftware.com>

eGain Communications
(CRM, eCUS)
<www.egain.com>

Envision Telephony (CIC, CRM)
<www.envisiontelephony.com>

Epicor Software Corporation
(CRM, MA)
<www.epicor.com>

e-solutions Software, Inc.
(CIC, CRM, MA, PRM, SA)
<www.e-solutions.com>

Exchange Applications
(CRM, eCUS)
<www.exapps.com>

Featherlite (CRM)
<www.featherlite.com>

File Tek (CRM, eCUS)
<www.filetek.com>

4SA, Inc. (CRM)
<www.4sainc.com>

Glyphica (CRM, MA, PRM)
<www.glyphica.com>

Goldmine Software Corporation
(CRM, MA, SA)
<www.goldmine.com>

Great Plains (CRM, eCUS)
<www.greatplains.com>

GWI Software, Inc. (CRM)
<www.gwi.com>

idEXEC (CRM, MA, SA)
<www.idexec.com>

iLux (CIC, CRM, eCUS)
<www.ilux.com>

IMR—Information Management Research (CRM, MA)
<www.imrgold.com>

Infotech Research International, Inc. (CIC, CRM, eCUS, MA, PRM, SA)
<www.infotechRI.com>

Intelligent Enterprise (CRM)
<www.iemagazine.com>

Knowledge Impact (CRM)
<www.kimpact.com>

MarketForce (CRM)
<www.marketforce-inc.com>

Mastery Marketing Group (CRM)
<www.masterymktgrp.com>

MEI Group (CRM, MA, SA)
<www.meicpg.com>

MicroStrategy, Inc. (CRM)
<www.microstrategy.com>

NetMoves (CIC, CRM, eCUS, MA)
<www.netmoves.com>

Norkom Technologies
(CIC, CRM, eCUS)
<www.norkom.com>

OAO Technology Solutions (CRM)
<www.oaot.com>

On!contact Software Corporation
(CIC, CRM, MA, PRM, SA)
<www.oncontact.com>

Onyx Software
(CIC, CRM, eCUS, MA, PRM, SA)
<www.onyx.com>

Optima Technologies, Inc. (CRM)
<www.optima-tech.com>

Pivotal Corporation
(CIC, CRM, eCUS, PRM, SA)
<www.pivotal.com>

Profit Solutions (CRM)
<www.profitsolutions.com>

Questra Corporation (CRM, MA)
<www.questra.com>

Recognition Systems (CRM)
<www.recsys.com>

Remedy Corporation (CRM)
<www.remedy.com>

Repository Technologies (CRM)
<www.custfirst.com>

RightNow Technologies
(CRM, eCUS)
<www.rightnowtech.com>

Sales Authority, Inc.
(CIC, CRM, eCUS, MA, PRM, SA)
<www.salesauthority.com>

SAS Institute Inc. (CRM)
<www.sas.com>

Search Software America (CRM)
<www.searchsoftware.com>

Siebel Systems
(CIC, CRM, CSA, MA, PRM, SA)
<www.siebel.com>

Sky Alland (CRM, eCUS)
<www.skyalland.com>

SpeechWorks International (CRM)
<www.speechworks.com>

SPLASH-NET
(CIC, CRM, eCUS, PRM, SA)
<www.splash-net.com>

Targetbase Interactive (CRM)
<www.targetbase.com>

Thinque Systems (CRM, SA)
<www.thinque.com>

YOUcentric, Inc. (CRM)
<www.youcentric.com>

Customer Service Automation Software (CSA)

Baan Company
(CRM, CSA, MA, SA)
<www.baan.com>

Siebel Systems
(CIC, CRM, CSA, MA, PRM, SA)
<www.siebel.com>

Database Software

IBM
<www.ibm.com>

Microstrategy
<www.microstrategy.com>

Infomix
<www.infomix.com>

Oracle
<www.oracle.com>

Microsoft
<www.microsoft.com>

Data Analysis Software

eHNC
<www.ehnc.com>

SAS Institute, Inc.
<www.sas.com>

Net Genesis
<www.netgen.com>

E-customer and Lead Generation Management (eCUS)

Allegis Corporation
(CRM, eCUS, PRM)
<www.allegis.com>

ClickAction, Inc. (CRM, eCUS)
<www.clickaction.com>

Artificial Life, Inc. (CIC, eCUS)
<www.artificial-life.com>

eGain Communications
(CRM, eCUS)
<www.egain.com>

Aspect Communications
(CIC, eCUS)
<www.aspect.com>

Entice
<www.multiactive.com>

BoldFish, Inc. (eCUS)
<www.boldfish.com>

Epiphany (eCUS)
<www.epiphany.com>

Cincom Systems, Inc. (eCUS)
<www.cincom.com>

eShare Technologies (eCUS)
<www.eshare.com>

Exactium, Inc. (eCUS)
<www.exactium.com>

Exchange Applications
(CRM, eCUS)
<www.exapps.com>

GoldMine
<www.goldmine.com>

Great Plains (CRM, eCUS)
<www.greatplains.com>

Harte-Hanks (CRM, eCUS, MA)
<www.hartehanks.com>

Idiom, Inc. (eCUS)
<www.idiominc.com>

iLux (CIC, CRM, eCUS)
<www.ilux.com>

Kana Communications
(formerly Silknet) (eCUS)
<www.kana.com>

MarketFirst
<www.marketfirst.com>

NetMoves (CIC, CRM, eCUS, MA)
<www.netmoves.com>

Norkom Technologies
(CIC, CRM, eCUS)
<www.norkom.com>

Onyx Software
(CIC, CRM, eCUS, MA, PRM, SA)
<www.onyx.com>

Personify (eCUS)
<www.personify.com>

Pivotal Corporation
(CIC, CRM, eCUS, PRM, SA)
<www.pivotal.com>

Primus (eCUS)
<www.primus.com>

RightNow Technologies
(CRM, eCUS)
<www.rightnowtech.com>

SalesLogix Corporation
(CIC, eCUS, MA, PRM, SA)
<www.saleslogix.com>

Saratoga Systems, Inc.
(CIC, eCUS, MA, SA)
<www.saratogasystems.com>

Servicesoft Technologies
(eCUS)
<www.servicesoft.com>

Sky Alland (CRM, eCUS)
<www.skyalland.com>

SPLASH-NET
(CIC, CRM, eCUS, PRM, SA)
<www.splash-net.com>

Support.com (eCUS)
<www.support.com>

Targitmail.com (CRM, eCUS, MA)
<www.targitmail.com>

Unica (eCUS)
<www.unica-usa.com>

Upshot
<www.upshotonline.com>

Marketing Automation Software (MA)

Applix, Inc. (CRM, MA)
<www.applix.com>

Baan Company
(CRM, CSA, MA, SA)

Epicor Software Corporation
(CRM, MA)
<www.epicor.com>

e-solutions Software, Inc. (CIC, CRM, MA, PRM, SA)
<www.e-solutions.com>

Glyphica (CRM, MA, PRM)
<www.glyphica.com>

Goldmine Software Corporation
(CRM, MA, SA)
<www.goldmine.com>

Harte-Hanks (CRM, eCUS, MA)
<www.hartehanks.com>

idEXEC (CRM, MA, SA)
<www.idexec.com>

IMR—Information Management Research (CRM, MA)
<www.imrgold.com>

Infotech Research International, Inc. (CIC, CRM, eCUS, MA, PRM, SA)
<www.infotechRI.com>

MEI Group (CRM, MA, SA)
<www.meicpg.com>

NetMoves (CIC, CRM, eCUS, MA)
<www.netmoves.com>

On!contact Software Corporation
(CIC, CRM, MA, PRM, SA)
<www.oncontact.com>

Onyx Software
(CIC, CRM, eCUS, MA, PRM, SA)
<www.onyx.com>

Pageflex, Inc. (MA)
<www.pageflexinc.com>

Questra Corporation (CRM, MA)
<www.questra.com>

Sales Authority, Inc.
(CIC, CRM, eCUS, MA, PRM, SA)
<www.salesauthority.com>

SalesLogix Corporation
(CIC, eCUS, MA, PRM, SA)
<www.saleslogix.com>

Saligent Software (MA)
<www.saligentsoftware.com>

Saratoga Systems, Inc.
(CIC, eCUS, MA, SA)
<www.saratogasystems.com>

Siebel Systems
(CIC, CRM, CSA, MA, PRM, SA)
<www.siebel.com>

Targitmail.com (CRM, eCUS, MA)
<www.targitmail.com>

Partnership Relationship Management Software (PRM)

Allegis Corporation
(CRM, eCUS, PRM)
<www.allegis.com>

ChannelWave Software, Inc.
(PRM)
<www.channelwave.com>

Click Commerce (PRM)
<www.clickcommerce.com>

e-solutions Software, Inc.
(CIC, CRM, MA, PRM, SA)
<www.e-solutions.com>

Glyphica (CRM, MA, PRM)
<www.glyphica.com>

Infotech Research International, Inc. (CIC, CRM, eCUS, MA, PRM, SA)
<www.infotechRI.com>

Metrix Matrix, Inc.
(CRM, eCUS, PRM)
<www.metrixmatrix.com>

On!contact Software Corporation
(CIC, CRM, MA, PRM, SA)
<www.oncontact.com>

OnDemand, Inc. (PRM)
<www.ondemand.com>

Onyx Software
(CIC, CRM, eCUS, MA, PRM, SA)
<www.onyx.com>

Partnerware (PRM)
<www.partnerware.com>

Pivotal Corporation
(CIC, CRM, eCUS, PRM, SA)
<www.pivotal.com>

Sales Authority, Inc.
(CIC, CRM, eCUS, MA, PRM, SA)
<www.salesauthority.com>

SalesLogix Corporation
(CIC, eCUS, MA, PRM, SA)
<www.saleslogix.com>

Siebel Systems
(CIC, CRM, CSA, MA, PRM, SA)
<www.siebel.com>

SPLASH-NET
(CIC, CRM, eCUS, PRM, SA)
<www.splash-net.com>

Sales Automation Software (SA)

AIT—Advanced Information Technologies (CRM, SA)
<www.advaninfo.com>

Baan Company
(CRM, CSA, MA, SA)
<www.baan.com>

e-solutions Software, Inc.
(CIC, CRM, MA, PRM, SA)
<www.e-solutions.com>

Goldmine Software Corporation
(CRM, MA, SA)
<www.goldmine.com>

idEXEC (CRM, MA, SA)
<www.idexec.com>

Infotech Research International, Inc. (CIC, CRM, eCUS, MA, PRM, SA)
<www.infotechRI.com>

MEI Group (CRM, MA, SA)
<www.meicpg.com>

On!contact Software Corporation
(CIC, CRM, MA, PRM, SA)
<www.oncontact.com>

Onyx Software
(CIC, CRM, eCUS, MA, PRM, SA)
<www.onyx.com>

Pivotal Corporation
(CIC, CRM, eCUS, PRM, SA)

Sales Authority, Inc.
(CIC, CRM, eCUS, MA, PRM, SA)
<www.salesauthority.com>

Siebel Systems
(CIC, CRM, CSA, MA, PRM, SA)
<www.siebel.com>

SalesLogix Corporation
(CIC, eCUS, MA, PRM, SA)
<www.saleslogix.com>

SPLASH-NET
(CIC, CRM, eCUS, PRM, SA)
<www.splash-net.com>

Saratoga Systems, Inc.
(CIC, eCUS, MA, SA)
<www.saratogasystems.com>

Thinque Systems (CRM, SA)
<www.thinque.com>

ADDITIONAL SOFTWARE APPLICATION CATEGORIES

Transaction Processing

First Virtual Holdings, Inc.
<www.fv.com>

Terisa Systems
<www.terisa.com>

GlobeSet, Inc.
<wwwglobeset.com>

Transport Logic
<www.transport.com>

ICVERIFY
<www.icverify.com>

VeriFone
<www.verifone.com>

InfoDial
<www.infodial.com>

VeriSign, Inc.
<www.verisign.com>

Web Site Analysis Software

Accrue
<www.accrue.com>

NetGenesis
<www.netgen.com>

Web Site Content Management Software

Art Technology Group
<www.atg.com>

Net Perceptions
<www.netperceptions.com>

BroadVision
<www.broadvision.com>

Vignette
<www.vignette.com>

LikeMinds
<www.likeminds.com>

TECHNOLOGY AND INTERNET PUBLICATIONS

The Internet provides a wealth of information about eCRM issues, technological solutions, and expert commentary. Many of these online publications have e-mail newsletters that provide snapshots of the latest eCRM news and information about upcoming online and offline events.

Bitpipe.com
Bitpipe.com is a Web marketing and distribution channel that distributes company white papers and case studies to prospects and industry analysts.

Beyond Computing Magazine Online
Beyond Computing magazine helps top-level executives align their technology investments with their business strategies. In every issue, you'll get advice on everything from Internet security to enhancing customer loyalty to Y2K solutions.

Call Center Coach
Call Center Coach, LLC, is dedicated to providing call center professionals with a comprehensive resource package that contains the latest information affecting the customer relationship management industry.

CIO.com Strategic Resources for Information Executives <www.cio.com>
Online magazine for executives interested in information technology applications

ComputerUser.com
ComputerUser, a monthly magazine focusing on computers and technology, is available in cities across the United States and India.

Computerworld
Computerworld is a complete information services company for IT leaders, providing print and online publications, books, conferences, and research services.

CRMXchange
The CRMXchange is a place on the Internet for an exchange of information on customer relationship management (CRM), sales, call center, and telemarketing issues.

DIRECT Magazine (MA) <www.directmag.com>
DIRECT offers readers expert insight on the latest trends, innovative ideas, winning strategies, market analysis, and ideas on how to build successful customer relationships.

ECNet
ECnet is the leading e-market for the high-tech manufacturing industry, supporting high-tech manufacturers in components and semiconductors, communications and networking, computers and peripherals, consumer electronics, and contract manufacturing.

eCRM Magazine (CRM)< www.sffaonline.com>
eCRM provides a road map of how the Internet impacts a company's relationship with its customers, suppliers, and internal business units, and how to integrate new technologies to extend the enterprise.

DMNews.com—Your Direct Marketing Network
DM News offers news reporting, plus a selection of focused sections providing in-depth coverage of specialized market niches.

e-Summit International: Call Center Summits
MW Productions produces the Call Center Summits, senior-level conferences focused on strategies to create call center and corporate success.

Faulkner & Gray
Faulkner & Gray is a publisher of award-winning magazines, newsletters, books, CD-ROMs, and electronic products in the areas of banking, card systems technology, mortgages, accounting, biometrics, and health care technology.

Front Line Solutions (PRM) <www.frontlinehq.com>
Front Line Solutions specializes in partner relationship management consulting and research.

Information and Ideas for Call Center Design and Performance
<www.telemkt.com/design.html>
Article about the design and performance of call centers

InfoWorld.com
Daily technology news and editorials

International Telework Association and Council
The International Telework Association and Council is a nonprofit organization dedicated to promoting the economic, social, and environmental benefits of teleworking.

Internet Statistics (Explore the Internet, Library of Congress)
<lcweb.loc.gov/global/internet/inet-stats.html>
A page of external links to Internet information on the topic of Internet statistics

Internet Traffic Report
The Internet Traffic Report monitors the flow of data around the world. It then displays a value between 0 and 100. Higher values indicate faster and more reliable connections.

ISM Customer Relationship Management Consultants: The Guide
ISM Inc. is a CRM marketing and analysis firm specializing in sales, customer service, and marketing automation.

Pen Computing Magazine (SA) <www.pencomputing.com>
Pen Computing is dedicated to those interested in pen technology, wireless communications, and mobile computing.

Planning a European Call Center <www.telemkt.com/tel_plan.html>
Article about creating a European call center

Sales & Marketing Automation Online <www.sffaonline.com>
Publication written for management in today's enterprises as a source of information designed to successfully help businesses implement and manage their technology-enabled sales and marketing workforces.

Sales & Marketing Executives <www.smei.org>
Sales and Marketing Executives International meets for the exchange of ideas, a channel for new techniques in marketing, and an opportunity to develop sales and marketing skills through information seminars, workshops, and conferences.

Selling Power Magazine <www.sellingpower.com>
The editorial mission is to provide sales management with techniques and technology solutions that increase productivity and improve the operating efficiency of their sales organizations.

Software Business Magazine <www.infowebcom.com/software>
Software professionals turn to *Software Business* for valuable editorial coverage on CEO strategies, sales and marketing, software replication, product development, financial reports, electronic distribution, and packaging/fulfillment.

SolutionCentral <www.solutioncentral.com>
SolutionCentral is a searchable, Web-based resource for IT professionals looking for technical courses and events, as well as expert knowledge.

The Standard: Intelligence for the Internet Economy
<www.thestandard.com/>
The industry Standard is a source for critical, timely information about the Internet economy. It delivers sophisticated coverage of the people, companies, and business models shaping the Internet, as well as insightful news analysis, business model reviews, personality profiles, industry metrics, and executive recruiting.

TelePlaza: Call Center, Customer Service and Telemarketing Portal
<www.teleplaza.com/>
TelePlaza is an organized and categorized directory of call center industry-related Web sites, with over 750 links to customer service, CRM, telesales, and e-commerce information worldwide.

TMCnet.com <www.tmcnet.com/>
TMCnet is a publishing and trade show company that is focused only on the fields of telecom/datacom convergence and today's technical call center.

Web Marketing Today Info Center <www.wilsonweb.com/webmarket/>
Web Marketing Today Info Center links to thousands of online articles about effective Web marketing and online resources for business.

Women in Technology International <www.witi.com/index-c.shtml>
Women in Technology International offers a vertical portal site on the Internet for women who have a high reliance on technology in both their careers and their businesses.

ZDNet
News, product guides, downloads, games, and a searchable database of articles from all major Ziff-Davis PC magazines

TECHNOLOGY THINK TANKS AND RESOURCES

Technology thinks tanks and similar resources are the place to go for the data and research statistics you'll need to get started. Your organization may want to begin with secondary market research from these organizations to profile potential online customers.

Aberdeen Group—IT Consulting and Market Research
Aberdeen Group provides IT consulting and market strategy advice to the IT supplier community. Aberdeen focuses on answering clients' critical business and technology questions in the context of the Internet economy and across the product life cycle.

The Association of Support Professionals <www.asponline.com/articles.html>
The Association of Support Professionals is an international organization dedicated to the advancement of the technical support profession and a community where individual members can share ideas, insights, and experiences with their colleagues.

Computer Sciences Corporation News and Events
<www.csc.com/news/index.html>
The corporate purpose of Computer Sciences Corporation is to be preeminent in the solution of client problems in information systems technology, making a commitment to excellence in contract performance and products.

Forrester Research
Forrester is a leading independent research firm that analyzes the future of technology change and its impact on businesses, consumers, and society. Companies use the research as a source of insight and strategy to guide their business technology decisions.

Help Desk Institute

HDI provides targeted information about the technologies, tools, and trends of the help desk and customer support industry, as well as customized training and certification programs for both the individual and site support organization.

Internet World Statistics Toolbox <www.iw.com/daily/stats/index.html>

Internet World is a provider of global real-time news and information resources for Internet industry and Internet technology professionals, Web developers, and experienced Internet users.

Meridien Research—Providing Detailed IT Research for Financial Services

Meridien publishes in-depth research reports and briefs on carefully selected topics within each research focus. Clearly written and illustrated, these analyses include case studies detailing how financial institutions are applying specific combinations of technology, why they chose the solutions, and how successful the investments have proven.

META Group, Inc.: The Bottom Line IT Research You Need

Offering advisory services, consulting/benchmarking, and publications that span the full spectrum of IT, META Group addresses the latest technologies, industry trends, and business challenges.

ServiceScan <www.servicescan.com/index.html>

ServiceScan is an information service dedicated to service, support, and training organizations and suppliers in the computing industry. Through weekly updates (fax or e-mail), ServiceScan keeps service, support, and training management efficiently up-to-date on relevant innovations, trends, partnerships, competitive announcements, management strategies, and service management technology reports published in the computer industry media and service press.

Technology Review: MIT's Magazine of Innovation

Technology Review provides readers with the broadest possible perspective on technological innovation.

TechWeb: The IT Network

News, reviews, special features, and a searchable archive from CMP Publications

Glossary

advertising networks Companies specializing in amassing profiles of Internet users based on their online browsing and shopping behaviors

affiliates Companies geared to drive targeted traffic from their own Web sites to another site via hyperlinks between the two. Affiliates generally reap a percentage of the sales generated at the merchant Web site, while providing extra service to visitors of their own Web sites.

artificial intelligence (AI) The simulation of human intelligence by computers, such as learning, reasoning, game playing, responding to human languages, and reacting to external stimuli

browser Client software that retrieves, displays, and prints information and HTML documents from software such as Netscape or Internet Explorer

business-to-business (B2B) Defined as the communications and transactions between two business entities via the Internet

business-to-consumer (B2C) Defined as the communications and transactions between a business and a consumer via the Internet

business models Business models are used to create or redefine and capture a market. An example of a business model is the advertising model, where the content is free and mixed with advertising that supports the Web site. In contrast, the community model is often supported by a combination of subscription fees for premium services and advertising revenue.

chat A form of interactive communication that enables users to have real-time conversations with others who are also online. Chats include text chat, which uses text messages instantly relayed to others online, and voice chat, which allows users to communicate via speaking into their computer's microphone and listening to the chat via their computer's speakers.

click-and-mortar A combination of a traditional store and a Web site, where customers can order merchandise online and possibly tie the Web to a physical store via an in-store kiosk

click-through The act of an Internet user clicking a link to another Web site. For example, an affiliate posts your ad banner, and an Internet user clicks on the banner to go to your Web site. (Click-through rates are often used to measure the effectiveness of different types of promotions.)

click stream The path of pages and links followed by an Internet user during a visit to your Web site

clickstream analysis The analysis of a user's movements through your Web site by monitoring browser clicks

cluster analysis Defined as the process of dividing data into groups (clusters) to meet the objectives of a particular application

clustering Dividing a dataset into mutually exclusive groups in such a way that members of each group are as different as possible from one group to the next

collaborative filtering software Defined as a technological solution for sifting through customer profiles or usage patterns to make customer recommendations based on the purchasing behaviors or other preferences of customers with similar characteristics

computer telephony integration (CTI) Defined as the merger of traditional telecommunications equipment and computer applications; for example, the use of caller ID to automatically retrieve customer information from computerized databases

conversion A customer conversion is the process of converting a prospect to a customer. Conversions are often measured in different ways, depending on the goals of the Web site. A conversion may be the completion of a registration form, completion of a loan application form, participating in a chat forum or online discussion, downloading trial software, or requesting more information.

cross-selling A method of increasing the value of a customer; often based on analysis of the customer's profile

customer acquisition Involves convincing an Internet user who has been reached to engage with your company for the first time. This first engagement can be a visit to the Web site, calling on the telephone, sending an e-mail message, etc.

customer interaction solution (CIS) Traditional call centers are "morphing" into customer interaction centers. The software used integrates customer contact (phone, fax, e-mail, Web, voice over the Web, text chat, and other marketing technologies). Often, the chief function of CIS is to be the portal through which customers receive company information.

customer loyalty Generally, customers who are bound to your company or products intellectually or emotionally

customer notification Customers can sign up for automatic e-mail alerts, subscribe to newsletters about promotions, and are contacted via cell phone, wireless handheld devices, e-mail, fax, or direct mail, or receive targeted content the next time they log on to your Web site.

customer optimization A CRM approach that optimizes customer value across product or service lines and customer touch points. The focus is on continuous improvement of customer value, instead of maximizing return on individual marketing campaigns.

customer profile A categorization of a customer, based on his or her customer type and buying pattern

customer profiling The process of assembling a comprehensive database about customer shopping behaviors, motivations, and product or service preferences. Information is captured from online and offline transactions. This information is often used for target marketing.

customer relationship management (CRM) Encompasses sales, marketing, customer service, and support applications

customer retention The goal of marketers that seek to maintain high levels of customer satisfaction. The cost of retaining customers is often significantly lower than the cost of acquiring new customers. Definitions of retained customers vary. To be considered a retained customer, the user may have to make two purchases within a specific time period. (See *retention*.)

customer segmentation Allows companies to divide their customer bases into small, very specific audience segments. Customer segmentation usually makes it possible to identify your best customers, for example, customers who recently visited your Web site, return often, and make purchases.

customer touch point Any facet of the company that interacts directly with the customer. Examples include Web sites, e-mail, field sales, customer support centers, branch offices, and point-of-sale locations.

customized web content Web sites that allow users to modify the look and feel of their Web site by selecting different page layouts, color schemes, and ways information is presented

data analysis software Technological solutions that look for actionable patterns and statistical information in customer information

database Where raw data is stored

data mart A data mart is a subset of a data warehouse or a process of deriving information from a data source. Data marts are generally used for a specific purpose or for a major data subject to support business needs.

data mining A technique using computer applications to discover patterns that reveal insights into a company's business and customers. Data mining is the process of sifting through large amounts of data to adjust or enhance business strategies.

data warehouse An informational database or database server that stores sharable data collected from a variety of different sources. Typically, companies tap into the data warehouse for operational data for tracking and responding to business trends and to facilitate forecasts, planning, and customer communication efforts.

digital or electronic cash Often an electronic cash account, stored on the customer's computer, for purchasing products or services online or offline

duration The measurement of the time spent on a particular activity; for example, repeat customers may have an average duration of five minutes per visit, new customers an average duration of three minutes.

e-business Defined as a new environment from communications, interactions, and transactions. It is based on the Internet (that is IP-based networks); links any server, network, or device to any other, anywhere in the world; enhances relationships; and touches large enterprises as well as new Internet start-up companies.

e-commerce Automated business transactions, including both the transfer of information and funds, via computers. E-commerce is often defined as the buying and selling of products or services to consumers or other businesses over electronic systems, usually the Internet.

eCRM (electronic customer relationship management) Gives companies the means to conduct interactive, personalized, and relevant communications with customers across electronic and traditional channels. Also defined as a set of decisions that assist the company in developing relationships with customers. Customer buying profiles, targeted online campaigns, and personalized Web content are examples of activities that can significantly affect the value of relationships between customers and the company.

e-mail Private messages sent electronically via computer. Messages are usually text, sent from one person to another. E-mail can also be sent to large numbers of individuals automatically.

enterprise relationship planning (ERP) Software that links back-office computer systems, such as manufacturing, financial, human resources, sales force automation, supply chain management, data warehousing, document management, and after-sales service and support

frequency   How often a user visits your Web site to perform certain activities; for example, frequency can be the number of purchases during a predetermined time period or how often a user visits your Web site.

frequently asked questions (FAQs)   The most commonly asked questions (and answers) that a specific group of Internet users, researchers, bargain hunters, or others ask on a newsgroup, mailing list, or Web site. FAQs provide basic and necessary information so that users can make purchase decisions while at your Web site.

fulfillment   The process of completing a transaction, such as a purchase, request for information, or redemption of promotional offers

high-value customer   An economic view of a customer that measures how profitable the customer is to the company, instead of measuring the profitability of product or service lines. Customer relationship management is geared towards optimizing the value of each customer.

hit   Single entries in the host server log file. This entry is generated when a user requests a Web site resource. Each Web page has an arbitrary number of files that can result in a number of hits. Consequently, this data is not good for comparison analysis.

impression   The single display of a given banner ad to an individual Internet user

information capture   Online customers register, enter a contest, or complete a form and provide the company with personal information, which is stored in a database.

interactive call centers   (See *Web-based call center.*)

interactive voice response (IVR)   Defined as systems that provide recorded messages over telephone lines in response to user input in the form of spoken words or Touch-Tone dialing; for example, brokerages that allow you to place trades via your Touch-Tone phone

kiosk   Usually a stand-alone, boxlike unit that houses a computer and monitor for public display

knowledge discovery tools   Data mining software that locates patterns and suggests rules your company can act on

lifetime customer value (LTV)   The forecasted financial value of a customer over a predetermined period of time

loyalty   Building a relationship with the customer that encourages repeat sales. (See *customer loyalty.*)

mass customization   Often defined as the division of the production or manufacturing process into modules that allow the firm to change product or service elements to meet a customer-stated preference; for example, manufacturing a Motorola pager with the specific options a customer desires

one-click shopping A process introduced by Amazon.com that allows credit card customers to place an online order by clicking one single button instead of completing multiple steps and forms to place the online order

page view A request for a document (instead of an online image, movie, or audio file) on your Web site

personalization For marketers, it is the gathering of specific customer information and sending individual customers tailored messages at the right moment.

personalized Web content Often defined as the company using e-customer and personalization software that selects individualized Web content to be sent to the Internet user

portal A gateway Internet surfers use as a jumping-off point for their journeys through cyberspace. Portals allow users to access their e-mail or to connect to another Web site or search engine to find specific information.

privacy statement A company's promise to Web site users in which it guarantees them the freedom from unauthorized intrusion

recency A measurement of when the customer last interacted with your Web site in a recorded event, such as a visit to the Web site, a purchase, a call to the customer contact center, and so on. Recency is usually considered the strongest predictor of future buyer behavior.

recency/frequency/monetary value (RFM) analysis An approach to building effective database marketing strategies based on customer information

referring URL A page on another Web site from which a user follows a link to your Web site

retention Defined as customers making repeat transactions. Internet users may be considered retained customers if they make frequent Web site visits, purchase regularly, or often post comments to message boards.

return on investment (ROI) A finance term that measures the value of a project by what benefits (return) the company can accrue from its investment of resources or capital

rules applications Web site content applications apply the rules created by CRM applications to provide e-customers with targeted or individualized Web content.

rules creation CRM applications create rules that facilitate customer relationships.

sales automation software (SA) Application software process for managing sales activities

scalability The ability of an information system to grow, expand, and provide adequate performance support as greater demands are placed on it

security technology A broad-based term to describe various systems that are designed to either protect the integrity of your Web site or to allow for secure customer transactions over the Internet

server A software application that responds with requested information or executes tasks on the behalf of a client application (such as a browser); also, a network host or any computer that allows other computers to connect to it

spam Unsolicited e-mail messages (junk mail) that are usually sent to large numbers of recipients.

stickiness A word often used to describe Web sites that make you want to stay or encourage repeat visits

target marketing A business technique for isolating the most likely set of potential customers for a given product or service

user A person who logs onto your Web site. A user may frequently access your Web site. The clickstream data of a specific user can be followed for an individual visit.

value-added proposition Managing and enhancing the value to both the customer and the company within the relationship

visit An online session at your Web site that ends when the user logs off or clicks away to another Web site after a certain length of time

Web-based call center Often defined as the central repository for all the company's data on individual customers. Includes customer support and service via e-mail, fax, phone, text-chat, or voice over the Internet. When a customer makes contact, the customer service agent has access to the customer's purchase history, profile, and other relevant information for better customer service and improved customer satisfaction.

Web enabled A technological solution that is designed to operate via the Web in one or more functional areas

Index

About the Author

Kathleen Sindell, Ph.D., is an adjunct faculty member at the Johns Hopkins University MBA program and the author of numerous popular, academic, and professional articles, Web sites, and books, including the bestselling *Investing Online for Dummies.* A dynamic consultant, speaker, writer, and scholar, Sindell is regularly tapped as an e-commerce expert on CNNfn, *The Nightly Business Report,* and at popular online and print outlets.

Sindell is the founder of a firm that provides consulting and authoritative publications about management, finance, and real estate in the e-commerce environment. She and her colleagues work with organizations to deliver effective solutions for new ways of conducting business and managing finances in the emerging electronic environment. She is also the former associate director of the financial management and commercial real estate programs for the University of Maryland, University College Graduate School of Management & Technology.